D0428853

The History of the JEWISH PEOPLE

Volume I
The
Antiquity

Books by Moses A. Shulvass

DIE JUDEN IN WÜRZBURG WÄHREND DES MITTELALTERS 1934

ROME AND JERUSALEM (HEBREW) 1944

CHAPTERS FROM THE LIFE OF SAMUEL DAVID LUZZATTO (HEBREW) 1951

THE JEWS IN THE WORLD OF THE RENAISSANCE (HEBREW VERSION) 1955

IN THE GRIP OF CENTURIES (HEBREW) 1960

BETWEEN THE RHINE AND THE BOSPORUS 1964

FROM EAST TO WEST 1971

THE JEWS IN THE WORLD OF THE RENAISSANCE (ENGLISH VERSION) 1973

JEWISH CULTURE IN EASTERN EUROPE 1975

THE HISTORY OF THE JEWISH PEOPLE 1982–

The History of the JEWISH PEOPLE

Moses A. Shulvass

Volume I
The Antiquity

REGNERY GATEWAY

Chicago

The Antiquity (Vol. I, *The History of the Jewish People*)

Library of Congress Catalog Card Number 81-85564
ISBN 0-89526-660-1 (Vol. I)
ISBN 0-89526-652-0 (5-vol. set)

Regnery Gateway
360 West Superior Street
Chicago, Illinois 60610

To the memory of grandfather
Benjamin Schenker
of Cracow, Poland
(1865–1943)
Died as a Martyr of the Holocaust on
6 Adar B, 5703 – March 13, 1943

CONTENTS

PREFACE

The plan of writing this five-volume *History of the Jewish People* evolved over decades of studying and teaching Jewish history to undergraduate and graduate students and lecturing to audiences of educated laymen. To my students, I recommended the available textbooks; in my research, I used the various multi-volume histories written during the past 150 years of Jewish historiography. My students and I greatly benefited from the perusal of this vast Jewish historiographical library.

And yet I gradually became convinced that a work of intermediate length was needed as a reference book for the well-educated general public and as a textbook for undergraduate students of Jewish history. I realized that the multi-volume histories, with all their virtues, cannot be used effectively as textbooks due to their size. One-volume histories, conversely, are simply too short to convey to student and reader an adequate picture of the millenia-old and world-wide past of the Jewish people. Some histories offer brilliant general descriptions, but lack what Samuel David Luzzatto called "the philosophical richness of detail." Other books offer detailed chronicles of events at the price of overlooking the great continuum which encompasses events, dates and personalities. A five-volume work seems to me to be a proper framework for the presentation of the totality of Jewish history with adequate space for both detail and synthesis whenever they seem necessary for an intelligent and reasonable elucidation of the Jewish past.

In writing this work I guarded against defining courses of events as known beyond doubt. All too often the historian faces a set of sources that yield no clear-cut picture of the events, but are still strong enough to lure the researcher into a false sense of certainty. I believe that to qualify the results of such research by the addition of cautionary words such as "possibly" or "probably," or "it seems that" would greatly add to the credibility of the picture presented and to the understanding of the true nature of historical happening.

Jewish historians have made remarkable efforts to identify certain basic laws which determined the unusual, and often bizarre historical course of the Jewish people in its dispersion. Trends and ideas previously hidden have been uncovered. New light was shed on many events, which led to new insights into, and evaluations of, major phenomena in the Jewish historical experience. But these efforts have not led to a convincing interpretation of the history of the Jews in *all* its ramifications. The "philosopher's stone" which would explain all that had happened to Israel among the nations has not yet been found.

A description of Jewish destiny would, however, greatly benefit by using the various results obtained by earlier researchers in their quest for the "prime mover" of the Jewish past. He who describes the Jewish past in all its aspects will find that although the "prime movers" do not each explain everything, together they shed a great light on the course of Jewish history and lead to a closer understanding of many uncertainties.

The question of how to divide the Jewish past into epochs is still a matter of debate. Although a division into an Antiquity, Middle Ages, and New Times appears to be a workable framework, an attempt to identify these three epochs chronologically with the same epochs in world history, would create severe difficulties. For example, it would be both artificial and misleading to use one date as the conclusion of Antiquity in all Jewish communities from the Persian Gulf to the Atlantic and from Southern Arabia to Northern Europe. Instead, I believe that, although no system of periodization is beyond challenge, different dates for the completion of each period in different areas should prove a fructifying factor in making Jewish historical events and processes more comprehensible.

Hebrew words and names have been transliterated in the usual manner, with a view to simplifying the transliteration as much as possible. Diacritical marks, therefore, have been omitted. Although an attempt was made to be consistent, some exceptions were made. For example, while the Hebrew letter *kof* is generally transliterated by the letter *q*, the letter *k* is used in cases of accepted different transliteration in widely used words, such as *kabbalah* or *kehillah.* Biblical names are given in the form usual in English translations of the Bible. Words in a language other than English are printed in italics.

I wish to express my profound gratitude to my wife and coworker Celia A. Shulvass. Her encouragement and support in all phases of writing this work were immensely helpful. And so were her opinions in our many discussions on the problems and challenges that I confronted as an author.

Special thanks are due to Attorney Elisa Spungen for ably assisting me in formalizing the publication arrangements. As before, Benita Masters, my daughter Phyllis Gelman, and Samuel Cherniak made many felicitous linguistic and stylistic suggestions. Several grants from the Rosaline Cohn Scholars Fund of Spertus College of Judaica provided technical assistance in the collection of source material. Jacqueline Bocian and Maryse Manelli prepared the index. Leon Pasko and David G. Singer assisted in the proofreading. Ann Gran of Spertus College of Judaica secretarial staff has prepared the typescript. To all of them go my sincere thanks.

Moses A. Shulvass

Spertus College of Judaica
Chicago, Illinois
11 Nisan, 5742–April 4, 1982

Section I

EARLY ISRAELITIC HISTORY

Chapter 1

Israelitic Origins and Sojourn in Egypt

The Jews belong to the family of Semitic peoples, whose homeland is the Near East. The original dwelling place of the Semites in pre-historic times is unknown. There is a likelihood that they first appeared in North Africa, from where they emigrated to the Near East.

Abraham, the ancestor of the Jewish people, who lived during the Bronze Age, originated from an Aramean family; he was born in Mesopotamia, modern Iraq. It seems that the family of Terah, Abraham's father, was still partly nomadic. Although the clan occasionally engaged in commercial enterprises, and in farming, its main occupation was the raising of cattle, which made it necessary for it to perpetually wander with its flocks in search of good grazing areas. From Mesopotamia the family emigrated to the northwest, and sojourned in the area known as the Fertile Crescent.

The family of Terah worshipped *Sin,* the moon god, as is indicated by the names of several of its members. At a certain point in his life, Abraham abandoned moon worship to turn to the belief in an invisible God who was eternal, omnipresent, just, and omnipotent. He envisaged himself and his family as having an eternal covenant with his God. The cult of this religion was based on a simple sacrificial service.

Following his break with the religion of his father, Abraham separated himself from the clan and went southwestward to the land of Canaan, on the shores of the Mediterranean. He and his family considered the land of Canaan as having been promised to them by God. However, when he arrived in Canaan, Abraham realized that large parts of the country, especially in the north, were settled by other peoples and tribes. He therefore went southward to the sparcely settled Negev. The area bounded by Hebron, Beer-sheba and the Dead Sea then became the place where he spent most of his life. His son Isaac also lived there his entire life. An attempt by his grandson Jacob to settle in Shechem in the north, proved unsuccessful. Although in comparison with other segments of the population, Abraham's family was small in number, it nonetheless succeeded in taking firm root in the country, even to the degree of intervening in conflicts among various states in the area.

The country in which the Abraham clan lived was poor in water resources and always dependent on the rainfall. In times of drought the clan had to move, at least temporarily, to neighboring Egypt, where the Nile river always supplied ample quantities of water. Other tribes living in the Negev, such as the Edomites, likewise went periodically to Egypt. Thus, Egypt, especially its northern regions, became a familiar ground to Abraham and his descendants.

An opportunity for a prolonged sojourn in Egypt presented itself to the Hebrews, or Israelites, as Abraham and his family were often called, when a mass movement of Asiatics resulted in the establishment of the kingdom of the Hyksos in northern Egypt. The Hyksos, meaning *foreign rulers,* or *shepherd kings,* were probably mostly of Semitic stock and therefore welcomed the arrival of additional groups of Semites into Egypt. Under these circumstances, and due to economic stress, Abraham's descendants found it advantageous to leave the Negev and settle in northern Egypt. One of them, Joseph, even attained a high position in the royal court. In addition, other Hebrews related to them settled in Egypt at the same time or possibly even earlier. The Hebrews lived mostly in the northern part of the Nile Delta, in a region known as Goshen, probably identical with the city of Avaris and its environs.

As long as the Hyksos ruled northern Egypt, the Hebrews

were treated well. However, when the Hyksos were expelled in the middle of the 16th century B.C.E. ("before the common era"—equivalent to B.C.), the lot of the Hebrews changed radically. As Semites they were treated with suspicion, and ultimately made slaves of the state. Large numbers of them were used as construction workers in the building of the city of Tanis. The Hebrews, for many generations shepherds by profession, found construction work very hard and backbreaking.

The sojourn of the Hebrews in Egypt lasted several hundred years. During this time they developed from a clan into a people. Their special status as state slaves tended to keep them apart from the native population. Moreover, they were kept together by memories of a common distinct historical past. There is even a possibility that they possessed written records describing the lives of Abraham, Isaac, and Jacob, whom they considered founders of their people. The memory of their former link to the land of Canaan also helped to keep them alive as a distinct group. Above all, it was their faith in the invisible, eternal, and just God, inherited from their ancestors, that sustained them and ultimately led them to freedom.

Chapter 2

The Exodus from Egypt and the Conquest of Canaan

Exodus and Sojourn in the Sinai Desert

At a certain point in the thirteenth century B.C.E., there arose among the Israelites a leader, Moses, who began to propagate among them the idea of leaving Egypt. Moses' propaganda met with a quick and favorable response among the oppressed Israelites, and they escaped from Egypt at an opportune time. One theory has it that the exodus took place under Pharao Merneptah (ca. 1224–16 B.C.E.), when the Egyptians were busy suppressing uprisings in Libya to the west, and in Canaan to the northeast. The starting point of the exodus was the city of Tanis. At the very beginning of their march the Israelites encountered an Egyptian force, which however, was not able to stop them and which drowned in the nearby waters. After overcoming this first obstacle, the Israelites could continue unhampered in their march towards freedom. Although their goal was no doubt the land of Canaan, vivid in their tradition as the land of their ancestors, they chose to enter the desert rather than to proceed along the shores of the Mediterranean. The Mediterranean coast was part of the main caravan route and was patroled by Egyptians, which made it unsafe for the Israelites. Marching in the desert, the escapees, now obviously organized in a variety of tribal units, attempted to keep close to oases and places which were known to have a supply of water.

There is an enormous discrepancy between the biblical tradition and many modern-day scholars regarding the number of Israelites who left Egypt. According to the Bible, the number of the able-bodied warriors among the Israelites was over 600,000. The total number of the Israelites thus must have been about one and a half million. Such a large population could be fed in the desert only in a miraculous way by collecting the *manna,* "bread from heaven," and quails for meat. Modern-day scholars, however, who do not believe in miracles, estimate that only between 7,000 and 25,000 Israelites escaped under Moses from Egypt, since this was the number of people which could sustain themselves in the Sinai desert by collecting the honey-like white secretion from small insects that live off a sort of acacia shrub native to arid regions, the manna. In addition, large numbers of quails migrating in the spring from Africa northward to the Balkan countries, which rest exhausted in the Sinai desert and can be collected by hand, also served as food for the Israelites.

Some time after the exodus, the Israelites were led by Moses to Mount Sinai, where they experienced a religious event of decisive magnitude. The exact location of Mount Sinai is not known. The name Sinai is probably derived from the fact that bushes named in Hebrew *sneh* grew on its slopes. The experience at the holy mountain entrenched itself in the tradition of the people as a theophany, a re-affirmation of their closeness to God and of the covenant concluded between God and the Patriarchs. This God now became known to them by His name YHWH, the awe inspiring name which had to remain ineffable. Now, after the hundreds of years from Abraham to Sinai during which they had worshipped this exclusive God in practice, the oneness of God became clear to them as an idea. YHWH was conceived as a universal God, creator of the world, who shapes its destiny, but has a special, covenantal relationship with the people of Israel. From this covenant derives the authority of the Israelitic Law, centered around the Ten Commandments. It is profoundly ethical and represents the moral force central in Israel's faith. Following the theophany, a religious practice was introduced, which was in its nature sacrificial; it centered around a portable sanctuary with an organized priesthood, led by Aaron, the first high priest.

After the experience at Sinai, the Israelites continued to wander in the desert and in the Negev during the entire lifetime of the generation of the exodus. A group of spies sent into Canaan found that most of the cities were fortified to a degree that would make it impossible for the militarily untrained and virtually unarmed Israelites to occupy the country. An invasion into Canaan thus had to be postponed, and Kadesh Barnea, a large oasis in the western part of the Negev, possibly captured from the Amalekites, became the center of the Israelite tribes for several decades. During this time, the Israelites kept on multiplying, and their numbers further grew by the admission into their midst and to the YHWH religion of certain other Semitic groups who lived a nomadic life in the regions adjacent to southern Canaan. As a result, Kadesh Barnea and the other oases could no longer sustain the Israelites. The only possibility for survival now, a generation after the exodus, was to make the long-hoped-for invasion into Canaan, the land of the ancestors.

Invasion into Canaan

The situation in Canaan at this time, close to the year 1200 B.C.E., was favorable for the invading Israelitic tribes. The rather small country was divided into no less than 31 states. In addition,

Egypt on whom the Canaanite states were dependent, and whose help against the invaders they could have expected, was busy repelling an attack from the North by the "people of the sea" (Cretans, Philistines). The invasion of the Israelites was, furthermore, sudden and unexpected, and this left the Canaanite states with little time and opportunity to join forces for an effective common defense.

For reasons unknown to us, the Israelitic tribes divided in order to invade the country from several directions. One group of tribes marched around the southern part of Transjordan, and ultimately occupied its northern part known as Gilead. Another group of tribes under the leadership of the tribe of Judah attacked the country from the south and occupied the region later known as the Mountains of Judah. The largest group of tribes, however, led by Joshua, of the tribe of Ephraim, crossed the Jordan from the east near the northern shore of the Dead Sea and occupied a large part of the west bank of the Jordan, a territory roughly identical with the later state of Samaria.

These three invasions, although not fully simultaneous, seem nonetheless to have been executed according to a common plan. They resulted in the occupation by the Israelites of what was basically mountainous country. The Mediterranean coast and most of the valleys, however, remained under Canaanite control. Here the Canaanites could deploy their chariotry to effectively thwart the assault of the untrained and poorly armed Israelites. In the mountainous regions, where chariots could not be used, and the fight was between man and man, the Israelites won. Their very survival depended on their success, and they fought heroically and bitterly against the more civilized Canaanites, whom they considered heathens who had to be destroyed together with their gods and their abominable idolatry.

It seems that the Israelitic attack lasted a relatively short time. The population of the conquered cities was exterminated or expelled, and its place was taken by the invaders. Some cities succeeded in arriving at an agreement with the Israelites by which they could continue to exist as Israelitic dependencies. Their population was ultimately absorbed by the Israelitic tribes. The rest of the Canaanite states remained unconquered, and hostile to the invaders. As a result, the map of the land of Canaan after the conclusion of the wars of the conquest looked like a chessboard, with Canaanite "pockets" within Israelitic territory, and Israelitic "pockets" among the Canaanites. The Israelitic tribes settled and lived permanently each in its own territory, probably allotted to it in the general plan of the conquest. The sole exception was the tribe of Dan which, several generations after the conquest, left its original territory in the southwest of the country and settled in its northern-most region.

Chapter 3

The Period of the "Judges"

Tribal Confederation and "Judges"

When the Conquest was concluded, it became clear that the Israelites were not able to establish in Canaan a unified Israelitic state. The still distinct tribal structure of the people, the lack of territorial continuity, and the nomadic tradition were obstacles which could not be overcome. In addition, the transition from a nomadic to an agricultural economy was difficult, and preoccupied the average Israelite to such a degree that not much energy and interest remained for state building. Also, the wars which the Israelites had to fight between 1200 B.C.E. and 1100 B.C.E., were limited in scope and number and could be handled by temporary coalitions of two or three tribes.

It seems that as long as Joshua was alive, he was the recognized head of the people now known almost exclusively by the name of *Israel.* We do not know his duties and prerogatives. We may assume that the city of Shechem, on the border of the tribes Ephraim and Manasseh, was his residence. The intertribal authority of elders which came into being during the sojourn in the desert, seems to have continued to exist after the Conquest. Within this loose organization, each tribe seems to have had virtually full independence under the rule of its elders, although it is likely that the tribe of Ephraim claimed a status of leadership among them. It is not possible to determine with certainty if the intertribal organization of the Israelites was an amphictiony, that is, a confederation, the center of which was a common holy shrine. With the erection of the Temple in Shilo, however, the confederation of the tribes may have assumed, de facto, the nature of an amphictiony.

This loosely organized tribal confederation existed for several generations without any visible change. Only in times of war, did affected tribes show an inclination to yield their primitive democracy to the temporary rule of a forceful individual. Such individuals are called in the Bible, "judges." The exercise of judicial authority was one of the main prerogatives of any ruler in ancient times, and "ruler" and "judge" became synonymous concepts. The "judge" was a charismatic personality in the area of political life, similar to the prophet in the area of spiritual life. We do not know very much about the life of a "judge" prior to his appearance. In a critical moment he emerges out of anonymity, fulfills his task, and disappears into oblivion. One thing, however, must be supposed as certain: before assuming his assignment, the "judge" must have proved his prowess as a military leader. It was this military skill which made him eligible for the post, and for which the tribe or tribes which submitted to his leadership were ready to accept him.

The first of the wars of this period was fought in the North between a group of Israelitic tribes and the neighboring Canaanite king of Hazor. We do not know the reasons for the outbreak of this war. It is possible that after the thrust of the Conquest was over, the Canaanites gained some kind of sovereignty over the neighboring Israelitic tribes, and that the war was fought for the abolition of this sovereignty. The Israelitic victory under the prophetess Deborah and Barak, the son of Abinoam, makes it plausible that the strength of the Isrealites in the region was growing and that they were able to overcome a Canaanite force in a place where they had been unable to do so at the time of the Conquest. Of a similar nature must have been the war fought in Transjordan between the Israelitic tribes in Gilead and their Ammonite neighbors to the south. Here, Jephtah, an outcast, was called back by the very tribes which had rejected him, to win for them a victory over their enemies.

Of a somewhat different nature was the war fought against the Midianites. This people, living around the Gulf of Aqaba, invaded the country as far as the valley of Esdraelon. A coalition of four nearby tribes opposed them under the "judge" Gideon, and the Midianites were beaten. It may also be assumed that Gideon was supported by the Canaanites who were threatened by the Midianite invasion as much as were the Israelites.

After the war between the Israelites and the Canaanites in the north of the country, Canaanite resistance to the "Israelization" of the country waned. Except for a few cities, such as Jerusalem (Jebus), no independent Canaanite cities continued to exist. The Canaanites became a second-class population, and they were kept in this low status even as late as Solomon's reign, about 200 years later. At the same time, a rapproachment between Isrealites and Canaanites began, which was promoted by frequent cases of intermarriage between members of the Israelitic tribes and inhabitants of neighboring Canaanite settlements. Since most of the Canaanites had survived in the North, the Israelitic population of this region ultimately became heavily intermixed with Canaanite elements, while the population of the South retained to a much greater degree its original Israelitic character.

The Religious Life

The religious life of the Israelites was deeply affected by the transition from a nomadic to a sedentary way of life. There was no longer a need for a portable sanctuary, and a place had to be found for the erection of a permanent temple. It was certainly due to the influence of the tribe of Ephraim that the Temple was built in Shiloh, on its territory. While the process of settling in Canaan was still in progress, the "tent of meeting" was set up in Shiloh in the presence of "the whole congregation of the children of Israel" (Joshua 18:1). Shiloh was thus in practice designated from the very beginning as the place for a future permanent sanctuary. The sanctuary was probably built a few decades later, when the wars of the Conquest were concluded. Its priests were no doubt descendants of Aaron, the first high priest of the portable sanctuary in the desert. About 600 years later the prophet Jeremiah, himself of priestly origin, was still aware of the importance of the Temple in Shiloh, which he considered the First Temple (Jeremiah 7:12). It is likely that local temples or altars were built on the territories of other tribes as well.

Although the Shiloh Temple and its service dedicated to YHWH were held in high esteem, both as a holy shrine and as a unifying factor in the intertribal confederation, other forms of religious life began to appear as well. The progressive shift of the Israelites to farming and the rapproachement with the Canaanites in the North directed their attention to the various fertility cults practiced by the Canaanites inside Israel and by the peoples on its borders. The book of Judges preserved a solid tradition about many Israelites turning to the fertility cults. An opportunity for practicing the fertility cults was available in the many pagan shrines which escaped destruction during the Conquest. In addition, there were Israelites who had statues made for themselves to serve as their housegods. It is likely that a grandson of Moses served as priest in such a private sanctuary containing a statue.

With all the importance attached to the sacrificial service in Shiloh and elsewhere, it was the festivals, agricultural and historical, which occupied a place of centrality in the life of the individual Israelite. The Sabbath was a permanent, weekly religious experience which distinguished the life of the Israelite drastically from the life of his non-Israelitic neighbor. It was a purely Israelitic institution which did not resemble any of the Canaanite holidays. The three major festivals, Passover, Pentecost, and Tabernacles did have their roots in the seasonal experiences of the farmer, as the Festival of Spring, the Festival of the First Fruits, and the Festival of Harvest. But in the religion of YHWH they were given an overwhelming religio-historical content as festivals which commemorated the exodus, the theophany at Sinai, and the prolonged sojourn in the desert. Each Israelite was expected to make pilgrimages to Shiloh to celebrate the festivals there. It is hard to determine to what degree the average Israelite lived up to this expectation, but there is evidence that the pilgrimage to Shiloh was practiced at least on an annual basis.

After the great religious events at Mount Sinai and during the

Conquest, the Israelites experienced in Canaan a definite decline of their covenantal commitment. The hardships of the adjustment to the routine of farming turned this time into a lackluster period, devoid of great events and religious enthusiasm. The resistance to the fertility cults was therefore weak and so was the resistance to the moral depravity which came with it. Acts of inhumanity toward fellow Israelites, and even the practice of human sacrifice appear to have occurred more than once.

Yet within the unfavorable conditions, the lofty Sinaitic ideals were kept alive. All through the period a prophetic circle was vigorously promoting adherence to the concept and ways of pure YHWHism. In addition, it constantly demonstrated a patriotic Israelitic and vigorously anti-Canaanite zeal. It was the prophetess Deborah who inspired the people in the war against the king of Hazor and led it to victory. Numerous bands of "sons of the prophets," that is, groups of young men aspiring to, and training for, a prophetic career were crisscrossing the country and untiringly admonishing the people to live up to high moral and religious standards. It was these bands of young prophets, and above all the towering personality of the prophet Samuel which helped the people to free themselves to a great degree from the evil of pagan assimilation and to withstand the greatest danger to their future, the onslaught of the Philistines.

The Philistine Menace and the Prophet Samuel

We have seen how the Philistines, called "People of the North" or "People of the Sea," tried to invade Egypt at the time of the Israelitic invasion into Canaan. When it became clear, however, that they were not able to occupy the Egyptian sea coast, the Philistines turned to the shores of Canaan. They were warriors who came from Crete and the Aegean islands, and were in possession of metal weapons at a time when such military equipment was still very rare among the Israelites. Thus, hardly encountering serious resistance, they occupied the southernmost portion of the sea coast. In the Greek fashion they organized themselves as a confederation of five city-states. Initially, the Philistines controlled a stretch of the coast between Gaza and Jaffa, and their inland expansion went only as far as the city of Gath. Gradually, however, they began to expand eastward and northward, pressing hard upon the neighboring Israelitic tribes.

It was this continuous state of border war which, in all likelihood, compelled the tribe of Dan to abandon its original territory and emigrate to the northern border. These events all took place before 1100 B.C.E. With the advent of the eleventh century B.C.E., the situation of the Israelites further deteriorated. The Philistines imposed their rule over most of the country, and only the region of the northern-most tribes (Galilee and Gilead) remained free of the Philistine yoke. By the year 1050 B.C.E. Philistine garrisons were stationed in a number of key cities, and Shiloh was destroyed. The Philistine occupation of the country was thus accompanied by the disappearance of the only existing center of the intertribal Israelitic confederation.

By and large, however, the occupation was not too severe. The Philistines were a small group of warrior-aristocrats, and their occupation of the country on a continuing basis by necessity had to be of a lenient nature. There seems to have been no attempt to suppress the YHWH religion, as pagans only rarely oppose the exercise of another religion. The destruction of Shiloh was not intended as a blow to the religious center of the Israelites, but rather to their political center. The spirit of freedom was thus continuously kept alive among the Israelites by the YHWH religion, which was born as an act of liberation from bondage, and whose festivals were a constant reminder of the liberation of the people in the past. In addition, an example of Israelites living in freedom existed in Galilee and in the Gilead. It also seems that the Philistines did not limit the freedom of movement of the bands of the "sons of the prophets" who were continuously fanning the patriotic zeal for liberation.

Above all, it was the prophet Samuel to whom all the people looked for leadership. He was at the same time a prophet and a "judge." He lived in Ramah, equally close to Ephraim and Judah, the two leading tribes. Unlike the previous "judges," he did not confine his activities to one or two tribes, but was obviously recognized as a leader by all the tribes of Israel. The Philistines may have been aware of his activities, but did not see in them a threat to their domination. At any rate, they did not restrict

Samuel's movements among the tribes. Samuel's activities and the impact of the other factors described here thus worked to prepare the people for a war of liberation and hastened its outbreak.

Section II

THE UNITED KINGDOM

Chapter 1

The Unification of Israel under King Saul

The Need for a Unified State

We have seen how at the time of the Conquest conditions were unfavorable for the establishment of a unified state, and all that could be achieved was a loose confederation of the tribes. The authority of the "judges," like the ministry of prophets, was limited to their own lifetime, or a part of it, and was never hereditary. An attempt by a son of the "judge" Gideon to establish himself as king by gaining recognition from both parts of the population, Israelites and Canaanites, was short-lived and ended in a complete failure.

However, in the last quarter of the eleventh century B.C.E. there appeared both an urgent necessity and a realistic possibility for the establishment of a unified state, headed by a king. The inadequacy of the intertribal confederation to cope with the Philistine menace was obvious, and the liberation of the country was clearly dependent on the ability of the tribes to organize a viable unified state. Also, the old obstacles were now gone, or at least weakened. Although tribal differences still existed, some of the tribes (as for instance Simeon) were absorbed by larger tribes. Also, for various reasons, many Israelites left their homesteads in their own tribal territories to settle among other tribes.

Of still greater importance was the progressive amalgamation, through mutual infiltration and intermarriage, of Israelites and Canaanites in the northern regions of the country. On the positive side, Samuel's activities throughout the country proved that the people were ready for unified leadership. The example of a number of neighboring countries, ruled by monarchs on a hereditary basis, was also enticing. The idea of a decisive constitutional transformation from a loosely organized primitive democracy to a tightly knit country under a king was gaining solid support.

It is probable that as long as Samuel was able to lead the people with full vigor, no formal demand for the establishment of a kingdom was voiced. But when Samuel began to age, the problem became acute. Samuel's two sons were interested in public office but were dishonest and unpopular and could not be considered as heirs to their father's role. Consequently, the elders requested from Samuel that he choose for them a king. His status as a "man of God" and his unequaled glory as "judge" made it impossible to choose a new leader without his consent.

When Samuel was confronted with the demand for a king, he was shocked. He was a prophet to whom the old ideals of a people under God's kingship were very dear. He saw in the appointment of "judges" on a temporary basis and for a specific task the ideal form of government, which did not impose any burdens upon the people. He therefore attempted to dissuade the people from asking for a king by describing to them in simple but forceful words how a king would oppress them and impose upon them a heavy burden of taxation, especially in the form of forced labor. Significantly, Samuel's speech against the idea of a monarchy was widely used by American preachers in the period of the Revolutionary War, when they spoke out against George III and in favor of a republic. Samuel's words, however, did not impress his contemporaries. Samuel's world was waning and the hard facts of life in Israel demanded the formation of a kingdom. The old prophet thus had to bend to the will of the people and choose for them a king.

Saul's Early Reign

Saul, the man whom Samuel chose and anointed king of Israel about 1020 B.C.E., was of the tribe of Benjamin. Benjamin was a small tribe, and the selection of a king from among its members was a felicitous act by which neither of the two giant tribes, Ephraim and Judah, was offended. In addition, the tribe of Benjamin was dwelling in a wedge-shaped territory between Judah and Ephraim, and a town located there could be a logical choice for a capital of a king of all Israel.

Prior to his elevation, Saul belonged to the prophetic circles, and his appointment as king was by prophetic designation. The symbolic act of anointment by Samuel made him the legitimate king of Israel, and there seems to have been no popular opposition to his elevation. The town of Gibeah in his native territory of Benjamin became his capital. We must assume that Saul had some kind of military experience prior to his anointment, since he was able, early in his reign, to give effective relief to an Israelitic city across the Jordan, besieged by the Ammonites. His prowess in warfare, however, unfolded fully when he began shortly thereafter a systematic campaign to expel the Philistines from the Israelitic territories held by them.

His success was due to a number of factors. To begin with, Saul's elevation to the kingship may have been unnoticed by the Philistines, to whom he may have appeared a mere successor to the prophet-"judge" Samuel. We may also assume that after having occupied Israel for almost a century without having encountered any real opposition, the garrisons kept by the Philistines in Israel were not very numerous or very alert. Saul surely could expel these garrisons without great difficulty. And when the Philistines finally mustered a large army against Saul, the battles were fought mostly in the mountains where chariots could not be deployed.

We do not know how it happened, but Saul must have succeeded in raising an army rather speedily, equipping it and making it ready for successful warfare. Some of his soldiers, and especially the crown prince Jonathan, showed during the battles resourcefulness, courage, and even heroism. Unknown to us is the military background of Saul's commander-in-chief and uncle,

Abner, and his actual role in the campaigns. The result of the campaign against the Philistines was the liberation of the mountainous regions of southern and central Israel. The Philistines had to withdraw to the coastal plains. Besides the Philistines, Saul also fought the Amalekites to secure the southern borders of the country against their recurring attacks.

Saul achieved most of his military victories during the first five or six years of his reign. What he did during this period in domestic matters and for the organization of an officialdom, is largely unknown.

It seems that at the beginning relations between Saul and Samuel were such that no open conflict developed between them. In view of Saul's successes, Samuel may have given up his basic opposition to the monarchy. But after some time relations between the king and the aging prophet began to deteriorate. The reasons that lay at the root of the clash are not very clear. But it was most likely an attempt by Saul to perform the sacrificial service which brought the conflict into the open. To be sure, men of non-Aaronid origin were tacitly permitted to officiate at sacrificial services up to the time of the erection of the Solomonic Temple. Saul's attempt thus was not a "religious offense" as such. But Samuel saw in it an attempt by the king to concentrate all authority, temporal and spiritual, in his hands, thus putting a definite end to the last vestige of democracy, the separation of the royal power from the priestly establishment.

The prophet's ultimate break with the king came when the latter failed to execute the captured king of the Amalekites and saved some of the spoils which he was supposed to destroy utterly. Amalek was considered the arch-enemy of Israel, against whom eternal holy war was to be conducted. Saul, an anointed king who showed mercy to an Amalekite King, therefore forfeited his right to Israel's throne. It is significant that when Samuel decided to declare Saul unfit for the kingdom, he did not attempt to restore the old democratic order, but anointed another man to be king. Obviously, Samuel had by then given up his basic opposition to the monarchy.

Saul's Last Years

After the break with Samuel, Saul's situation continued to deteriorate in many ways. A mental illness ("an evil spirit from the Lord") befell him, possibly as a result of his traumatic experience with Samuel. In addition, he became suspicious about the intentions of his son-in-law David, and spent most of the remaining years of his life pursuing him.

David, the son of Jesse, was a young shepherd from Bethlehem in the territory of the tribe of Judah. During the wars with the Philistines he came by chance to Saul's headquarters and was presented to the king. Soon thereafter, he rose to a position of great importance. He became the most popular hero in the war against the Philistines, and was credited with killing a Philistine giant by the name of Goliath. David was also a talented musician, and the ailing king became more and more dependent on his musical renditions to calm his tormented soul. Simultaneously, a great, sincere friendship developed between David and the crown prince Jonathan. It was thus natural, that Michal, the king's younger daughter, was given to David as a wife.

Little by little, however, the relations between Saul and David began to deteriorate. Saul become jealous of David's immense popularity with the masses. There is a possibility that the young hero's real name was Elhanan, and the name David, meaning "the beloved one" was given to him by his countless admirers. In addition, it was David whom Samuel secretly anointed as a replacement for Saul. It was, of course, inevitable that before long this fact became known to the king.

Saul's reaction was natural. Considering David's consent to be anointed an act of betrayal and rebellion, Saul decided to put him to death. But help came from Jonathan. David seemed to have had an agreement with Jonathan that after Saul's death he would be king and Jonathan a sort of viceroy. Jonathan therefore forewarned David and he was able to escape. The young fugitive felt that the most secure place for him would be his home territory of Judah. There he gathered a gang of several hundred people, composed of his kinsmen, outlaws, and men otherwise disillusioned with the government, thus creating for himself a sort of military force. The role played by David's gang is not very clear. It seems that it fulfilled a positive need of protecting the southern border regions from recurring invasions from the neighboring states. On the other hand, however, the gang exacted "protection money" from the Israelitic landowners. Being afraid that Saul might do harm to his parents in Bethlehem, David sent them to safety in Moab, whence his great-grandmother Ruth, the Moabite, had come. He himself, for reasons unclear, made the dubious step of surrendering as a vassal to the Philistine king of Gath, and receiving in return the town of Ziklag as a residence.

Some time during the last decade of the eleventh century B.C.E. the relations between Israel and Philistia became more strained, and a new war became imminent. The Philistines knew of the sad state of affairs in Israel resulting from the king's illness, and the rift between him and David. This moment, when David became their ally, may have seemed to them opportune for an attempt to recapture the Israelitic territory from which Saul had expelled them earlier in his reign. The place chosen for the decisive battle, a valley in the vicinity of Mount Gilboa, was favorable for the Philistines with their chariotry. When the king of Gath moved northward to the encounter with the Israelites, his vassal David accompanied him with his men. But before the battle began, the Philistines ordered David to return to Ziklag. Evidently they were not fully sure of his loyalty, and were afraid that in the decisive moment David might defect and rejoin his Israelitic brethren.

It turned out that even without David's help the Philistines were able to decisively defeat Saul's army. In the disastrous debacle, many Israelites lost their lives, including the crown prince Jonathan. Saul himself, who entered the battle with the feeling that he was going to lose, was now in utter despair and committed suicide. A group of Israelites from Jabesh-Gilead, mindful of the rescue of their city by Saul from an Ammonite siege, now came to Beth Shean, where the Philistines had placed Saul's body, and carried it away to Jabesh for burial.

What David's true intentions were when he marched up with the Philistines to Mount Gilboa, will never be known. But it was of the utmost importance that at the time of the Israelitic disaster, David's gang constituted de facto an Israelitic military force of some kind. The Israelitic population thus was not completely at the mercy of the victorious Philistines. Now, with Saul dead, David could consider himself, on the basis of the anointment by Samuel, the legitimate king of Israel. His gang thus also became the legitimate army of Israel.

Chapter 2

The Reign of David

The Beginnings

It was a critical moment for David and for the Israelitic people. His own future as king and the independence of the country were at stake. The action which he took was cautious and designed to give him time to solidify his position. He could not remain in Ziklag, because this would have been tantamount to a formal continuation of his status as a Philistine vassal. It therefore seemed wise for him to enter the city of Hebron and reside there.

Hebron was located high in the mountains in David's home territory of Judah, and fairly distant from the borders of Philistia. It could be easily defended in case of a Philistine attack. It also had an old tradition of holiness, as the burial site of the Patriarchs. All this made it a good choice for a temporary capital. In addition, David's wife Abigail could be considered an heiress to the city of Hebron, and the Philistines could be made to believe that by setting up his residence there, David had no specific political plans. Once entrenched in Hebron, however, David was anointed king of Judah. Not only was he no longer a Philistine vassal, but their enemy, committed to preventing them from reaping the fruits of their victory at Mount Gilboa.

David, however, was not the only king in Israel. Abner, Saul's commander-in-chief and uncle, came out alive from the Mount Gilboa disaster, and began to promote the claims of Saul's only surviving son, Eshbaal (Ish-bosheth), to the throne of Israel. He took him to Mahanaim in Transjordan, a safe distance from both David and the Philistines, and there he set him up as king. Abner seemed to have effectively controlled the northern and Transjordanian parts of Israel, while David remained in control of what was basically his home tribe of Judah. For a period of seven years the two kings, David and Eshbaal, fought for control of the entire country. Although David was getting stronger and Abner weaker, the war situation remained basically a stalemate. There is the possibility that David tried to avoid excessive bloodshed, hoping that after the death of Abner, who by then must have been advanced in years, Eshbaal's kingdom would collapse.

When both sides realized that the situation was that of a stalemate, the time seemed ripe for negotiations. Abner knew that in the long run Eshbaal was no match for David and was now ready to give up his cause and to make peace with David. In return for this, Abner probably expected to be appointed commander-in-chief of David's army. David received Abner in a friendly manner and the unity of the country was restored. The unprovoked murder of Abner by David's commander and nephew Joab was a tragic setback, but did not break up the newly established unity. The elders of the northern tribes came to David, and he was anointed king of all Israel. Eshbaal was murdered by two of his officers of his own tribe of Benjamin and the cause of Saul's dynasty was lost.

The division of the country into two groups of tribes, led by Judah and Ephraim, which resulted from the separation of the tribes during the Conquest, did not disappear with David's recognition as king over the entire country. Under Saul, who was of the "neutral" tribe of Benjamin, these differences may have temporarily lost much of their intensity. But David was of the tribe of Judah, Ephraim's perpetual rival. The differences thus reappeared, and David's recognition as king over "all Israel" was therefore tantamount to the establishment of a united kingdom, with David serving simultaneously as king of two countries. In fact, the constitutional framework of his rule was different in Judah from that in the North. In Judah he was a hereditary, almost absolutist ruler, while in the North he was king on the basis of a "covenant," that is, an agreement between him and the representatives of the people with regard to the limits of his power. It was this basic constitutional character of his rule over the North, which made it so easy for this part of the country to secede from the united kingdom after Solomon's death. This nature of the state found its expression in the various names by which it was known. The South was called *House of Judah* and the North *House of Israel* or *House of Joseph.* The united kingdom was called *All Israel, Israel and Judah,* or often simply *Israel.*

With the re-establishment of the united kingdom, Hebron became inadequate as a capital. It was not in the center of the country, and its location in Judah could offend the North, which was territorially larger and whose population was more than double that of the South. An unusual opportunity to establish a neutral and almost ideally located capital was now available. The city of Jebus in the territory of Benjamin remained one of the last Canaanite islands within Israelitic territory. David now set out to capture the city in order to turn it into his capital. The campaign in which Joab played a major role was short and successful. After its capture, Jebus was renamed the *City of David,* but became henceforth universally known as *Jerusalem.* Israelites of all tribes settled in it, thus demonstrating its national, supratribal character. The Ark of the Lord which was kept successively in various towns after Shiloh's destruction, was now brought to the capital and placed in a temporary sanctuary ("tent"), which David erected for it. After an altar for the sacrificial service was also built, the city became simultaneously Israel's political and religious capital. The establishment of the new capital of Jerusalem, about the year 1000 B.C.E., completed the foundation of the United Kingdom.

David's Wars and Conquests

During the years following the establishment of the new capital, David waged many wars. The Philistines were effectively neutralized after David captured the city of Gath and imposed upon them an annual tribute. Why he did not occupy all of Philistia cannot be said with certainty. Possibly he wanted a sort of buffer state to exist between Israel and Egypt. It is noteworthy that his palace guard in later years was composed of

Philistines and their Cretan kinsmen. Other non-Israelitic cities, especially those in the Plain of Esdraelon, were not occupied, and by this time practically all Canaan was under David's firm control.

Of the neighboring countries, only Phoenicia was chosen as an ally. It provided David with much-needed building materials and skilled workers. Also, its decisive role in maritime trade and traffic made it attractive as an ally rather than a vassal. All other neighbors, however, were reduced to the status of tribute-paying vassals. It took a lot of fighting to capture Ammon, located in the center of Transjordan, because the armies of various Aramean states which came to Ammon's aid, had first to be defeated. But once Ammon was captured, the way was open for a campaign into Syria, and the occupation of its southern region, including the city of Damascus. More easily Moab, across the Dead Sea, and Edom in the Negev were made tribute-paying vassals. No sufficient information is available about David's armed forces. It seems that the army was mostly composed of Israelites. When the wars were over, however, most of the warriors returned to their homes and farms. Only the palace guard, composed of Cretans and Philistines, served on a permanent basis.

After the conclusion of the conquests, Israel became the foremost nation on the Eastern Mediterranean coast. Some modern historians even speak of David's "empire." A policy of expansion was made possible not only by David's skill as warrior and diplomat, but also by the fact, that Egypt and Assyria-Babylonia, the great powers flanking Israel on the southwest and the east, were temporarily weak. Thus, a power vacuum was created into which Israel could step. The various parts of the empire, however, did not lose their own distinctiveness and liberated themselves as soon as conditions changed. Later talmudic tradition considered especially the occupation of Syria a temporary one. For the time being, however, the occupation of the neighboring countries was of decisive importance. Through the conquest of Edom David got hold of a region which was rich in ores, badly needed for the production of weapons. The control of Damascus, on the main Mediterranean caravan route, increased considerably the revenue from customs, bringing much wealth into the otherwise rather poor country. In addition, the army was camping most of the time in the conquered lands, and was no burden to the Israelitic taxpayers. This state of affairs lasted throughout David's reign.

David's Latter Years and the Problem of the Succession

David was a many-sided personality. As king, warrior, and diplomat he was by far superior to all his successors, both in Judah and Israel. When necessary he hit hard and swiftly, but whenever possible he was kind, considerate, and magnanimous. He was, in addition, blessed with great artistic talent as a harpist and poet. As the author of a large number of psalms, he stands out in world literature as a profound religious thinker who knew how to express his thoughts in some of the loftiest verses ever written. As a thinker, poet, and great king he ultimately became identical in Jewish tradition with the future King Messiah.

And yet, in his private life as a family man he often failed miserably. He married some of his wives in a manner not befitting a great man, let alone a religious thinker of such magnitude and profundity. His behavior could not but affect his children, who were thus dragged into situations leading to sin, rebellion, and intrigue. The crown prince Amnon abused one of his sisters and was killed by her brother Absalom in revenge. Absalom then fled, and could return to the court only after Joab persuaded the king to forgive him. Absalom, however, continued to be bitter, and his frustration increased when unmistakable signs began to appear that David was planning to promote a younger son, Solomon, as successor to the throne instead of Absalom, now the oldest. True, there was no precedent yet established regarding the succession to the throne of Israel. But the Pentateuchal law clearly favors the oldest son in all matters of inheritance. Absalom had therefore the right to consider himself the legitimate crown prince. Thus, in order to protect his rights against Solomon, Absalom rebelled and proclaimed himself king.

This was the saddest moment in the life of the already aging David. It looked as if the people of Israel, whom he had led to major victories and who sincerely admired him as a hero, had now abandoned him. Even some of his trusted advisers switched their loyalty to Absalom. Curiously, an attempt was made then to revive the claims of Saul's family to the throne of Israel. David had to flee from Jerusalem, and, ironically, to seek refuge in Mahanaim in Transjordan where several decades earlier Saul's son Eshbaal looked for protection against David. Absalom's uprising failed due to a number of tactical errors committed by him, and he lost his life. The question of the succession, however, remained unresolved.

Besides Solomon's ambitions, it was also David's long life and reign which made his sons impatient. David lived to be 70 years old, a life span unusual for those times. Longevity of a king always makes the heir to the throne impatient. So when David became old and possibly partly senile, Adonijah, who was next in line for the succession, decided to take action. Supported by a number of high officials, he made a feast to promote his claims to the throne. Whether at this feast he was actually proclaimed king cannot be said with certainty. But, Bath-sheba, Solomon's mother, upon learning of the events, presented herself to David in the company of Nathan the prophet and together they convinced David that Solomon should be enthroned immediately. By appointing Solomon co-regent during his lifetime, David gave a semblance of legitimacy to Solomon's succession. But what really decided the succession was the fact that Benaiah, the son of Jehoiada, the commander of the palace guard, sided with Solomon. We have seen that in David's latter years the palace guard was the only permanent military force in the country. When this group threw its support to Solomon, his accession to the throne was assured. David died some time between 970 and 965 B.C.E.

Chapter 3

The Reign of Solomon

Solomon's Foreign Policy

It seems that there was no negative reaction among Israel's population to the manner in which the succession to the throne was settled in the palace. A short while later the two main opponents, Adonijah and Joab, were executed, and the old high priest Abiathar was banished from Jerusalem. Some time later the man who during Absalom's uprising had urged the restoration of the Saulian dynasty was also executed. No other opposition to Solomon seems to have developed until late in his reign.

The inner tranquility of the country was accompanied by peace on the frontiers. Solomon was not a warrior, and was not interested in waging wars. His overall plan was to do everything, short of warfare, for the protection of the empire which he inherited from his father. As it turned out, he succeeded only in part, and by the end of his reign Israel's territory had diminished.

In order to carry out his plan, Solomon concluded a number of alliances. He renewed the friendship with Phoenicia established by his father, and during his reign the relations between Phoenicia and Israel became closer and much more meaningful. He also married a number of foreign princesses, including one from Egypt's 21st dynasty. Through these alliances he hoped to secure permanently the borders of the country. However, not being fully sure of the sufficiency of these arrangements, he built a well-organized professional army of charioteers to be used in case of foreign invasions. He bought chariots in Egypt, and horses he imported from Cilicia, in Asia Minor. He placed the chariots and their crews in Jerusalem and in a number of localities called "chariot cities." A review of the geographical distribution of the "chariot cities" clearly indicates that the chariotry was designed for defense, not offense. Significantly, several "chariot cities" were located on the roads leading to Egypt, ruled by his ally and father-in-law.

Solomon's reluctance to wage war led to the loss of Aram (Syria) and its capital Damascus. After the 21st dynasty was deposed in Egypt late in Solomon's reign, the alliance with this country seems to have come to an end, and Egypt began to support irredentism in Edom. Whether the dependency of Edom was consequently completely lost, is impossible to determine. What kept the other dependencies, Ammon and Moab, from seceding from Israel we do not know. Solomon's indifference towards the territorial integrity of his country was truly amazing when we consider the fact that late in his reign he ceded to Phoenicia 20 towns in Galilee in lieu of payments for supplies and labor. That, in spite of all this, the country remained under Solomon a viable state with a high degree of prosperity, at least during the first part of his reign, was due to the solid foundations given to it by David and the enormous wealth accumulated by him in the state treasury from tribute and customs.

Solomon's Building Projects

King Solomon devoted a great deal of his time and interest to a variety of building projects. The first to be built were probably the chariot cities, which were the backbone of his defense system. He built six such cities, if not more. Besides the stables for the many horses, he had to build homes for the horsemen and their families. This must have added up to a very large number of homes, since each chariot was serviced by a crew of three. Each chariot city also had a number of storage houses. In addition to the chariot cities, he also built a number of fortresses.

Of a different nature were the structures he built in Jerusalem. The city took on a new character under Solomon. A royal palace with all possible refinements was built, in addition to the many structures that had to house Solomon's numerous harem with its large number of servants. A special building, named "the house of the forest of Lebanon," probably housed the royal treasury. Other buildings for the royal administration also had to be erected to accommodate the many new officials appointed by him.

The most important structure which Solomon built was the Temple in Jerusalem. We have seen that upon occupying Jerusalem, David built an altar there. David gave much thought to the possibility of building a Temple, but was only able to do some preparatory work and to begin the accumulation of building material. When Solomon undertook the task of bringing to completion David's idea, he had mainly to rely on the cooperation of his Phoenician allies. They supplied large quantities of timber, unavailable in Israel, and they supplied most of the skilled labor for the work of construction. Although the Israelites had now lived in the country for a period of over 200 years, they had not developed their own architectural style. It is therefore understandable that the Phoenician architects, carpenters, and masons built the Temple of YHWH according to Canaanite and Aramean styles. Egyptian as well as Babylonian elements were also discovered in Solomon's Temple by historians of architecture. Significantly, decorations on the bases of the washbasins depicted various animals.

The altars, candelabrum, and the other holy vessels were placed in various courts and chambers. The most important chamber was called "Holy of Holies." This chamber housed the Holy Ark with the Tablets of the Covenant. The Ark was covered by the wings of the *cherubim,* called by some modern scholars winged sphinxes. Some of the vessels kept in the portable sanctuary in the desert were also housed in the Temple. The Temple, often called "The House of God," was built on a hill believed to be Mount Moriah. The description of the Temple in the Bible leaves no doubt that it was a magnificent building. It was also a very strong structure and lasted about 350 years, till it was destroyed by the Babylonians in 586 B.C.E. Every few decades the Temple was thoroughly repaired from funds accumulated from pious donations.

Religion and Culture under Solomon

With the erection of the Temple in Jerusalem, important changes took place in Israel's religious life. Prior to that, although sacrificial services were held in Jerusalem "before the Ark of the Covenant," the "great high place" was in the city of Gibeon. We may also assume that David's lifelong High Priest Abiathar officiated in Jerusalem and not in Gibeon. Furthermore, although the descendants of Aaron were considered to be the legitimate priests, non-Aaronides also officiated at Sacrificial services, as for instance David's sons, or his friend Ira the Jairite.

Under Solomon all this changed. True, for several hundred years more the Israelites continued to sacrifice on local altars all over the country. But the centrality of the Jerusalem Temple in the life of the people became more and more conspicuous. It was this Temple to which everybody felt obliged to make a pilgrimage. With Abiathar's expulsion from Jerusalem, Zadok, who already in David's times performed priestly duties, was installed as high priest of the new Temple. The office became hereditary in his family, and in the period of the Second Commonwealth the Rabbis insisted that only his descendants should be considered legitimate high priests.

With all the enhancement given to the worship of YHWH by the Temple in Jerusalem, the attraction exerted by the fertility religions had not subsided. On the contrary, it may even have increased. During the reigns of David and Solomon numerous Canaanites were absorbed into the Israelitic population, and this could not help but bring their cults closer to the attention of the Israelites. The alliance with Phoenicia and the occupation of Ammon, Moab, and Edom further contributed to the strengthening of the position of the gods and goddesses of these nations among the Israelites, and of the temptation to serve them alongside the God of Israel. But it was possibly the wholesale induction of foreign women into Solomon's harem, and his liberal attitude toward their idolatrous practices, which were mainly responsible for the popularity of Astarte and her companion gods and goddesses in the latter years of Solomon's reign. On a mountain near Jerusalem he built altars for them which existed for several hundred years. The Bible even directly accuses Solomon of having become a victim of the idolatrous aberration himself. Also, the possibility should not be overlooked altogether that Solomon's promotion of the pagan cults was at least in part designed to limit the power of the Zadokite priesthood, which may have become too strong and something of a menace to the power of the throne.

The general intensification of life during the period of the United Kingdom was also accompanied by an upsurge in the area of literature and art, especially under Solomon. Periods rich in historical happening manifest an interest in historical literature. Thus parts of the books of Samuel and Kings, notably those describing David's life and deeds, were written in Solomon's reign. Similarly, biographies of the prophets Samuel, Nathan, and Gad, no longer extant, were written and known in the same period. The interest in literature was certainly enhanced by the fact that both David and Solomon were very talented authors. David's greatness as a poet was only partly matched by his son. While it is doubtful whether Solomon authored the Song of Songs and Ecclesiastes, it is certain that at least part of the book of Proverbs was written by him.

Equally notable was the interest in the fine arts. While the development of the visual arts may have been limited due to the negative attitude of the YHWHist religion to the depicting of the human or animal form, music was cultivated with enthusiasm. We have seen what a large role music and dance played in the circles of the "sons of the prophets." King David, who played the harp, was only one among a host of contemporary musicians. But it was in the Solomonic Temple that music attained major importance, as part of the service. While some degree of foreign influence existed in the area of music, pure Israelitic creativity prevailed in it more than in the other areas of the fine arts.

Solomon's Fiscal Policy and the Decline of the Kingdom

During Solomon's reign governmental expenditures increased enormously. The army of charioteers, the extensive building projects, the large bureaucracy, and the luxurious personal life of the king were far too costly for a nation of basically poor farmers. In addition, the loss of Damascus cut off an important source of income, the revenue from customs of the caravan route.

At the beginning, the problem of financing the expenditures

of the government was not too serious. The wealth accumulated under David could now be spent. In the course of time, however, Solomon had to look for other sources of income. He then turned to the lucrative maritime trade, which he could conduct with the help of his allies, mostly the Phoenicians. Although it is not possible to determine to what degree Solomon retained control over Edom, it is certain that he had access to the Gulf of Aqaba and could make its ports a basis for extensive international trade. His Phoenician allies, the ancient world's great navigators, built a merchant marine for him there. The crews also consisted mostly of Phoenician sailors. The fleet first traded with various ports on the Arabian peninsula, where it bought spices and incense, which could be sold at a great profit. The visit at Solomon's court of the queen of Sabea ("Queen Sheba") points at close relations between Solomon and this south-Arabian country. Solomon's fleet, however, went further south also, to import gold, ivory, and other exotic articles from various countries on the east-African coast, such as Somaliland, and possibly even South Africa ("Ophir"). Even more lucrative was the trade in chariots and horses. Solomon bought the former in Egypt and the latter in Cilicia, both for the use of his own army of charioteers and for resale. The international trade was conducted as a state monopoly and brought much wealth into the royal coffers.

The vicinity of the Gulf of Aqaba is rich in various ores, and mining operations, especially copper mining, are known to have been conducted there thousands of years ago. Solomon, as we have seen, had ready access to the area. Whether he actually engaged in mining activities cannot be said with certainty, since the archeological evidence is inconclusive.

The income from Solomon's business enterprises did not suffice to cover all his expenditures. The king therefore established an elaborate system of taxation, based both on payments in kind and forced labor. Already under David the country was divided into 12 regions, with each region supplying the state with provisions and services one month during the year. Now Solomon developed this system more efficiently by placing a special official in charge of every region. A review of the geography of the tax regions reveals that they were cut out in a manner favorable to Solomon's home tribe of Judah, less favorable to the tribes in central and northern Israel, and very burdensome to the areas in which the remnants of the Canaanite population lived. Most Canaanites, as we have seen, underwent a process of amalgamation with the Israelites. Those who did not were strongly discriminated against during the period of the United Kingdom. Under Solomon they were singled out for forced labor and assigned a status not unlike that of the Hebrews in Egypt.

This system of taxation could not but evoke a deep dissatisfaction and opposition in the northern parts of the country, where most of the tribes and the remnants of the Canaanites lived. This opposition was joined by the prophetic circles who became disillusioned with Solomon due to his pro-pagan religious policies. The combined opposition ultimately turned into open rebellion led by a former high official, Jeroboam, the son of Nebat, of the tribe of Ephraim. Jeroboam was in charge of the forced-labor system in the northern part of the country, and we do not know why he became a leader of the rebellion. The rebels planned to dissolve the "covenant" which the central and northern tribes had concluded with David, and to establish an independent kingdom with Jeroboam as king. In this they were fully backed by the prophets, one of whom secretly promised Jeroboam the reign over the northern ten tribes. The armed rebellion, however, did not succeed, and Jeroboam fled to the now hostile Egypt.

We have seen that in spite of the problematic nature of Solomon's legitimacy as heir to the throne, he was accepted as king without any popular opposition. No doubt the people expected his reign to be a period of peace, prosperity, and justice. Solomon's fame as a man of superior wisdom and some of his judicial decrees show that among the people expectations ran high. His reign, however, turned out to be a period of decline. Fiscal oppression was widespread, the territory of the state diminished, and idolatry was openly promoted. The simplicity of Saul's and David's way of life was replaced by an elaborate and luxurious royal court, alien to old Israelitic tradition. The splendor of the palaces, and the newly created aristocracy drastically contrasted with the simple life of the masses. Unlike his older brothers, Solomon grew up at a time when the travails of the wars were over. The people were to him not comrades in arms, basically equal in their rights to the king whom they had chosen from among themselves, but subjects who could be governed and taxed without regard for their feelings. Dissatisfaction thus kept on growing and undermining the very foundations of the United Kingdom and ultimately led to its dissolution.

Section III

THE KINGDOMS OF JUDAH AND ISRAEL

Chapter 1

The Early History of Judah and Israel

King Solomon died some time between 930 and 920 B.C.E., and was succeeded by his son Rehoboam. It seems that Rehoboam had no difficulty in being accepted in Judah. However, when he went to Shechem, the unofficial capital of the North, to be crowned as king of Israel, he was confronted with a determined demand to ease the burden of taxation imposed by his father. Jeroboam, who had lived as a fugitive in Egypt, was now called back by the elders of the North to head the delegation which was to negotiate with Rehoboam. The choice of a man who had ambitions to become king himself precluded the possibility of an agreement. In addition, Rehoboam was advised by a group of his younger officials not to make any concessions, and the United Kingdom dissolved with a rapidity that certainly surprised Rehoboam and the country as a whole.

The events in Shechem were followed by Jeroboam's formal election as king over Israel. Thus, two separate states, Judah and Israel, the latter also known as Ephraim, replaced the relatively short-lived United Kingdom. While it is not possible to trace the exact boundaries between the two states, it can be said that by and large Rehoboam retained the tribe of Judah and the tribe of Benjamin, where the capital city of Jerusalem was located, and Jeroboam reigned over the rest of the country. Jeroboam's choice of Shechem as his capital was natural. Not only was the city located in the territory of his own home tribe Ephraim, but it also had major historical significance as Joshua's residence. Somewhat later Tirzah, northeast of Shechem, also began to be used as a royal residence, and became under King Baasa the main capital.

While politically the northern tribes were ready to sever their relationship with David's dynasty, many were reluctant to give up their ties to Jerusalem as the seat of the Temple. To counteract these tendencies, Jeroboam built two new temples, one in Dan, in the northernmost corner of the country, and one in Beth El, quite close to the southern border. Both places had obvious geographic advantages, and had in addition an old cultic past. The Temple of Beth El had the special status of a royal sanctuary, and outlived the state of Israel by 100 years, until it was demolished by King Josiah of Judah.

The division of the kingdom had far-reaching political consequences. The fairly strong United Kingdom changed into two weak states of minor political and military significance. Their influence on the east Mediterranean political arena was henceforth felt only sporadically, and often they were not even able to retain their independence, let alone to control their vassals. The two states were further weakened by the recurrent warfare between them which lasted over half a century. At the same time Egypt and Aram (Syria) grew more aggressive, and became a real menace to both states.

The two Israelitic states were at war because each wished to annex the other. That this did not happen and that the situation remained a stalemate, was due to basic differences in the structure of both countries at the time of the division. While Israel was larger, wealthier in resources, and more populous, Judah had a more stable governmental structure, which made it possible for the Davidic dynasty to rule uninterruptedly up to the conquest of Jerusalem by the Babylonians in 586 B.C.E. Israel, on the other hand, kept changing its dynasties, and even had a line of individual usurper kings shortly before its fall. Also, Israel's population contained many Canaanite elements, while in Judah the population was purely Israelitic. All this made Judah a more tightly knit state, and it could resist Israel's attempts to overrun it.

The hostility between the two kingdoms made them vulnerable to attacks from the neighboring states. Aram kept on attacking the northern and Transjordanian regions of Israel and even succeeded in occupying some of them on a permanent basis. Even more devastating was an invasion of King Sheshonk I of Egypt about the year 918. Although this invasion did not result in a permanent occupation, it brought much misery when it swept over all of Judah, parts of Israel, and even over the Israelitic areas in Transjordan.

The dynasty established by Jeroboam ruled little more than two decades. It was overthrown by Baasa, whose dynasty was equally short-lived. Most of this time Judah was ruled by King Asa, who was either Rehoboam's son, or grandson. Only after Asa's death and the ascendance of a third dynasty in Israel, that of Omri, was peace restored between the two Israelitic peoples, bringing for both of them somewhat better times.

Chapter 2

Israel under the House of Omri

After the overthrow of the Baasa dynasty, a fight for the throne developed among various contenders. Omri ultimately emerged as the winner, and established the third dynasty in Israel some time between 882 and 876 B.C.E. During the first few years of his reign he resided in Tirzah, capital of the Baasa dynasty. This city, located fairly close to the Jordan valley, seems later to have become inconvenient as a capital due to Aramean pressure on the nearby region of Gilead. Omri therefore built a new capital, Samaria, also in central Israel, but much closer to the sea coast.

The Omri dynasty developed a new, more active foreign policy than the preceding two dynasties. Its cornerstone was peace and friendship with the sister state of Judah, and the renewal of the alliance with Phoenicia, which seems to have been terminated by neglect after Solomon's death. In the Solomonic manner, both alliances were cemented by marriages. Omri's son king Ahab married the Phoenician princess Jezebel, and Athaliah, who was either Ahab's daughter or sister, was given as wife to the crown prince of Judah. The new policy reintroduced Israel into the wider political arena of the Near East. This is fully demonstrated by the fact that the Assyrians began to call Israel "House of Omri," and the name prevailed even as late as 100 years after the fall of the Omri dynasty.

The immediate result of the new policy was the reacquisition of Moab, which was lost after the dissolution of the United Kingdom. Now it was even possible to settle a certain number of Israelites in Moabite territory. The alliances, however, were not able to check the Aramean pressure upon Israel, even though Judah gave it active military assistance. All through the reign of Omri and during the first years of his son Ahab, Aram had the upper hand in the conflict. About the year 853 B.C.E. a change in the situation took place and Ahab was able to defeat Aram's army and to take its king into captivity.

But then the unexpected happened. Ahab released his captive and concluded with him a treaty of mutual defense. This dramatic reversal in the relations between Israel and Aram was caused by information received by Ahab that the Assyrian army was marching westward. It was an avowed perpetual goal of Assyria's foreign policy to create an empire which would stretch from her home base on the rivers Tigris and Euphrates (present-day Iraq) to the shores of the "Great Sea," that is, the Mediterranean. This goal could be achieved by subduing Aram, Phoenicia, and Israel. Whenever Assyria had inner troubles, or was menaced by her eastern or northern neighbors, the Mediterranean states felt secure and could fight among themselves for the control of the region. But in times when Assyria had inner tranquility and peace on her borders, her westward drive was immediately renewed.

Now, in 853 B.C.E., an Assyrian army was again moving westward, and the perpetual foes Aram and Israel had to unite with their neighbors to face the Assyrians. A great battle indeed took place near the city of Karkara in Syria. This battle, in which Ahab participated with a respectable contingent of chariots, was not decisive. As a result, Assyria again withdrew temporarily, and the war between Israel and Aram resumed.

Under king Ahab, who ruled about 20 years (probably between 871 and 852 B.C.E.), great religious and social tensions developed in the country. His Phoenician wife Jezebel was a forceful personality who interfered in all matters of government and society. She was not satisfied with merely having the freedom to continue to practice her pagan religion in her new home. Her desire was to make her Phoenician cult the official religion of Israel. Coming from an absolutist monarchy, she had, in addition, no understanding of the principles and manifestations of the Israelitic covenantal law, which gave to the average Israelite broad guarantees for the protection of his life and property. To her it meant nothing to frame an innocent man, and accuse him of blaspheming God and cursing the king, in order to bring about his execution and to confiscate his property. Her behavior and Ahab's acquiescence, however, evoked unrest and anger among the people.

Despite the erection of the temples in Dan and Beth El, the religion of YHWH continued to have many adherents in Samaria. These circles strongly resented the presence of the priests of the Phoenician Baal in the country and the disregard for the old Israelitic covenantal law. When Jezebel's abuses became flagrant, the anger of the people reached its peak. It was then that the prophet Elijah appeared before the king and fearlessly threw into his face the accusation: "Hast thou killed, and also taken possession?" (I Kings 21:19).

When the war with Aram became more and more tedious and seemed to have no end, the dissatisfaction in the country became so deep that the time seemed ripe for a decisive change. The task of bringing about this change was undertaken by the prophet Elisha, Elijah's pupil and successor, who, like Samuel long before him, was a prophet of action, rather than a preacher. He was convinced that the rule of the Omri dynasty should be terminated, and therefore designated for king a man who, he believed, would do away with the Phoenician idolatry and the social injustice accompanying it.

Chapter 3

From Jehu's Revolt to the Fall of Israel

Shortly after the battle of Karkara, Ahab was killed in an encounter with the Arameans and was succeeded by two of his sons, first Ahaziah and then Jehoram. All the time the war dragged on with little success for Israel, and it seems that the commanders of the army blamed king Jehoram for the recurring defeats. Elisha, who had a penetrating understanding of the political and military situation of the country, no doubt knew of the mood prevalent in the army. In 842 B.C.E., obviously being sure of the army's cooperation, he sent one of the "sons of the prophets" to the headquarters with instructions to anoint as king a high officer by the name of Jehu. As soon as the officer corps learned of the event, it acclaimed Jehu as king.

This was followed by an expedition during which Jehu personally assassinated King Jehoram of Israel, while other officers killed his relative, King Ahaziah of Judah, who was visiting with him. The dowager queen Jezebel was killed soon afterward, and all the princes of the Omri family were murdered in a brutal massacre. The astonishing ease with which the extermination of the Omri dynasty was carried out indicates that by then it no longer had the backing of the country, and that Jehu was a welcome replacement for Jehoram.

Prophetic designation, which had been extended to Jehu in secret, was now openly manifested when a man by the name of Jehonadab, the son of Rechab, joined Jehu in his chariot on his way to Samaria. Jehonadab belonged to a unique family which refused to reconcile itself with the sedentary and urban way of life and continued to live a "nomadic" life by dwelling in tents rather than in houses, and by abstaining from tilling the soil and drinking wine. The family thus manifested the viability of the "desert ideal" so dear to the prophets. Jehonadab's approval of Jehu was thus tantamount to public prophetic recognition.

Jehu did not fulfill the expectations of the circles which promoted him to the throne. He conducted the war against Aram with no greater success than King Jehoram whom he had assassinated. In fact, the situation became even worse due to the loss of Israel's two staunch allies, Judah and Phoenicia. A man who had slaughtered Jezebel's family could not expect assistance, either from Phoenicia, or from Judah, where the Omrid queen Athaliah had taken power by force. Consequently, Jehu lost to Aram a great part of his land, and was compelled to become its vassal.

Nor did Jehu fulfill the hopes of the prophetic circles. True, he banned the worship of the Phoenician gods and put to death their priests, thus saving the nation from possible assimilation with the Phoenicians. But he did not lead the country in a full return to the religion of YHWH. He "followed the sins" introduced by Jeroboam, probably for the same purpose of keeping the people of Israel from loyalty to the Temple in Jerusalem. Nonetheless, the dynasty which he established became the most stable and lasting of all dynasties in Israel.

Israel's weakness continued through the reign of Jehu's son, Jehoahaz, who died about the year 800 B.C.E. But then the tide began to turn in Israel's favor. Assyria, although not yet in her full strength, became enough of a menace to Aram to weaken the latter's pressure upon Israel. Under these circumstances Israel's power began to recover during the reign of King Jehoash (800–784), and under his son Jeroboam II (784–748) it experienced a sort of golden age. The new strength of Israel became evident when Jehoash was challenged to war by King Amaziah of Judah. He defeated him easily and captured his capital Jerusalem. Significantly, the reality of two separate Israelitic states had now become so fully accepted, that Jehoash did not use the opportunity for reuniting them.

Under Jeroboam II, Israel had recovered not only its own full territory, but also the vassal states Ammon and Moab. She again controlled the main caravan routes, and, as in David's time, great wealth was streaming into the country from custom revenues. The development of cities, begun on a large scale under Ahab, now reached its peak. An urban population and an overgrown aristocracy and officialdom pursued a luxurious way of life, far removed from the old Israelitic simplicity and from the desert ideals of the prophets and Rechabites. But as the standard of living of the aristocracy was rising, the lot of the peasantry, the bulk of the population, was getting worse. There is a likelihood that

Jeroboam employed a fiscal system not unlike that of Solomon, with all the suffering that it brought to the common people. It was then that the first "literary" prophets appeared and cried out loudly against the oppression of the poor and the grave moral decay which came with it.

About two years after Jeroboam II died, Tiglath Pileser III (746–728 B.C.E.), often called the true founder of the Assyrian empire, ascended the throne. With him the impact of Assyria on the eastern Mediterranean states became decisive and fatal. The old goal of the Assyrian kings to occupy these states on a permanent basis in order to get hold of their timber and mineral resources, as well as their outlet to the sea, began to be pursued again in an energetic and brutal manner. By organizing a professional officers corps and by building a network of roads, the Assyrians gained a major strategic advantage over their prospective victims. Tiglath Pileser III also introduced the practice of mass deportations of the subjugated peoples in order to prevent possible uprisings. It was this brutal practice which caused the prophets to compare Assyria to the beast which carries away its victim to consume it in another place.

The unmistakable threat which was hanging over the Near Eastern nations evoked a state of anarchy in Israel. Much in the way that Solomon's empire collapsed after his death with astonishing rapidity, the magnificent governmental and economic structure erected in Israel by Jehoash and Jeroboam II lay in ruins as soon as Jeroboam was dead. His son and successor Zechariah was assassinated after a reign of only a few months. Five usurper-kings now followed each other during the last 25 years of Israel's existence. First to be annexed by Assyria were the Gilead and parts of Galilee. Their inhabitants were the first Israelites to be forcibly deported to Assyria. A last effort to oppose Assyria was made by Aram and Israel, accompanied by an attempt to force Judah into the anti-Assyrian coalition by deposing its king Ahaz and replacing him with another man, possibly an Aramean. This coalition, too, failed, and soon all Aram with Damascus were under firm Assyrian control.

Israel still existed another ten years, but its territory and strength kept on diminishing. Ultimately, in 722 or 721 B.C.E., the capital city of Samaria was captured by the Assyrian forces and

Israel disappeared from the map of the nations after an existence of 200 years. Additional thousands of Israelites were deported to Assyria bringing the total of the exiles to possibly over 50,000. The bulk of the population, however, remained in the country, and Israelites continued to live in various cities, including Samaria. Nonetheless, the deportation gave rise in the Middle Ages to the legend of the Ten Lost Tribes, dwelling in a hidden place and destined to reveal themselves at the time of the coming of the Messiah. In replacement of the deported Israelites, the Assyrians settled in Israel thousands of people from other regions of their sprawling empire. It was this infusion of non-Israelites into the already mixed Israelitic-Canaanite population that gave rise to a new people, the Samaritans.

Chapter 4

Judah under the House of David

The First Two Hundred Years

After one of the longest reigns in Judah's history, King Asa died about 870 B.C.E., and was succeeded by his son Jehoshaphat. Jehoshaphat was one of the wisest and most devoted kings on Judah's throne. It was his initiative, probably, which led to the reconciliation with Israel. The marriage of his son Jehoram with Athaliah, Ahab's sister or daughter, cemented the new alliance. Significantly, although decisively devoted to the religion of YHWH, Jehoshaphat was not deterred by Ahab's and Jezebel's open promotion of idolatry from a close alliance with them. One even gets the impression that Judah manifested more interest in the alliance than Israel, although the latter was its main beneficiary.

Jehoshaphat's rule was also beneficial in Judah's domestic affairs. He introduced a far-reaching reform of the judicial system. He appointed royal judges in a number of key cities to function alongside the local elders, who traditionally performed judicial duties. In addition, he established in Jerusalem a sort of court of appeals. The reforms helped to speed up the judicial process, and to make it independent of local influences, and probably earned him the name Jehoshaphat, which alludes to judicial activities. When, as a result of the reconciliation with Israel, he could use his forces to strengthen Judah's hold over Edom, he made a serious attempt to renew the country's maritime trade. His plans did not succeed however, since the fleet which he built in the Gulf of Aqaba was destroyed by the elements.

The marriage of his son Jehoram to Athaliah may have seemed to Jehoshaphat a step destined to be advantageous to the country. Ultimately, however, it brought about a great misfortune to his family. When the dowager Athaliah learned of Jehu's, coup d'etat and the assassination of her son king Ahaziah, she usurped the throne in Jerusalem for herself, attempting simultaneously to assassinate all members of the royal family and to impose the religion of Baal upon Judah. Only Ahaziah's one-year-old son Joash escaped death when an aunt, the high priest's wife, hid him in the Temple. Athaliah ruled Judah with an iron hand for a number of years. When Joash became seven years old, the high priest thought the time ripe to present him to the country. Athaliah was then overthrown with the help of the *am haaretz,* " the people of the land," probably a parliamentary institution, or assembly of the landed gentry.

The reigns of King Joash (837–800 B.C.E.) and his son King Amaziah (800–783 B.C.E.) turned out to be a stormy period in Judah's history. The conduct of both these kings evidently evoked dissatisfaction and led to their assassination by groups of rebels. Amazia did have to his credit the occupation of Sela, thus solidifying Judah's hold over Edom. But his adventure against King Jehoash of Israel brought about, as we have seen, the fall of Jerusalem and a substantial loss of the wealth of the country, paid to Israel as tribute. What exactly was behind the conspiracies that led to the assassination of these two kings, we do not know. But it is significant that the assassinations did not lead to the replacement of the Davidic dynasty by another. Unlike Israel, where each assassination of a king led to the emergence of a new dynasty, in Judah, David's house was so deeply entrenched that no one could overthrow it.

Amaziah's son Azariah, also called Uzziah (783–742 B.C.E.), was one of the good kings produced by the Davidic dynasty. He cared with equal zeal for the military strengthening of the country and the betterment of the life of the people. He reorganized the army, developed new weapons, and fortified the walls of Jerusalem. He strengthened Judah's position in Edom by building a number of fortresses in the southern desert. He demonstrated an interest in farming and dug many wells which could be used for irrigating farmland.

Azariah ruled during the period preceding the new aggressive policies of Assyria. Under his skillful and benevolent rule, Judah thus experienced, like Israel under Jeroboam II, a period of political tranquility and economic prosperity. It was therefore a grave blow to the country when the valiant king, at the height of his success, was stricken with leprosy, and thus compelled to live in isolation for the rest of his life. His son Jotham ruled first as regent, and after the father's death as king. Neither he nor his son and successor Ahaz (735–715 B.C.E.) possessed Azariah's wisdom and energy, and their reigns were a lackluster period in Judah's history. At the time when the leper king died, Tiglath Pileser III had already ascended Assyria's throne and the dark shadow of the robber nation began to cover the Kingdom of Judah also.

Under the Shadow of Assyria and Babylonia

Almost from the beginning of his reign Ahaz realized, probably more than other contemporary kings in the Near East, that Assyria's might was decisive. He therefore willingly accepted the status of a vassal, and paid tribute to Assyria at a time when Aram and Israel still attempted to fight for their independence. His basically timid character thus helped to save Judah from an Assyrian onslaught that could have resulted only in complete disaster.

Ahaz' son Hezekiah (715–687 B.C.E.) was quite different from his father. He was courageous and ready to risk war even against Assyria in order to secure his country's independence. To be sure, his times were more favorable for an anti-Assyrian policy. Rebellion was raging in various parts of the Assyrian empire, and Egypt, the only other major power in the region, was undergoing a process of resurgence of its military strength. At the beginning, Hezekiah, one of the greatest personalities in the Davidic dynasty, undertook various actions designed to strengthen the country from within. He introduced various economic reforms, and built a subterranean acquaduct to solve Jerusalem's perennial problem of water shortages. He also undertook to record Judah's literature, probably to save it from oblivion.

Hezekiah's attempt to free his country from the Assyrian yoke seems to have been well prepared. He concluded alliances with the Babylonians and the Egyptians, both potential powerful opponents of Assyrian expansion. Nonetheless, when in 705 B.C.E., against the advice of the prophet Isaiah, he openly rebelled against the Assyrians together with other small nations in the region, he lost. He could consider himself very lucky when the Assyrians agreed to leave him on Judah's throne in return for a heavy tribute and the delivery of a number of important hostages. And yet late in his reign he again rebelled against the Assyrians. King Sennacherib then sent his army to besiege Jerusalem. The situation seemed hopeless, but unexpectedly the Assyrians one day lifted the siege. An epidemic, possibly the bubonic plague, as well as rumors of unrest in Assyria, caused the sudden retreat. An old Greek tradition has it that it was an invasion of field mice which compelled the Assyrians to withdraw.

The futility of opposing Assyria at the time her might reached its peak became fully apparent during the long reign of Hezekiah's son Manasseh (687–642 B.C.E.). Not only did he never make any attempt to free himself and the country from Assyrian yoke, but he handed over Judah into Assyrian hands to a degree no king ever did before or after. His willingness to serve the Assyrians was accompanied by a massive introduction of Assyrian priests into the country and a decisive promotion of Assyrian idolatry in Judah. So great was Manasseh's betrayal of the religion of YHWH that talmudic tradition excluded him from participation in the world to come, together with the two great sinners on Israel's throne, Jeroboam, the son of Nebat, and Ahab. The possibility should, however, not be overlooked that Manasseh's total submission to, and cooperation with, Assyria was the only way in which he could save his nation from total destruction or deportation.

It was not before Manasseh's grandson Josiah (640–609 B.C.E.) ascended the throne that a possibility presented itself for Judah to become free again. There was not even a need to rebel against Assyria. That empire simply began to disintegrate under the blows given to it by a coalition of Media and Babylonia. The pressure upon Assyria's northern borders by the Scythians, a people which at that time came from the Caucasus, further weakened the former giant. Josiah cleverly used the new situation, not only to throw off the Assyrian yoke, but even to annex parts of the former state of Israel, including the Gilead. Had Josiah lived longer, he probably would have restored the United Kingdom. Of utmost importance was the king's energetic and thoroughgoing removal of all vestiges of idolatry and of the "high places," after a holy book, "the book of the Torah," hitherto unknown to him was found in the Temple. Following this, the covenant with YHWH was renewed and the law of the Torah was formally proclaimed the law of the land.

After Nineveh, the capital of Assyria, fell in 612 B.C.E., Babylonia began to emerge as the new power in the Middle East. This situation brought about a reversal of the alliances, and Egypt, hitherto Assyria's mortal enemy, was now ready to come to her rescue. It was with this in mind that King Necho II of Egypt led his forces in 609 B.C.E. up the Judaean coast, on the way to Mesopotamia. Josiah probably was convinced that an Egyptian victory over the Babylonians would leave Judah at the mercy of Egypt. He therefore decided to make an attempt to stop the Egyptians near Megiddo, where so many important battles had taken place in the past. How Josiah could hope to defeat the army of a major power like Egypt is hard to understand. And, indeed, Josiah was mortally wounded at Megiddo in an encounter the nature of which is quite obscure.

Josiah's death placed Judah for all practical purposes under Egyptian control. But, when a few years later Necho was decisively defeated by Babylonia's crown prince Nebuchadnezzar in the great battle of Carchemish, Judah stood before the agonizing decision of whether to remain in Egypt's corner, or submit to

Babylonia. This was Judah's burning political problem throughout the following two decades. As never before, the country was sharply divided into a pro-Egyptian and a pro-Babylonian party.

Under these circumstances two of Josiah's sons and a grandson, Jehoiachin, followed each other on the throne. Finally, in 598 B.C.E. the forces of King Nebuchadnezzar II (605–562 B.C.E.) appeared at the gates of Jerusalem, thus demonstrating that it was Babylonia, and not Egypt, upon which Judah's destiny would henceforth depend. The gates of the city were therefore opened, and young King Jehoiachin surrendered, to be deported to Babylonia. Together with him many government officials, military commanders, and skilled workers also were deported in order to strip the country of the possibility of rebelling. Josiah's third son, Mattaniah was now put on the throne, after he pledged loyalty to Nebuchadnezzar.

Had the new king, who upon his elevation to the throne was renamed Zedekiah, been a man of steadfast character, Judah probably could have lived peacefully under a fairly light Babylonian yoke. But indecision was the main trait in Zedekiah's character, and the years of his rule thus turned into a period of continuous oscillation between a pro-Egyptian and a pro-Babylonian policy. One of the main advocates of a policy of loyalty to Babylonia was the prophet Jeremiah, then in the prime of his life and preaching ministry. More than anybody else Jeremiah appreciated Babylonia's decisive position in the region and the basically benevolent nature of her sovereignty over Judah. Whenever Jeremiah had the king's ear, the latter was easily convinced to remain loyal to Nebuchadnezzar. But, as soon as pro-Egyptian officials and patriots from the nobility succeeded in removing the king from Jeremiah's influence, they were able equally easily to sway him to an anti-Babylonian policy.

Ultimately, the pro-Egyptian officials prevailed, and Zedekiah discontinued paying the annual tribute, which was tantamount to open rebellion. A Babylonian force then reappeared at the walls of Jerusalem early in 587 B.C.E. The hoped-for Egyptian intervention either did not materialize or was ineffective, and in the mid-summer of 586 B.C.E. Jerusalem was captured by the Babylonians. About one month later, on the 9th of Ab, the

Babylonians burned the city, including the Temple which had served as a sanctuary for over 350 years. Zedekiah was taken into captivity while attempting to flee. Nebuchadnezzar's revenge for Zedekiah's breach of loyalty was cruel. After his sons were slain before his eyes, Zedekiah was blinded and deported to Babylonia, to be jailed for the rest of his life. Most of Judah's population was deported to Babylonia, and only the poor were permitted to remain in the devastated country. Of the about 250,000 people who had lived in Judah, now probably less than a half remained in the country.

Despite their experience with Zedekiah, the Babylonians still believed in the possibility of the existence of a state or province of Judah governed by Judaeans and loyal to them. They knew of the existence of the pro-Babylonian party and of Jeremiah's insistence on loyalty to them. In fact, while Jerusalem was besieged, many people, dissatisfied with the king's policies, left the city to join the Babylonians.

It was all of this which prompted the Babylonians now to appoint as governor of the country Gedaliah, the son of Ahikam, a high official in Zedekiah's government and a member of an aristocratic family. Jeremiah, whom the Babylonians gave the choice of staying in Judah or going to Babylonia, remained in the country with the purpose of aiding Gedaliah in the effort of rebuilding the land. Gedaliah chose Mizpah, to the north of Jerusalem, as his residence. At the news of his appointment, refugees who had fled to neighboring countries began to return. Remnants of the army with their commanders who were hiding in the countryside to escape capture by the Babylonians, now came to Mizpah, thus creating what in effect was a nucleus of a new Judaean army. An altar, and possibly some sort of edifice called "House of the Lord," was erected either in Mizpah or in Jerusalem, at which a limited sacrificial service was practiced. The peasants who remained in the country began to till the soil and the land seemed to be returning to normalcy.

All this went on for two to three years. Gedaliah's success was apparent, and it was perhaps possible to gain the impression that under him a new Judaean dynasty was emerging. It was probably this that prompted a member of the royal family, Ishmael, the son of Nethaniah, who found refuge in nearby Ammon, to return and assassinate Gedaliah. Even then Jeremiah still believed that the Babylonians would permit Judah to continue to govern itself. He was, however, unable to convince the commanders of Gedaliah's small army to stay in the country. The commanders decided to leave for Egypt and took the prophet along against his will. Thus, "the last burning coal" of Judah's statehood was extinguished. It would be about 40 years before a new Judaean state came into being.

At the time the Judaean state fell, an Israelitic diaspora had come into being, and a sizable number of Israelites now lived permanently in other countries. The causes for this emigration were mostly economic, but in part also political. The extensive business enterprises which Solomon developed in cooperation with Phoenicia and Egypt must have resulted in the settlement of some Israelites in both these countries. Jeroboam's flight to Egypt after the collapse of his rebellion against Solomon, and a few other similar cases recorded in the biblical writings, clearly indicate that emigration for political reasons was not uncommon in Judah and Israel. When the defeated King Ben-Hadad of Aram said to Ahab "thou shalt make streets for thee in Damascus" (I Kings 20:34), he probably conceded to the king of Israel the right of establishing in Aram's capital a colony of Israelites. All this brought about the establishment of a diaspora of minor proportions. In the ninth and eighth centuries B.C.E., when social oppression increased and a landless proletariat came into being, larger numbers of people began to emigrate.

The forced deportations of Israelites and Judaeans when these two states fell brought enormous masses of them to foreign lands. Many others fled in various directions to avoid capture by the Assyrians or Babylonians. One may therefore venture to say that about the year 584 B.C.E., when Gedaliah was assassinated, a majority of the Israelitic people lived in the diaspora. Although a part of the exiles afterwards returned to Judaea, a sizable number of them, and possibly the majority, remained permanently in the diaspora. The diaspora thus became an accomplished fact and a permanent reality in the history of the Jewish people.

Chapter 5

Religious Life in the Period of the First Commonwealth

Temple, Provincial Shrines, and Idolatry

A review of the religious life of the Israelites from Saul's elevation to the throne to the destruction of Jerusalem in 586 B.C.E. reveals a picture of confusion coupled with many aberrations. On the one hand, the religion of YHWH was professed and practiced throughout the period to a greater or lesser degree. In times when it seemed rejected and abandoned, its staunchest representatives and defenders, the prophets, held its ideals alive and vibrant. In addition, there is evidence in the Bible that many laws and customs later recorded in the *Halakhah,* the Jewish oral law, were known and operative in this period. Furthermore, it seems that some of the prophets conducted prayer gatherings, and that a certain form of the *amidah* (a chief part of the Jewish liturgy) was known in those times. On the other hand, customs and practices not endorsed by the representatives of the YHWH religion, the priests and the prophets, continuously attracted many of the people. Furthermore, from time to time the gates of the country were widely opened to the most drastic forms of idolatry. Not only were foreign wives in the royal courts permitted to worship their idols, but even in Saul's court, which by all indications was faithful to YHWH, the king's daughter Michal, David's wife, kept *teraphim,* a sort of housegods. In general, however, though the people often deviated from the ways of God, they often also solemnly returned to Him in a dramatic way.

The Temple in Jerusalem was the dominant center of religious life. Even though the people continued for centuries to sacrifice to YHWH at provincial shrines, called "high places," the centrality of the Temple was never questioned in Judah. In time, the sacrificial service outside of Jerusalem began to be regarded as sinful, and kings described by biblical writers as having "walked in the ways of God," were again and again castigated for having tolerated it. The uniqueness of the Temple was further stressed by the general recognition that only the priesthood descended from Aaron was legitimately qualified to perform the service there.

Against the background of the emerging centrality of the Temple in Jerusalem, King Jeroboam I of Israel set up rival temples in Dan and Beth El. In addition, he cut off Israel's people from Judah's religious calendar by decreeing that the feast of Tabernacles should be celebrated a month later than heretofore. The reasons for his actions were not religious, but political. He was apprehensive lest continuous ties to the Jerusalem Temple would awaken among the people of his state feelings of loyalty to the Davidic dynasty reigning in Jerusalem. In Jeroboam's temples golden calves were placed, reminiscent of the calf made during the sojourn in the desert.

A number of people in the state of Israel evidently considered the temples in Dan and Beth El illegitimate or even idolatrous, and emigrated to Judah to remain loyal to the Temple in Jerusalem. The biblical writers unanimously condemned the two temples as places of idolatry, and the sages of the Talmud proclaimed Jeroboam, their builder, unworthy of living in the world to come.

Modern scholars are not so sure that Jeroboam wanted to introduce idolatry. They do not consider the calves as deities, but rather pedestals which served, like the *cherubim* in the Jerusalem Temple, as God's "throne." The religion of YHWH, they argue, was practiced in the temples at Dan and Beth El, although in a somewhat diluted form. Had Jeroboam's religion been a total deviation from the way of YHWH, it would probably have encountered stiff opposition among the population. Furthermore, even King Jehu who was elevated to the throne for the avowed purpose of eliminating idolatry from Israel, left the two temples intact. Curiously, the use of names which included two or three letters of the ineffable Name of God were quite common in the kingdom of Israel, and appeared even in Ahab's immediate family.

Manifestations of exclusive adherence to YHWH were also common in the state of Israel. It seems that except for the period of Jezebel's pagan innovations, these "fearers of the Lord" were not persecuted. "Sons of the prophets" and prophets of YHWH could be found in large numbers, and presumably could move around in the country, preaching freely. When King Hezekiah undertook to revive the celebration of Passover, he distinctly invited the people of *all Israel,* from Beer-Sheba to Dan, to participate in the celebration (II Chronicles 30:1–5). Obviously, he did not regard the Israelites of the North as pagans.

There were, however, times when the worship of foreign gods was officially imposed upon both countries, Israel and Judah. In Israel it happened in the times of Ahab, whose wife Jezebel had a missionary zeal for the Phoenician deities Baal, Melqart, and Asherah. This period of idolatry, grave as it was in Israel's religious history, was short-lived. But even when the period of official idolatry came to an end, some of its vestiges remained. Even though Jehu had wiped out Baalism from the country, his dynasty seems to have tolerated the Asherah, Baal's goddess-mate.

Judah experienced two periods of official idolatry. The first was firmly introduced by Athaliah after traces of Baalism had appeared earlier under Jehoram. She proclaimed Baalism the official religion and built a "house of Baal," so named in imitation of the Temple, called "House of the Lord." However, she seems to have abstained from banning the religion of YHWH. The High Priest Jehoiada remained in control of the Temple, and was able to rid the country of both Athaliah and Baalism fairly easily after only a few years.

Much more serious was the period of idolatry introduced by Manasseh. It lasted over 40 years, during which the Temple was a place of worship of the Assyrian gods. Only outside of Jerusalem were sacrificial services to YHWH possibly performed on "high places." The "high places," to be sure, were abolished by Manasseh's father, Hezekiah. They were restored, we may assume, in Mannasseh's reign by Judaeans who desired to sacrifice to YHWH. The gravity of the situation was further strengthened by the fact that the official adherence to the Assyrian religion was a symbol of Judah's loyalty to Assyria. Under these circumstances, the Assyrian idolatry could be removed only when Assyria began to weaken and her grip over Judah to lessen. One could even speculate that Manasseh, the son of the truly pious King Hezekiah, was not a sincere devotee of the Assyrian gods, but rather a victim of a tragic political situation.

With the weakening of Assyria, Judah could free herself both from Assyrian domination and the Assyrian gods. When Manasseh's grandson Josiah ascended the throne in 639 B.C.E., the country was still deeply engulfed in all forms of idolatry which entrenched itself during Manasseh's long reign. But when the boy king grew up to manhood, he set out to give a decisive blow to the idolatrous establishment and to restore the Israelitic religion to a position of full domination. To be sure, opposition to idolatry and idols began to develop almost 100 years earlier under Josiah's great-grandfather Hezekiah. The teachings of the prophets about a God who prefers loving kindness to sacrifices began to create among the people a new understanding of the relationship between man and God. Above all, the deep contrasts between the God of Israel and the idols of other nations became apparent with ever greater clarity. It is thus understandable that the *nehushtan*, the brazen serpent, to which "the children of Israel offered," was removed from the Temple by Hezekiah, even though Moses himself had made it.

Hezekiah, however, did not stop at this point. He set out to demolish the "high places" all over the country, although the sacrificial service performed there was mostly dedicated to the God of Israel. Possibly he discovered at the "high places" paganizing tendencies. But there is also the possibility that Hezekiah knew the "Book of the Covenant" found in the Temple 100 years later. It is in this book that instructions appear to concentrate all sacrificial service exclusively in the Temple.

Why the "high places" were again in existence at a later time, we do not know with certainty. Possibly, as mentioned above, they were erected in Manasseh's times by people who remained faithful to YHWH and were reluctant to frequent the Temple in Jerusalem because of the hold the Assyrian priests had over it. Be this as it may, the final destruction of the "high places" and the definitive concentration of the sacrificial service in the Jerusalem Temple was accomplished under King Josiah. This was coupled with the most thorough removal of idolatry, its altars, statues, and other paraphernalia, ever undertaken by a Judaean king. Josiah was moved to his actions by a two-fold reason. He desired to do away with the Assyrian idolatry, because it was a symbol of Assyrian domination over Judah, but he was motivated more by the discovery in the Temple in 623 B.C.E. of a holy book unknown to him. The book was called "the Book of the Law" or "the Book of the Covenant." Modern scholars assume that it was the book of Deuteronomy and that it was brought to Jerusalem from Samaria at the time of the latter's fall about 100 years earlier.

After reading the book, the king went out with his soldiers and destroyed and defiled every structure and every object connected with idolatry. He also destroyed the temple built by Jeroboam in Beth El, although it is possible that the golden calves were removed from it more than 100 years earlier. The "high places" met with a similar fate. All priests of the foreign gods present in the country were put to death. After concluding the act of destruction, Josiah returned to Jerusalem and solemnly proclaimed the renewal of the covenant between the people and God.

Josiah's action, sometimes called the Josian puritanical reform, seems to have come at a time when the people were ready for a basic change in their religious attitudes. The interest in the foreign gods was waning and idolatry never again returned to Judah. It is also possible that as a result of the abolition of the provincial shrines the synagogue came into being. With the establishment of cultic centralism and with no local altars in the towns and villages, other institutions had to be created in a framework in which the Judaean could find a contact between himself and his God. The teachings of the prophets also encouraged the process. Their perpetual admonitions not to rely solely on sacrifices, but to live a just and moral life, greatly helped in the transition to the personal religious experience offered by the synagogue.

The Prophets

A unique phenomenon in the realm of Israelitic religion was prophecy. Its representatives had no official status of the kind enjoyed by the priesthood. It had nevertheless immeasurable influence not only on religion proper, but also on society and on the course of political events. It was indeed an establishment in itself, whose members derived their authority not from a great ancestor as was the case with the priesthood, but from God Himself.

The prophet was a "man of God," and as such accompanied the people of Israel from its very inception. Biblical tradition has it that the Patriarchs experienced a direct contact with God, and thus were prophets. From then on the prophet underwent many metamorphoses. Sometimes he was only a "seer" and was expected to help people in their daily life by revealing things unknown to them. At other times prophets, like Samuel and Elisha, were leaders active in the political life of the country. They finally became great preachers, destined, often against their will, to reveal to the people the word of God and the ultimate fate of the nation. But whether they were seers or preachers, they were men believed to have been chosen by God for a close relationship with Him that was denied to ordinary mortals. With all the influence prophets of action like Samuel and Elisha had, it was the preacher prophet, often called classical prophet, or literary prophet, whose life and ministry made of prophecy a potent force in contemporary society and to all mankind thereafter.

Prophecy could not be inherited nor could one be trained for it. True, the bands of "sons of the prophets" were groups of mostly young people who aspired to become prophets. But it was ultimately an act of special grace by which a prophet was chosen for his ministry. Once chosen, the prophet clearly knew his task. Whether he was a prophet of action, or the "literary" prophet, who delivered his oracles in polished lofty verses, his task was to guard the Israelitic people from straying away from "the ways of God" and to constantly admonish it to return to the Sinaitic covenant. In practice, this meant that the people should unconditionally reject the enticing attraction of the foreign gods, who were close, tangible and more easily understood than the remote, invisible YHWH, sternly watching the moral behavior of His followers. It also meant the voluntary submission to limitations upon oneself for the purpose of conducting a just and moral life.

To achieve this, the prophets of action used such mundane means as deposing kings and dynasties. Idolatry, and the inhuman conduct that came with it, could be terminated by the removal of kings and dynasties. Aberrations of common men could best be healed by acts of teaching and preaching. The masses had to be taught that sacrifice and ritual are pleasant in God's eyes only when accompanied by a remorseful heart and a decision to do good. To say that the prophets were opposed to the sacrificial service would be incorrect. After all, Jeremiah and Ezekiel, two of the greatest prophets, belonged to priestly families themselves. What the prophets fought against was the popular belief in the fetishist nature of the sacrifices and the Temple itself.

The ideal society envisaged by the prophets was one similar to that of the Israelites sojourning in the desert. Theirs was a simple way of life, devoid of the vices and injustice generated by urban civilization. In this society all Israelites had equal rights, and there was neither a royal court nor an overgrown aristocracy to violate them. This envisaged society was, in short, the youthful, innocent Israelitic people, among whom God's presence was permanent. In comparing the contemporary societies in Israel and Judah with their ideal desert society, the excessive consumption of wine in the palaces of the aristocracy and of the officialdom became to the prophets the symbol of all the moral corruption and injustice which they so hated. The clan of the Rechabites which clung stubbornly to the desert ideal by living in tents and abstaining from tilling the soil and drinking wine, was to the prophets a living example of the viability of a return to a simple way of life. In the warnings of the prophets that the sins of the people will bring about an invasion of a fierce enemy who will lay waste the land and turn it into a desert, it is often possible to discover a ray of hope that the devastation will produce "desert-like" conditions which will lead the people back to the simple way of life and to their God. Thus the visions of the prophets contained both castigation and consolation, and predictions of horror intertwined with hope and love.

The number of prophets was very large. Before the "classical" period of prophecy began with Elijah in the 9th century B.C.E., many names of prophets are mentioned by the biblical writers. But many many more remained anonymous, and many died as martyrs for the cause which they were preaching. With Hosea and Amos in the 8th century B.C.E., the lofty sermons of the prophets began to be recorded into a literature which probably has never been surpassed in greatness, beauty, and holiness. Besides the large collections of prophecies of Isaiah, Jeremiah, and Ezekiel, the prophecies of a number of "minor" prophets also survived. They are called minor prophets because only a small number of their prophecies came down to us, while in reality they may have produced many such sermons in the course of their ministry. The period of the literary prophecy lasted about 250 years, and ended, for reasons not sufficiently clear, some time after the return to Zion of a part of the exiles from Babylonia. A modern theory has it that the cessation of prophecy was due to the canonization of the Pentateuch at that time. Now it was possible to know the will of God by interpreting the Pentateuch, and there was no more the need to resort to prophecy for this purpose.

Besides the men universally recognized as prophets, there were many others termed by the biblical writers "false prophets." The biblical writers, our only source of information about the false prophets, unanimously condemned them as impostors who did not speak the word of God but misled the people with false, optimistic promises. However, the information about the false prophets is scanty and too fragmentary to make it possible for us to understand their true nature.

Section IV

JUDAEA UNDER PERSIA

Chapter 1

The Beginnings of the Second Commonwealth

Little is known about the situation in Judaea after Gedaliah's assassination. The one thing we can be sure of is that the country was largely depopulated. As a result, people from the neighboring countries began to pour into Judaea and to occupy the ownerless land. The Edomites, for instance, moved up northward as far as Hebron.

In 538 B.C.E. a radical change took place. King Cyrus I of Persia, who the year before had conquered the Babylonian empire, initiated a policy of permitting peoples deported by the Babylonians to return to their native countries. The Judaean exiles in Babylonia became beneficiaries of this new policy when in the same year Cyrus issued a decree permitting them to return to Judaea. Simultaneously the Persian king ordered that the Temple be rebuilt in Jerusalem at government expense, and that the holy vessels removed in 586 B.C.E. from the Solomonic Temple to Babylonia, now be returned to Jerusalem. The haste with which this decree was issued suggests that by returning Judaeans to their homeland Cyrus wanted to establish near the Egyptian border a community friendly to him.

As many as 40,000 exiles possibly made use of Cyrus' offer. Their number, however, seems to have dwindled by the time they arrived in Judaea. The status of the new Judaean community, as well as that of its leader, is not fully clear. Originally it was probably planned to restore to the country the old principle of dual leadership. The House of David was to be in charge of the temporal power and a high priest was to head the Temple. It is thus understandable that the returnees were led by a member of the Davidic dynasty, and by a grandson of the last high priest of the Solomonic Temple. It is not possible to determine whether the names Sheshbazar and Zerubabel refer to the same prince of the House of David, or whether there were two Davidic princes who served successively as governors of the new province. It is equally impossible to know with certainty whether Judaea was given the status of a separate province, or that of an autonomous part of the province of Samaria, the former state of Israel.

Although Cyrus' decree clearly ordered the rebuilding of the Temple, it is not sure whether or not the work was undertaken upon the group's arrival in Jerusalem. If so, it was soon interrupted, for reasons unknown to us. It is possible that the Samaritans intrigued in the Persian imperial court against the building of the Temple after the Judaeans denied to them the right to participate in the work. The Samaritans were a sort of a separate people which possibly emerged from an amalgamation of Israelites of the North with non-Israelitic settlers brought by the Assyrians after the fall of Israel. Although the Samaritans were nominally adherents of the Israelitic religion, theirs was in reality a syncretistic faith, composed of both YHWHist and pagan elements. The returnees brought along from Babylonia a purified Jewish faith into which the Samaritans did not fit.

In the year 520 B.C.E. a climate favorable to the Judaeans developed again in the Persian court and King Darius I renewed Cyrus' decree to rebuild the Temple. At that time, Zerubabel, King Jehoiachin's grandson, whether identical with Sheshbazar or not, was governor of Judaea.

Encouraged by the prophets Haggai and Zechariah, Zerubabel laid the foundations for the Temple. It took five years for the building to be completed. When it finally was consecrated in 515 B.C.E., many were disappointed, since it was much smaller than, and lacked the splendor of, the Solomonic Temple. Neither the Holy Ark nor the *Cherubim* were there, as they had disappeared or were hidden under circumstances not fully clear to us. Nevertheless, the completion of the Temple was of great significance. It manifested that the re-establishment of the autonomous province of the Judaeans was an accomplished fact, and that Judaea was again a "normal" community. The fact that Joshua, grandson of the last high priest of the Solomonic Temple, was installed as high priest of the rebuilt Temple, was also of major importance. It manifested the continuity of the adherence of the Jerusalem Temple to the God of Israel. The consecration of the new Temple also signified to the people the end of God's wrath over Israel, which by then, according to Zechariah, had lasted 70 years, from the destruction of the Solomonic Temple in 586 B.C.E. till 515 B.C.E. Like the Solomonic Temple, the new edifice was called "House of the Lord." Later it became known under other names such as "Holy House" or "Sanctuary."

With the completion of the Temple, a far-reaching constitutional transformation took place in Judaea. Up to this time the principle of dualism prevailed in the leadership of the new community. The prophets Haggai and Zechariah again and again addressed themselves to Zerubabel and the High Priest Joshua together as the leaders. One could speculate that had conditions continued to develop favorably, Zerubabel would have ultimately become king of Judaea under Persian sovereignty. It so happened, however, that sometime after the consecration of the Temple Zerubabel disappeared, for reasons and under circumstances unknown to us. Again Samaritan intrigues may have caused Zerubabel's dismissal, or possibly execution.

In the vacuum thus created, the high priest became the sole source of authority. A theocratic regime, sometimes characterized as Aaronid absolutism, thus established itself. The people, prepared for such a development by some post-exilic prophets, seemed to have accepted the new order without opposition, and it remained Judaea's form of government for a period of about 70 years. The high priest united in his hands both the spiritual and temporal power. Judaea thus became a "temple state," not unlike various other territories of a similar nature within the confines of the Persian empire. A sacrifice and prayers offered daily in the Temple for the Persian king manifested the latter's sovereignty over the country. Since the new community was called Judaea because it centered around Jerusalem, the people began to be called universally *Judaeans* or *Jews,* and the ancient name Israelites ceased to be used.

Chapter 2

Life in the Restored Homeland

The Reforms of Nehemiah and Ezra

The high hopes which the returnees from Babylonia had for the future of the old-new homeland Judaea did not materialize. The removal of Zerubabel was a great blow to the political strength of the country. The high priest, preoccupied with the Temple, could not care for the strengthening of the country in the manner a secular ruler would have been able to. Thus, Judaea remained for the following 75 years a tiny political entity without significance. The high priests did not care for the proper maintenance of Jerusalem's walls, and by the middle of the fifth century B.C.E. they lay in ruins. Consequently, the impact of the neighboring states upon Judaea became increasingly great.

On the economic front, too, the new community achieved little success. While the returnees of 538 B.C.E seem to have been a group of well-to-do people, their descendants underwent a process of impoverishment. By the middle of the fifth century, the community was composed of a thin layer of wealthy aristocrats and a mass of poor peasants and proletarians.

Equally discouraging was the situation in the area of religious life. While the sacrificial service in the Temple seems to have been practiced regularly, a definite departure from the observance of the Jewish religious law took place. Intermarriage with the neighboring peoples was widely practiced, even among the priesthood. The Sabbath was flagrantly violated by vendors of produce, as if it were a regular weekday.

The sad situation in Judaea did not remain unnoticed among the Jews in the Persian empire, where in the meantime a large, wealthy, vibrant, and influential Jewish community had come into being (see further, Sec. VIII, Chap. 2). About the year 440 B.C.E. a certain Hanani returned to the Persian capital Suza from a pilgrimage to Jerusalem. Hanani was a brother of the king's cupbearer, Nehemiah. Hanani evidently was deeply concerned about the conditions he found in Jerusalem and reported them to his brother. Nehemiah, a truly pious man, was saddened by the report, and decided to give up his high position in the court in order to remedy the situation in Judaea. He therefore had himself appointed by the king as governor of Judaea. He knew well that his efforts would be met by opposition and intrigue on the part of Judaea's neighbors, especially the Samaritans, and therefore set out on his way to Jerusalem concealing the fact of his appointment as governor.

When Nehemiah arrived in Jerusalem, his first task was to rebuild the walls. In order to acquaint himself with the conditions of the wall ruins, he made a dramatic nocturnal journey around the city, after which he began energetically to organize the work of reconstruction. He evidently succeeded in persuading many people to do the work with great speed, always alert to the danger of an imminent attack on the part of neighbors. To further strengthen the defensive capabilities of the city, Nehemiah ordered a part of the people who lived on the land to settle permanently in Jerusalem.

Nehemiah's term of office, during which he did not accept any remuneration, lasted 12 years. He introduced many improvements in the administration of Judaea, which was no longer a part of Samaria, but a separate province. He also took strong action to bring relief to the poor. It seems, however, that he was not able to improve single-handedly the religious and moral life of the people. He carried out this task together with another important emissary from Persia, Azariah, or Ezra the Scribe. It is not possible to determine whether Ezra preceded Nehemiah or came with him when the latter returned to Jerusalem from a visit to Persia. Ezra was a learned man, who was mostly concerned with the religious situation in Judaea. He was officially appointed by King Artaxerxes I to go to Judaea for the purpose of teaching the people the Jewish law and establishing it as the law of the land. This was in line with the general policy of the Persians to permit the many peoples in the empire to live by their own laws. Nehemiah's and Ezra's appointments thus complemented each other and resulted in a successful transformation of life in Judaea.

When Ezra came he was accompanied by several thousand new Jewish settlers from Persia. We may assume that these new settlers were, like Ezra, pious men who left their homes not for economic or political reasons, but in order to fulfill the ideal of living in a land that came to be considered by Jews as holy. These new immigrants thus contributed by their very presence to the success of Ezra's religious mission.

Within the period of only one year, probably 428 B.C.E., Ezra succeeded in greatly strengthening the religious life of the Judaeans. In the month of the high holidays, when many Judaeans congregated in Jerusalem, Ezra read in solemn assembly the Pentateuch in order to acquaint the people with the law he had come to make obligatory upon them. He also convinced the people that marrying non-Jewish women was sinful, and he undertook a thorough action to make Judaeans divorce their foreign wives. It is remarkable how great Ezra's and Nehemiah's prestige was in that this action—which caused many family tragedies—was accepted by the people with almost no opposition. A modern theory has it that at that time an unknown author composed the Scroll of Ruth in defense of the non-Jewish wives. This author hoped that the marriage of Ruth the Moabite to an Israelite, a descendant of whom was no less a man than King David, would convince the people that intermarriage is not necessarily bad in itself. If this was so, the Scroll of Ruth had no influence upon the course of events, and intermarriage henceforth came to be considered among Jews as highly undesirable and even dangerous.

Additional steps were taken by Nehemiah and Ezra to establish a system of taxation which would insure sufficient income for the Temple and make it possible to conduct the sacrificial service uninterruptedly. The people also promised to pay regularly the tithes prescribed in the Jewish law. Special measures were also taken to strengthen the observance of the Sabbath as a day of rest in a more strict manner than hitherto. Finally, the release of debts and slaves, as well as abstention from tilling the soil, prescribed in the law for every seventh year, was henceforth to be observed scrupulously.

After the events of the year 428 B.C.E., Ezra and Nehemiah "disappeared." The reminiscences written by both men tell of their activities, but not of their lives thereafter. Thus a curtain went down over their latter years, much in the way the lives of the "judges" and prophets remained unknown after the completion of their missions and ministries.

Somewhat more is known about the general conditions in Judaea. The relations with the Persian court seem to have continued to be friendly. The country enjoyed the status of a semiautonomous commonwealth with the right to issue coins. It was administered by a succession of governors, some of whom were Jews. We do not know, however, to what degree the governors of Judaea limited the powers vested in the high priest in pre-Nehemiah times. The religious and moral standards introduced by Nehemiah and Ezra were not fully maintained. By and large, however, the people did not return to the way of life found so objectionable by the two great visitors from Persia. The various towns and villages were now to a greater degree populated by Jews, and the countryside was thus made more securely a part of Judaea. The economy seems to have expanded, and a new class of artisans came into being besides the older classes of the nobility and the peasants. Judaea could thus more vigorously withstand the conflict with the Samaritans, which became more and more serious, and which ultimately led to a complete breach with the former sister-state.

The Cultural Scene

During this period a number of changes could be discerned in the culture of Judaea. To begin with, the Aramaic language established itself more and more as the language of the people. To be sure, very little can be said with certainty about the linguistic conditions of the Israelites in pre-exilic times. Presumably, some Aramaic dialect was the original tongue of the Israelites at the time of their formation as a people. We have seen that indications are that the Patriarchs were of Aramaic stock, and lived prior to their emigration to Canaan in countries inhabited by Arameans. No information, however, is available regarding the time when the Israelites switched from Aramaic to the language which may be called "biblical Hebrew." A modern theory even has it that biblical Hebrew was never spoken by the Israelites, but only used as a means of literary expression, much in the way Latin was Europe's literary language in the Middle Ages. Instead, the Israelites of the biblical times used in their daily life the Hebrew dialect known to us from the Mishnah. This dialect is much closer to Aramaic than biblical Hebrew. Thus, when in post-exilic times "imperial Aramaic," the dialect used by the Persian bureaucracy, began to spread all over the Middle East, the Judaeans could adapt themselves to it without great difficulty. Simultaneously, the old Hebrew script in use in pre-exilic times was now abandoned. Instead, the square script, often called the Assyrian alphabet, became widely used. The returnees from the Persian empire were accustomed to the new script, and it was natural for them to continue using it after their settlement in Judaea.

Basic changes took place also with regard to calendation. The Pentateuchal calendar reveals clear traces of both a solar and lunar year. It seems, however, that in pre-exilic times a solar calendar was mostly in use among the Israelites. In the Persian empire the exiles became accustomed, under local influences, to a lunar calendar and the returnees continued using it in Judaea. As a result, a combined luni-solar calendation system established itself permanently among the Jews. Henceforth, the months were no longer designated by numbers, but by names adopted from the Babylonians.

While most cultural influences thus came from the Persian empire, Greek culture too began to penetrate from the West. In their perpetual expansion, Greek traders established themselves along the entire eastern shores of the Mediterranean long before Alexander the Great set out to conquer them. Greek pottery thus came to be used in Judaea in this period. Athenian influence can also be found in contemporary Judaean coins.

Against the backdrop of these influences from East and West some of the most important biblical writings were written. While modern research is by no means unanimous as to the dates when the various biblical books were written, it is fairly certain that some books of the category of the Hagiographa, the Wisdom Literature, belong to the Persian period in the history of the Jews. Certain scholars are also of the opinion that some biblical books, including Jonah, the Scroll of Esther, Ecclesiastes, and Chronicles, were originally written in Aramaic and entered the Bible about that time in Hebrew translation. Some of the apocryphal books, such as Judith and Tobit, were also written in this period. A modern theory has it that the Pentateuch, in the form in which it came down to us, was composed by Ezra. However, the fact that the Samaritans, Ezra's uncompromising opponents, accepted the Pentateuch with only minor changes points to the untenability of this theory.

While the 200 years of Persian domination over Judaea were by and large "silent centuries," the tiny and poor state of Judaea was nonetheless, as we have seen, undergoing many important changes. The Judaean people was thus not totally unprepared when, with Alexander's arrival in 333 B.C.E., it had its first great encounter with European culture.

Chapter 3

The Samaritans

There is no way to determine with full certainty how the sect of the Samaritans came into being. According to their tradition they descended from the two Joseph tribes, Ephraim and Manasseh. Their name "Samaritans," they assert, is not connected with the city of Shomron, located in western Israel, and they should not be called in Hebrew *Shomronim*, but rather *shamerim*, the keepers of the true Mosaic religion.

The Israelites who lived around the city of Shechem, located half way between the Mediterranean and the Jordan on the border between the tribes Ephraim and Manasseh, may well have developed some separate characteristics in pre-exilic times. When the Assyrians brought in non-Israelitic settlers after the fall of the kingdom of Samaria, these necessarily intermingled with the local population. Thus, when the Judaeans returned in 538 B.C.E. from their exile in Babylonia, the differences between them and the population living around Shechem were so striking, that they could not but consider the Samaritans a separate people. At that time the Samaritans numbered about 100,000.

Although the religious literature of the Samaritans does not contain any pagan elements, their religion was in practice a syncretistic faith. We have seen that pagan elements had penetrated the religion of the Israelites of the North as early as the period of the "Judges," due to their amalgamation with their Canaanite neighbors. The influx of non-Israelites into the country after 722 B.C.E. caused a further dilution of the religion of the Israelites of the North, so that it became, indeed, a syncretistic faith.

The Samaritans, nonetheless, considered themselves Israelites, and wished to participate in the building of the Second Temple. The returnees from Babylonia, however, must have discovered in the religious practices of the Samaritans rites familiar to them from pagan Babylonia, and rejected the offer. Thus the foundation was laid for a schism that grew wider and wider. According to other theories, however, Samaritanism emerged much later, and was originally one of a great variety of religious trends that asserted themselves within Judaism during the last three centuries before the common era.

The Samaritan religion in time developed along independent lines. Their Holy Scriptures consist only of the Pentateuch and the Book of Joshua. It is possible that the Samaritans did not reject the prophetic books but rather that these had never found acceptance in the North in the pre-exilic times. Furthermore, even the Pentateuch as accepted by them is in certain ways different from the text common among the Jews. The most striking difference can be found in the Ten Commandments, where the Samaritan text includes a lengthy exposition of the holiness of Mt. Gerizim, in the vicinity of Shechem. To be sure, Mt. Gerizim is given a certain religious importance in the Jewish version of the Pentateuch, but in the Samaritan version it is the place where God dwells. Hence, rejected from participation in the building of the Jerusalem Temple, the Samaritans built their own temple on Mt. Gerizim. They could not do it immediately, however. According to Samaritan tradition, they became subjected to the Judaeans in the times of King Darius II (423–404). Under these circumstances their temple could not, of course, be built. However, an opportunity for this presented itself when in 333 B.C.E. Alexander the Great invaded Samaria and Judaea (see further, Sec. V, Chap. 1). The Samaritans sided with him to a greater degree than the Jews, and were rewarded by permission to build a temple. Thus in 332 B.C.E., the Samaritan temple was erected on Mt. Gerizim. The temple was headed by a high priest who claimed Aaronid descent, and in whose family the office remained till the beginning of the 17th century. The new dynasty that followed was of Levitic descent.

The religious beliefs of the Samaritans are based on the prophecy of Moses and the Pentateuch. Not having a roster of great prophets like those of the Jews, the Samaritans elevated Moses to a position of sublime holiness. He is the sole prophet, and the five books written by him are the only authoritative source for religious guidance and inspiration. No concept can be considered valid unless found in Moses' book. A Torah scroll probably written in the Middle Ages is believed by them to have been written only a few years after the conquest of Canaan, and is thus highly authoritative. The Jewish version of the Pentateuch they consider as having been deliberately altered by Ezra. Since the Samaritans never left their homeland and were not exposed, like the Judaean exiles, to the Assyrian script, they retained the old Hebrew script, and to this day their Torah scrolls are written in this script.

Curiously, despite Samaritanism's syncretistic nature, its God concept, as it emerges from its holy writings, is as uncompromisingly monotheistic as that of the Jews. The Samaritan religious law follows a rigid interpretation of the Scriptures and resembles to a certain degree that of the Sadducees and Karaites (see further, Sec. V, Chap. 4 and Vol. II, Sec. XIII, Chap. 7). The faith has a variety of holidays, and Passover, Pentecost and Tabernacles are, as in the Jewish religion, pilgrimage festivals. On Passover the Samaritans have continued down to our own times to sacrifice the Paschal lamb on Mt. Gerizim.

During the period of encounter with the Greek world the Samaritan religion underwent a process of further syncretization by adopting certain views, rites, and practices from the Greeks.

Later, in the first century C.E. (of the common era—equivalent to A.D.), a period of great religious fermentation, they adopted the ideas of resurrection and paradise. In the person of the *taheb,* the Returner, the Restorer, ultimately identified with Moses, the Samaritans have their own parallel to the Jewish Messiah. Joshua also attained an important place in the Samaritan tradition due to his appointment by Moses as his successor. In the course of time different religious trends appeared within the Samaritan religion which gave rise to the emergence of sectarian movements.

The attitude of normative Judaism to the Samaritans was one of rejection. But, while they were not recognized as genuine Jews, they were not considered pagans either, because of their belief in the God of Israel. In fact, the sages of the Talmud were deeply impressed by their piety, and stated that "every *mitsvah* which Cutheans (i.e., Samaritans) have adopted they observe with greater care than the Jews" (Qiddushin 76a).

During the period of Ptolemaic and Seleucid rule, the fate of the Samaritans was in general similar to that of the Judaeans. Their situation worsened, however, when Shechem and its region were captured by Judaea's Hasmonean ruler Johanan Hyrcanus in 128 B.C.E. and the temple on Mt. Gerizim was destroyed. The grief and anger of the Samaritans was equal to the joy of the Judaeans, who made the day of the destruction of the Samaritan temple a semi-holiday. It was then that the breach between the Samaritans and the Jews became final.

Under Roman rule the Samaritans were oppressed no less than the Jews. A tragic era in their history was the reign of the emperor Commodus (180–92 C.E.), when many of them lost their lives as a result of persecution. Nonetheless, about the year 200 C.E. some 300,000 Samaritans still lived in Shechem and its vicinity. Their numbers, however, began to dwindle rapidly under Christian rule due to persecution and forced conversions. In 529 C.E. they made a desperate attempt to rebel against the Byzantine emperor Justinian I. The revolt was suppressed and followed by new massacres and mass conversion. The survivors were henceforth treated as an almost outlawed religious sect.

The Arab conquest of the Holy Land in the 630s did not bring the Samaritans any relief. On the contrary, oppression was so harsh that many families converted to the Moslem faith out of fear. Quite similar was the situation of the Samaritans during the 12th and 13th centures, when the Holy Land was ruled by the Crusaders. Oppression and mass conversion, forced and "voluntary" out of fear, were recurring regularly also under Mamluk and Turkish rule, down to the beginning of the 19th century. In addition, access to Mt. Gerizim was often forbidden. Under the Turks the Samaritan population had dwindled to a mere few thousand.

In the early 19th century the British consulate in Jerusalem began to protect the remnants of the Samaritans against oppression by the corrupt Turkish officials. Nevertheless, the sect continued to diminish due to the small number of women in its midst. Only in the 1920s, when the Samaritans began to intermarry with Jews, did their number begin again to increase. This coincided with a basic improvement in their general situation under the British mandate and in the State of Israel. The latter extended to them recognition as Jews, which gave them full citizenship rights. By now their number has increased to about 500.

In various times Samaritan communities had existed outside of Shechem, both in the Holy Land and elsewhere. The most important communities were those of Alexandria in Egypt, established in Alexander's times, and in Damascus. In these communities no sacrificial service was practiced. Instead, synagogues were built where worshippers prayed in the direction of Mt. Gerizim. All these communities, however, went under due to oppression by Byzantines and Moslems, and their few survivors found refuge in the mother community of Shechem.

We have seen that at the time of the emergence of the Samaritan sect, Aramaic became increasingly the language of the entire Middle East. It was therefore natural that this language and, notably, one of its western dialects became the language most prevalent among the Samaritans. In this language and in Hebrew most of their literary works were written. During the Hellenistic period some of their writings were composed in Greek, into which their Pentateuch was also translated. In the Middle Ages under Arab domination the use of Aramaic was discontinued and replaced by Arabic.

Against the backdrop of their unfortunate history, the literary creativity of the Samaritans was remarkable. At times their literary center was in Shechem, at times in the Diaspora. During the 13th and 14th centuries literature flourished in the Damascus community, where poetry, Hebrew grammar, and biblical exegesis were equally cultivated. Most of their ancient literature, however, was destroyed during Roman and Byzantine domination.

Section V

ENCOUNTER WITH THE HELLENISTIC WORLD

Chapter 1

Judaea under Egypt and Syria

In 334 B.C.E. Alexander the Great, king of Macedonia, went to war against the Persian empire. Within a short time he had captured its western provinces and he appeared in Judaea in 333 B.C.E. Although at the beginning the high priest tried to remain faithful to Persia, Alexander nevertheless treated the Judaeans in a friendly way. It seems that he refrained from appointing for Judaea a Macedonian governor and confirmed the high priest as the sole ruler, as in the early Persian period.

Not much information is available about the events which took place in Judaea during the ten years she belonged to Alexander's empire and the subsequent ten years during which Alexander's generals fought among themselves for the control of his lands. When the wars were over, Judaea found herself controlled by Egypt, where one of the generals, Ptolemy, had established for himself a kingdom. During the period of more than 100 years when Judaea was under Ptolemaic control, Syria, where general Seleucus had established for himself an empire, tried to wrest it away from Egypt.

The Judaeans seem to have been divided on this issue. Most of them seem to have been satisfied with the Ptolemies. All sources indicate that the Ptolemies did not interfere too much with the inner life of the people. True, they built in Judaea a number of new Greek cities and brought, in addition, Macedonian settlers into older cities, to strengthen their hold over the country, but this evidently was not considered by most Judaeans as a menace, and no serious opposition to the Egyptian Macedonians developed during the entire period of their rule.

There were, nonetheless, Judaeans, including some of the high priests, who would have preferred their country to be part of Syria. The Syrians were in control of vast areas, especially Babylonia, inhabited by huge numbers of Jews. Ties with this Diaspora Jewry within the confines of one empire seemed to them to be very advantageous. Judaea was, indeed, as we have seen, in close contact with Babylonian Jewry for a period of over 200 years, and the separation from this Jewry, as a result of Ptolemy's conquest, must have been painful.

The Seleucids ultimately succeeded in occupying Judaea in 199 B.C.E. and making it part of their empire. The Syrian takeover, however, did not bring peace to the country. On the contrary, the inner tensions among the various Jewish factions increased due to the general policy pursued by the Seleucid kings with regard to the many peoples comprising their empire. Unlike Ptolemaic Egypt, the Seleucid empire was a conglomeration of many different peoples. It therefore was perpetually preoccupied with the problem of combating many centrifugal forces in order to keep the empire together. Consequently, it pursued a more aggressive policy of Hellenization than Ptolemaic Egypt. The new situation in Judaea was therefore favorable to those Judaeans who were ready to accept Greek culture to a noticeable degree.

The situation became critical when Antiochus IV ascended the Seleucid throne in 176 B.C.E. He was enamored of Athenian culture more than any of his predecessors and considered the radical Hellenization of his empire an absolute necessity for the state and the masses of its non-Greek subjects. Within only a few years he appointed and deposed several high priests in an attempt to bring about a quick and total Hellenization of Judaea. A gymnasium was erected in Jerusalem where athletic games were practiced. The majority of the people responded with stiff opposition, since the games were of a pagan religious nature. The Judaeans who did favor the establishment of the gymnasium considered it merely a step in transforming Jerusalem into a *polis,* a Greek city. These Judaeans so much desired the status of a *polis* for Jerusalem that they preferred to call themselves Antiochians of Jerusalem. Antioch was the capital of Seleucid Syria, and by calling themselves Antiochians they wished to stress their status as citizens of the Seleucid empire. It was therefore a hard blow to them when the true plans of King Antiochus became apparent.

In 170 B.C.E. Antiochus was defeated in one of the recurrent wars with Egypt. The undisputed control over Judaea, the buffer between Syria and Egypt, now became most vital to him. He therefore considered a struggle which broke out in Jerusalem between two factions of Judaeans as an uprising against him, and he acted swiftly and brutally. He entered Jerusalem, pillaged the Temple treasures, and massacred a large number of Judaeans. Circumcision was outlawed by penalty of crucifixion of the father and the circumcised infant. The Temple was made a sanctuary of Zeus, the daily sacrifices were discontinued, and a swine, the "detestable thing" (Daniel 12:11), was offered in 168 B.C.E. on the altar. The king also attempted to compel the Judaeans in other localities to abandon the Jewish religion and to sacrifice to the Greek gods.

The suddenness and brutality with which the new policy was enforced, at the beginning seems to have intimidated the majority of the people into submission. A number of Judaeans, however, were ready to sacrifice their lives rather than to obey the king's orders. This group of people, who entered history under the name of *hasidim harishonim,* the pious men of old, probably took up weapons against the Syrians. The Syrians, however, soon found out that their stubborn opponents were not ready to fight on the Sabbath, even when their lives were in jeopardy. Syrian soldiers therefore converged on the Sabbath upon the caves where the pious men hid, and killed about 1,000 of them. The readiness of the pious men to die for the sanctification of God's Name was due not only to their reluctance to violate the Sabbath by fighting the Syrians, but probably also to their belief that this was the last struggle between God and His adversaries, and that they were obliged to demonstrate by their martyrdom that they were decidedly on God's side.

Chapter 2

The Hasmonean Revolt

Contrary to the expectations of the Syrians, the revolt of the pious Judaeans did not end with the execution of the *hasidim* in the caves. There were other pious men who not only resisted Antiochus' decrees, but also began to attack his forces in Judaea. The new movement centered around a family of priests in Modin, a town in the hills of Judaea. Mattathias, the son of Johanan, of the priestly clan of the Hasmoneans, left Jerusalem with his family to escape the religious persecutions. When, however, Syrian soldiers appeared in his new hometown Modin to compel the people to sacrifice to Zeus, he and his five sons killed them and their Jewish collaborators. This happened in 167 B.C.E. and it marks the beginning of an uprising which lasted a quarter of a century and returned to the Judaeans not only freedom of religion but also political independence.

As soon as the news of the uprising spread over the country, many *hasidim*, now ready to take up arms against the Syrians, joined Mattathias. Consequently, the rebels, quite at home in the Judaean hills, were able to use guerilla tactics skillfully and to seriously harass the superior Syrian forces. A short time later Mattathias died, and his son Judah followed him as leader of the rebels. Judah was known as "the Maccabee," a word whose meaning is not fully clear. Possibly it means "the hammer," to indicate his successes in beating the Syrians, or it may refer to the shape of his skull. Judah, a great strategist and statesman, was successful in the war against the Syrians not only because of his unquestionable personal heroism and the growing support of the Judaean population, but also due to the many inner difficulties which the Syrian empire experienced.

Judah's struggle was also greatly helped by the death of Antiochus IV in 165 B.C.E. Jerusalem was recaptured in the same year, in the month of Heshwan (November). The re-dedication of the Temple was, however, postponed for one month in order to celebrate it on the 25th day of the month of Kislev, the third anniversary of the day when a swine was sacrificed on the altar.

Henceforth, and to this day, the Jewish people have been commemorating the Temple's re-dedication by celebrating an eight-day semi-holiday called Hanukah. After the Temple was purified, the daily sacrifices were reinstated. In addition, children born during the three years when the Jewish religion was prohibited, were then circumcised, even by force when necessary.

Although the Syrian government abolished Antiochus' decrees after his death, its continued domination of Judaea remained doubtful. Judah Maccabee clearly acted as if he were the country's ruler. He was then in command of a fairly large and enthusiastic army and was even able to wage a sort of offensive war against pagan Idumaea in the Negev. When Jews who lived in neighboring territories were oppressed by their Greek neighbors, he sent his soldiers to their rescue. Such Jews were removed from the dangerous areas and resettled in Judaea. But nothing pointed so much to Judah's status as a sovereign ruler as the fact that in 161 B.C.E. he concluded a treaty of mutual defense with the Republic of Rome. Though Rome was still a distant country, its influence began to be felt in the Near East. At that time, about 100 years before the appearance of Roman forces in Judaea, a treaty was still of advantage to both, the future ruler of the world and its tragic victim, Judaea.

A short time afterwards Judah was killed in a battle, and his youngest brother Jonathan succeeded him as leader. Then hard times came upon the Hasmonean brothers. Many of the *hasidim* left them, since religious freedom was restored and recognized by the Syrians. A Syrian army entered the country for the purpose of pacifying it by the capture of Jonathan and his remaining brothers. Jonathan then retreated to the Jordan where he hid in the wilderness with a small group of faithful companions.

To the Syrians and the Jewish Hellenists, the cause of the Hasmoneans may have seemed lost. In 153 B.C.E., however, a situation arose which made it possible for Jonathan to use his superior skill as a warrior and diplomat to bring about a dramatic change in his position. A certain Alexander Balas appeared on the scene as a pretender to the Syrian throne, and in the ensuing struggle between him and King Demetrius I, both began to compete for Jonathan's support. No doubt, in spite of their temporary withdrawal into the wilderness the Hasmoneans had become the only decisive force in Judaea. Jonathan succeeded, in spite of initial setbacks, in transforming his band of guerrillas into a regular army. His collaboration was of special importance, due to the fact that Judaea was the natural buffer between Syria and Egypt and Jonathan could thus help to prevent, or facilitate, possible Egyptian interference in Syria's dynastic troubles. The seemingly impossible thus happened and Alexander Balas, who claimed to be a son of Antiochus IV, appointed Jonathan first as high priest, and subsequently as civil and military administrator, that is, governor of Judaea.

Under Jonathan's rule the territory of Judaea began to expand, partly by conquest and partly by Syrian cession, and to include lands which belonged to the two Israelitic states in pre-exilic times. True, Judaea was not yet an independent country, and a Syrian garrison continued to be stationed in Jerusalem's citadel. But the actions of the two rivals to the Syrian throne gave for the first time a status of legality to the claim of the Hasmoneans to the high priesthood and the temporal control of the country. To manifest the independence of his country, Jonathan sent emissaries to Rome to renew the treaty concluded with the Republic by his brother Judah about 18 years earlier. In the same year, however, he, who knew how to maneuver so skillfully his way among the proliferating pretenders to the Syrian throne, was ultimately dragged into the struggle, and lost his life. He died either at the end of 144 or early in 143 B.C.E.

Now only one of Mattathias' sons remained, Simon, the oldest. It became immediately clear that by popular consent he was now to be the leader. The conditions in Syria were again favorable for Judaea, and in 143 B.C.E. King Demetrius II released the country from paying the annual tribute, which was tantamount to Syrian recognition of Judaea's independence. About one year later Simon captured the citadel of Jerusalem, after having starved the Syrian garrison into surrender. Thus, exactly 25 years after the outbreak of the Hasmonean revolt, the last vestige of Syrian domination was eliminated. In 141 B.C.E. the Roman Senate renewed the treaty of friendship with Judaea, which further strengthened the country's newly won independence. Another country with which Simon concluded a treaty was Sparta.

After a long, long time Judaea again had a ruler and high

priest who held these positions by virtue of Jewish popular consent and not by appointment by a foreign power. To give legality to Simon's position, a Great Assembly was convened in Jerusalem in the year 141 B.C.E. Although we do not know who sat in the Great Assembly, the institution seems to have represented the will of the people quite well. Simon was confirmed as high priest and *sar am El,* the prince of God's people. It seems that the Great Assembly had some doubts about investing with the high priesthood a man who was not of the priestly line of which the preceding high priests came. It probably was also uneasy about confirming as secular ruler of the country someone who was not of Davidic origin. It therefore qualified its decisions by the added condition that they were valid until such time "when a true prophet will appear," presumably to confirm or reject them.

The eight years during which Simon ruled were a period of tranquility and success in the country. The only military clash with the Syrians ended in their total defeat. Simon could continue Jonathan's expansionist policy, and without great effort he acquired for Judaea the important port city of Jaffa and the surrounding towns. In his domestic policies Simon was just and devoted to the people, and there seems to have been no faction opposing him. His fate was nevertheless similar to that of his four brothers, and he, too, died a violent death. A son-in-law, jealous of his might and success, murdered him together with some members of his family in 136 B.C.E.

Chapter 3

Judaea under Hasmonean Rule

Hasmonean Monarchy and Territorial Expansion

Judaea's independence won under Simon lasted for almost 80 years, during which the country was ruled by four members of the Hasmonean family. The first of them, Johanan, also named Hyrcanus I, was Simon's son. He successfully continued his father's policy of expansion, and during the 31 years of his rule (136–105 B.C.E.) Judaea's territory greatly increased. His army was largely composed of alien mercenaries, but commanded by Judaean officers. In the north, he captured the region of Samaria, including the cities of Beth Shean and Shechem. In the south he occupied Idumaea (Edom). In order to solidify the newly captured territories, Johanan compelled the Idumaeans to convert to Judaism. He made an attempt to further eliminate religious differences by destroying in 128 B.C.E. the Samaritan temple on Mt. Gerizim. However, by eliminating the temple considered a rival of the Jerusalem Temple, he only increased the anger and resentment of the Samaritan sister nation.

In his relations with Syria, Johanan was not always successful. Early in his rule (133 B.C.E.) the Syrians invaded Judaea, devastated large areas of the country, and laid siege to Jerusalem. Johanan was, however, saved from total defeat by the intervention of his Roman ally.

Constitutionally, Johanan Hyrcanus I was in a position similar to that of his father, high priest and "head of the people of God." To be sure, opposition to him as high priest surfaced from time to time since he was a priest not of the line of Zadok, the first high priest in the Solomonic Temple. But opposition became quite vocal in the Pharisaic circles when he attempted unsuccessfully, late in his life, to assume the title of king. The Pharisees believed that the only legitimate Judaean dynasty was that of the House of David, and thus considered Johanan an usurper. Johanan then broke his tacit alliance with the Pharisees and abolished many of the laws and ordinances introduced by them.

Upon Johanan's death his widow was supposed to succeed him as ruler of Judaea. His son Judah, however, an ambitious man, imprisoned her together with most of his brothers and assumed power. He even succeeded in proclaiming himself king, and Pharisaic opposition was not strong enough to prevent him from doing so. He continued his father's expansionist policies by completing the conquest of Galilee and by annexing to Judaea certain areas which were never before a part of Judah or Israel. When he captured Ituraea, in southern Lebanon, he compelled most of its inhabitants to convert to Judaism, in the manner his father had acted with regard to Idumaea. The further plans of King Judah, also known by the Greek name of Aristobulus, were cut short, however, by his sudden death in 104 B.C.E. He left no offspring, and his widow, Salome, was married to his brother Jannaeus (Jonathan) in accordance with the Jewish law on levirate marriage.

Jannaeus, also called in Greek Alexander, then ascended the throne of Judaea. His reign, which lasted 27 years, was the most turbulent time during the entire period of Hasmonean rule. Hated by his father, he was banned as a youth from the royal court and sent to Galilee, where he adopted from the Syrian neighbors a Greek outlook on life and Greek manners. He thus had little understanding for the aspirations of the Judaeans and plunged the country into indiscriminate warfare during the entire years of his reign. He often was close to defeat and disaster, but somehow succeeded repeatedly in extricating himself and continuing his wars of conquest. As a result, Judaea's territory increased during his reign mainly by the acquisition of most of the former Philistine coast in the southwest, and a large region on the east bank of the Jordan.

In spite of these successes, the opposition of the Pharisees and of the masses of the population kept on growing. They especially resented his insistence on being high priest, while it was questionable whether he was legally fit for the office. The democratically minded Pharisees may in addition have been apprehensive lest the control of both the secular and religious establishments by the same man endanger the freedom of the people. The quarrel between the king and the people reached such proportions that the latter even took the questionable step of calling upon the King of Syria to invade the country. Jannaeus' revenge was boundless. About 50,000 Judaeans lost their lives in this civil war which lasted from 90 to 85 B.C.E. Thousands of Pharisees fled to other countries. About 800 of the ringleaders of the rebellion were crucified and their wives and children slain before their eyes.

Despite this victory, Jannaeus began to realize that the Pharisees, and not his Sadducean supporters, represented the overwhelming majority of the people. He may also have regretted many of his cruel deeds, and began to seek a reconciliation with the people. He thus advised his wife Salome, whom he designated successor to the throne, to ally herself with the Pharisees. He died in 78 B.C.E. at the age of 49 years, as a result of illnesses contracted by a wild lifestyle.

Salome, also known in Greek as Alexandra, now ascended the throne. Why her oldest son, Hyrcanus, by tradition legitimate heir to the throne, was bypassed in his father's will, is unclear. Salome's presumed familial relation to the leader of the Pharisees, Simon ben Shetah, may have been the cause. Be this as it may, Salome turned out to be in wisdom and diplomatic skill far superior to both her sons Hyrcanus and Aristobulus. Although she possibly had a hand in many of her husband's evil deeds, as ruler of Judaea she restored to the country the inner peace it badly needed after 27 years of her husband's wild rule. Her skillful diplomatic maneuvering and the alliance with Rome averted an invasion from the North. Her nine years of rule with no war and with economic prosperity thus turned out to be one of the more felicitous eras during the period of the Second Commonwealth. Her sons, the apathetic Hyrcanus and the ambitious and aggressive Aristobulus, were involved in the service of the country, the first as high priest and the latter as commander-in-chief. Salome died in 69 B.C.E., and she was henceforth commemorated as a great queen in Israel.

In her will, Salome directed that her older son Hyrcanus should succeed her. But Hyrcanus II had ruled for only three months when his brother Aristobulus started a rebellion against him. Before the conflict between the brothers became too serious, however, a compromise was worked out between them. Hyrcanus abdicated the throne but kept the position of high priest. Aristobulus, who by nature was more qualified to handle difficult governmental affairs, became king.

The restored peace between the two brothers would probably have been a lasting one. But at this time a man appeared on Judaea's political scene whose actions threw the country into turmoil which did not cease for two full generations. He was a wealthy and influential man by the name of Antipater. His father, also named Antipater, served under Jannaeus Alexander as military governor of Idumaea, the province in the Negev annexed by Hyrcanus I. Antipater, the son, did not hold any official office at the time of Salome's death. But by then he probably had the ambition of maneuvering the Hasmoneans out, and usurping the throne either for himself or for one of his sons. He cleverly reasoned that by throwing his support to the ousted Hyrcanus, his design would have much better chances than under the energetic and ambitious Aristobulus.

Antipater seemed to have easily convinced Hyrcanus to renew his quest for the throne. He equally easily obtained for Hyrcanus military aid from Aretas, king of the neighboring Arab state of Nabataea. A full-blown civil war thus broke out between the two brothers, during which many ugly acts were committed by both sides. Before any of the sides attained a decisive victory, however, a new political factor of great magnitude appeared on the scene, and turned the conflict between the two Hasmonean brothers into an insignificant event. It also opened a new, tragic chapter in the history of the Jewish people.

In the year 63 B.C.E., Pompey the famous Roman general who was sent to conquer western Asia, arrived in Damascus. Everybody in Judaea was aware of the fact that Rome had become the decisive power in the region, and that he whom Pompey would back would rule the country. When, therefore, delegates of the two Hasmonean brothers appeared before Pompey in Damascus it was tantamount to a de facto surrender of the country to Rome. There was, in addition, a faction in Judaea, which was so disgusted with the Hasmonean rulers that it petitioned Pompey to remove the Hasmoneans altogether. Had Pompey granted this request, Judaea would have become a Roman province, probably governed in Rome's name by the high priest, as was the case when Judaea was part of the Persian empire.

At the beginning, indecision seemed to have delayed Roman action. But Aristobulus' erratic conduct of joining Pompey one day and trying to oppose him the next, swung Pompey definitely to Hyrcanus' side. After capturing Jerusalem and massacring thousands of people, Pompey reinstated Hyrcanus as high priest and ruler of Judaea under Roman sovereignty. The title of king of Judaea was abolished, and a considerable part of the country's territory was annexed to the Roman province of Syria. Aristobulus, his daughters and his sons, were led away to Rome where they marched in Pompey's triumphal procession.

Thus in the year 63 B.C.E. an end came to Judaean independence won by the Hasmoneans some 75 years earlier. The Hasmoneans started out as fighters for religious freedom and the liberation of their people, but after some time their descendants degenerated to become petty, tyrannical rulers. The disappointment with the Hasmoneans seems to have been so deep that few people mourned their demotion and some even preferred to live under direct Roman rule.

The State and Its Institutions

The Hasmonean state was known by the name *hever hayehudim,* the Commonwealth of the Judaeans, and this name of the state appears on its coins. There seems to have been no difference in the nature of governmental control the Hasmoneans exercised in any of the four regions of their kingdom: Judaea, Samaria, Galilee, and Peraea, the name then common for the Jewish area on the east bank of the Jordan. Theirs was an aristocratic regime, which in the course of time took on increasingly the character of a Hellenistic government, both in its civilian and military aspects.

We have seen that the Great Assembly, which in 141 B.C.E. confirmed Simon as high priest and "ruler of the people of God," made it known that its recognition of the legitimacy of the Hasmoneans was of a temporary nature, until such time "when a true prophet will appear." The constitutional basis of the rule of the Hasmoneans thus remained all the time in a state of fluctuation. This could clearly be seen in the unstable rules of succession. Twice Hasmonean rulers designated their wives as successors to the throne, rather than their oldest sons, as prescribed by tradition. There was also much uncertainty with regard to the status of traditional governmental institutions. It may, however, be said that by and large the Judaean state, in spite of temporary deviations, was popular-based and sage-directed, and resembled to a great degree in its character the Greek *polis.*

The oldest "representative" institution of the Second Commonwealth seems to have been the Great Assembly. It may have antedated Nehemiah and Ezra, or have come into being in the course of the reforms introduced by the latter. The number of its members seems to have varied from time to time. At times it had a membership of 100 and included representatives of the various classes of society, such as the priesthood, the community of the sages, the aristocracy, and the elders of the people. It usually was convoked by the high priest for action on important matters of national interest. Thus, the Assembly met at irregular intervals, and often many years elapsed between one session and the next. It seems that the Great Assembly also played a major role in structuring the synagogal service and in the process of canonizing the Bible (see further, Sec. VII, Chap. 2).

With the advent of the Hellenistic period, another institution emerged which bore the Greek name *Gerousia,* that is, Council of Elders. *The Gerousia* resembled by its character the council of elders of the city of Sparta and its function was mainly administrative. As a Hellenistic innovation, the *Gerousia* became a victim of the Hasmonean revolt and lost much of its significance, and possibly went out of existence.

The most important institution to emerge in the period of the Second Commonwealth was the Sanhedrin. It is likely that its original name was *Beth Din Hagadol,* The Great (or Supreme) Court. It is also likely that the *Beth Din Hagadol* was at first called in Greek *Boule,* and that it acquired the designation Sanhedrin *(Synedrion)* in the later Hasmonean period.

In spite of the major role which the Sanhedrin played as a legislative and judicial body in civil and religious matters during a period of several centuries, it is not fully clear how it evolved and what its precise composition and its prerogatives were. There is a possibility that the *Beth Din Hagadol* was instituted by the Great Assembly at its convocation in 141 B.C.E. It consisted of 69 members, and together with its two presiding officers became known as the Sanhedrin of 71. The president of the Sanhedrin was called *nasi,* and the title of the second presiding officer was *av-beth-din,* head of the court.

The name "Sanhedrin" probably began to be used during the rule of Johanan Hyrcanus I. As time went on, the name became so popular that governmental committees of different character began to be called "Sanhedrin." But the Sanhedrin which played a truly great role during the Second Commonwealth was the one of

71 members which met for its sessions in the Temple area. A modern theory has it that by nature this Sanhedrin resembled the Athenian Areopagus at the time of its grandeur. The members of the Sanhedrin were recruited from among the sages, and since the sages came from all strata of the population, the Sanhedrin represented a cross-section of the entire Judaean people.

Among the membership of the Sanhedrin were both Sadducees and Pharisees (see Chap. 4). Most of the time the Pharisees were the dominant element in the Sanhedrin, since most of the sages belonged to the Pharisaic group. Again and again, however, the latter Hasmonean rulers expelled the Pharisees from the Sanhedrin because their views conflicted with the interests of the dynasty, and in such times Sadducees became the decisive factor in the Sanhedrin. The Pharisees were, however, always recalled, as it was they who lent the Sanhedrin its prestige and true authority.

The authority of the Sanhedrin was far-reaching. Up to the time of King Herod (37 B.C.E.) it was both the country's legislative body and supreme court. It decided matters pertaining to religious life as well as matters of state, including war and peace. It had the sole authority of proclaiming the New Moon and so controlled the entire area of calendation. It had the prerogative of appointing local courts and thus supervised the entire judicial system. Its impact on the shaping of the Halakhah was decisive, and its work thus became all-important for many future generations of Jews, both in the Holy Land and the Diaspora. It continued to enjoy almost undisputed authority even after Herod's times, when it was robbed of its legislative power.

The Sanhedrin's existence was temporarily terminated at the time the Temple, its abode, was destroyed in the year 70 C.E. It was, however, soon resurrected to become an even more important institution in the life of the Jewish people, now devoid of statehood.

Population, Economy, and Taxation

Although it is impossible to estimate the exact size of the population in the Hasmonean kingdom, it is safe to say that it was quite large. Judaea with its conquered territories was, with regard to its population, quite different from tiny Judaea of the Persian period. Already in the fourth century B.C.E. Jerusalem had, according to a contemporary Greek writer, a population of 120,000. It should be assumed that the population of the other cities, and even that of the rural areas, had likewise increased. It is hard to determine whether the majority of the population was Jewish. But even if it was, the proportion of the pagan population was quite considerable. Large numbers of pagans lived in the region of Galilee, as well as in many of the newly conquered cities, such as the port city of Jaffa. The population of the new cities established in Judaea by the Ptolemies was, of course, also pagan. The sages were cognizant of the presence of these large masses of "strangers" in the country, and enacted many specific laws for their protection.

The heterogeneous population of the country consisted of distinct social classes. Besides the aristocracy and peasantry of the Persian period, new, ever-growing classes of artisans and traders came into being under the Hasmoneans. The bulk of the population, however, consisted of peasants, and agriculture was dominant in the Judaean economy. Most of the products of the fields consisted of grains, fruits, and vegetables grown for domestic consumption. Judaean agriculture, however, also grew choice dates and balsam which were in great demand abroad and became a major product for export. Judaean balsam was widely used in the production of cosmetics and medicines. Every seventh year, when in accordance with the biblical law all work in the fields had to be stopped, the authorities took measures to assure that the grain crops from the unattended fields should be properly distributed. For this purpose special officials gathered the grain and the fruit, placed it in communal storehouses, and distributed it free each Sabbath eve in quantities proportionate to the size of the families of the recipients. While most of the people probably prepared for themselves staples for the sabbatical year prior to its beginning, the free distribution of grain, even in small quantities, was of great benefit to the poor classes of the population.

Export, and maritime trade in general, greatly increased under the Hasmoneans. This was due in great part to the fact that under them Judaea acquired an outlet to the sea. Of vital importance was the conquest of Jaffa by Simon. We have seen that even before Alexander's arrival Greek trading posts were a familiar sight on the Judaean coast. When the Hasmonean rulers annexed the coast to their state, full use could be made of the already existing trading facilities. The country did not fully rely upon the Greek traders, of course, and a Judaean merchant marine of considerable size came into being. Besides the products of the Judaean fields and orchards, asphalt from the Dead Sea was a major article of export. Judaean asphalt became so widely used, that the Dead Sea became known among the Greeks as the "Sea of Asphalt." Most of the asphalt was, however, exported to Egypt, which bought it in enormous quantities. Judaean trade was further promoted by two major caravan routes which traversed the country. Besides the route leading from Mesopotamia to Egypt, which had existed for centuries in the pre-exilic times, Judaean roads were now frequented also by caravans traveling from the Arabian peninsula to Asia Minor.

While the increased trade brought much wealth into the country, and the standard of living was rising, the lot of the bulk of the population, the peasants, was not as fortunate. The peasants' main staples were still grains, fruits, and vegetables, while meat was consumed only occasionally. In addition, the peasants were plagued by perpetual shortages of water and recurrent locust invasions. The poverty of the peasants was matched by a low social status. They, and even the somewhat better situated artisans, could not be appointed judges or members of town councils. The term *ame haaretz,* applied to the peasants, assumed a derogatory connotation among their contemporaries, and as such survived in the Jewish folklore down to modern times.

The lot of the masses was further aggravated by a system of taxation which became ever heavier and heavier. Under the Seleucids, and possibly even earlier under the Ptolemies, most of the income of the peasant was taken away from him in the form of taxes. One-third of the crop and one-half of the fruits a farmer harvested he had to hand over to the government. In addition, he still was obliged by the Pentateuchal law to give to the priests and Levites the prescribed tithes. In Judaea, at the time of Nehemiah's arrival (about 444 B.C.E.), the farmers were trying to avoid paying the tithes. We may assume that this became an even more widespread practice under the Ptolemies and Seleucids, when little was left to the peasants after they delivered to the government its share of the crop.

It is possible that beginning with 143 B.C.E., when the Syrian government gave up its claim to an annual tribute from Judaea, the tax burden became lighter. If this was the case, the relief was only temporary. As soon as the Hasmoneans began to pursue a policy of war and conquest, the expenditures for the army rose immensely. True, the inhabitants of the newly acquired territories were no doubt heavily taxed, and the increased foreign trade and the caravan routes brought large amounts of money into the coffers of the state. But the maintenance of a sizable army, a considerable part of which was composed of mercenaries, increased the expenditures of the state to a hitherto unknown degree.

The backbone of the system of taxation became the tithes. One-third of the tithes was collected by the Hasmonean ruler, and this was justified by the fact that he belonged to a priestly family. *Gabbaim,* tax collectors, are often mentioned in the contemporary literature. In addition, a tax was levied on those who brought sacrifices to the Temple, and on all imported and exported merchandise. These sources seem to have provided the Hasmoneans with the funds necessary to cover their expenditures, and enabled them to amass a state treasure deposited for safekeeping in various fortresses in the south of the country. All this, however, became insufficient during the 27 years of Jannaeus' war-ridden reign. The king therefore imposed upon the people the most burdensome of all taxes, a poll tax. It was this onerous levy that angered the people to the degree of resorting to rebellion. They began to view the period when Judaea was ruled by a high priest who refrained from waging wars, as an ideal time. Thus to them it was not treason when they threw their support to the invading Syrian king, but rather an attempt to restore a lost, idealized past.

Chapter 4

Sadducees and Pharisees

The stormy events of the Hasmonean era resulted in the emergence of groups with divergent views on the national goals of the Jewish people and on the role of the Judaean state. During the period of the First Commonwealth the people were divided from time to time on two clear-cut issues: the religion of YHWH as against idolatry, and the question of whether the Israelitic states should align themselves with the powerful neighbor in the southwest (Egypt), or with the equally powerful neighbor in the northeast (Assyria-Babylonia). During the period of the Second Commonwealth, however, the life of the people and the issues confronting it became much more complex. The question of the legitimacy of the Hasmonean dynasty was complicated by the concentration of the spiritual and secular authority in the hands of the same person (high priest-king).

The proliferation of literature and the entrenchment of the synagogue as the house of worship alongside the Temple, put into focus the basic questions of the nature of religious life. To answer these questions two distinct groups emerged and attempted to identify the goals to which the Jewish people should strive. The two groups, Sadducees and Pharisees, gave different, often diametrically opposed, answers to the issues confronting the people, and their answers were clearly conditioned by the different political and economic strata of the population from which they drew their following.

The Sadducees were a group of people who considered the Temple and the sacrificial service the only legitimate center of the Jewish religion. They therefore favored for Judaea a hierocratic regime and wished the Jews to be a cult-oriented society. It is not known with certainty when the group began to organize itself, nor is the meaning of the name "Sadducees" fully clear. The most plausible explanation of the name seems to be that it derived from the name of Zadok, who was installed by Solomon as high priest in the Temple. The Sadducees were of the opinion that only Zadok's descendants were legitimately eligible for the position of high priest, and only they were to be accepted as rulers of Judaea. "Sadducean" tendencies may have surfaced as early as at the time of the Restoration, in the form of opposition to Zerubabel and his claims to the Judaean throne. The Sadducees do not appear, however, as an organized group until the time of the Hasmonean rebellion. At that time they, together with the rest of the people, opposed Antiochus' oppressive measures.

With the entrenchment of the Hasmoneans as rulers of Judaea, the Sadducean party became more active and its ideology more defined. They seem to have relaxed their opinion that only Zadok's descendants could be considered legitimate high priests, and threw their support decisively to the Hasmoneans, despite the fact that the latter were non-Zadokite priests. At that time the composition of the party began to crystallize as representing the priesthood, the officialdom, the military, the merchants, and the aristocracy.

While the Sadducees were thus clearly a minority party, their influence upon the destiny of the Hasmonean state was decisive. They were aggressive nationalists and enthusiastic supporters of the policy of expansion and conquest. Their religious views were well suited to the needs of the state. By promoting the idea that the sacrificial service in the Temple was the only legitimate form of divine worship, they gave a strong boost to the Hasmonean priest-kings and helped to enhance their status. They accepted the Pentateuchal law in its literal meaning, and thus limited in practice the position of religion within Judaean society. Much attention and energy could thus be diverted toward the secularist goals of building the state and expanding its borders. While they advocated strict adherence to the Pentateuchal law, their attitude to the other books of the Hebrew Bible was less positive. And, of course, they decisively rejected all the customs and folkways, many going back to old times, which precisely then began to take on more and more the character of an oral law. They consequently rejected many ideas, such as immortality of the soul and resurrection, which in the trying times of Antiochus' persecutions became very dear to the pious among the people.

Being the party favored by the government, the Sadducees were always represented in the Sanhedrin. In times when the

Pharisaic opponents of the crown were expelled from the Sanhedrin, the Sadducees became its controlling majority. The party continued to exist even after Judaea became a Roman dependency, and still controlled the priesthood and the Temple, as well as the civil administration of the country. But with the destruction of the Temple in the year 70 C.E. the Sadducees lost the last base for their existence as an organized group, and disappeared from the historical arena. Their basic religious idea of accepting the Written Law and rejecting the Oral continued, however, to find supporters, sometimes openly and at other times clandestinely. These attempts at a comeback met with a lesser or greater degree of success.

Totally different from the Sadducees in composition and outlook were the Pharisees. Their origin too, as well as the meaning of their name, are shrouded in mystery. "Pharisaic" tendencies, too, may have surfaced shortly after the Restoration in the form of opposition to the high priest as Judaea's secular ruler. Be this as it may, all through the period of the Second Commonwealth the Pharisees kept gaining in importance until they became a broadly-based distinct popular movement led by a class of scholars, ever increasing in number and prestige. When under Antiochus IV, the high priesthood became completely compromised by a sequence of corrupt men appointed to the office, Pharisaic sages attained a status of decisive importance. Their opposition to the priesthood was so strong that they chose to deny that the latter had had any role in the transmission of the religious law during the preceding centuries.

While the Sadducean group was practically always on the side of the government, the Pharisees had frequent conflicts with Judaean rulers on matters of religion and state. They only reluctantly tolerated the Hasmoneans as high priests and rulers, and were therefore repeatedly removed from the Sanhedrin and from influence on the matters of state. In times of fiscal oppression and mass executions by the Hasmonean rulers, the Pharisees were even ready to prefer foreign domination tolerant to Jewish religious life over the rule of a corrupt Jewish king. They were by no means opponents of Judaean statehood and independence, but they were not in favor of harnessing all the energy and resources of the nation for the cause of endless territorial expansion. In their view the state should have been a framework for a peaceful existence of a people dedicated to the service of God, the study of the Law, and social justice. The never-ending military campaigns of the Hasmonean rulers not only did not promote these goals, but severely limited the prospects for their attainment. Herod's reign (37 B.C.E.–4 B.C.E.) and the subsequent brutual Roman rule (see Chap. 6) convinced the Pharisees that a state as such does not secure the tranquility and future of the nation, and that only a life fully devoted to the service of God can insure the uninterrupted existence of the people and save it from assimilation. These views were shared by the vast majority of the Jewish population.

While the religious ideas of the Sadducees were rigid and limited in scope, those of the Pharisees were comprehensive and refined, and had a decisive impact on the religious life of the Jew for many generations to come. Like the prophets, the Pharisees were not opposed to the Temple cult. On the contrary, they encouraged the laity to attend Temple services as often as possible, and even endeavored to introduce into the Temple folk customs not found in the Pentateuch. But, like the prophets, they did not wish to limit the religious experience of the people to the Temple cult, which was vicarious by nature. Their goal was to fill the life of the Jew with religious experience, independent of the Temple. They therefore began to stress the validity of the Oral Law, a body of rules and customs not recorded in Scripture, but much alive in the religious practice of the people. At the same time, however, the Pharisees endeavored to purify the oral tradition of all traces of superstition, and to convey to the people a concept of God who is not anthropomorphic, but incorporeal and intangible, and who has attributes instead of names. This God, although having chosen the people of Israel, was nevertheless a universal God, a God of all mankind. He gave to man the power of reasoning and of free choice. He holds man accountable for his acts in this life, and rewards or punishes him in the hereafter in accordance with his deeds.

To teach the people the two-fold Law, the Written and the Oral, the Pharisees resorted to a program of preaching and teaching. The synagogue was a natural base for their activities and for the non-cultic religious life of the people. Although of earlier origin (cf. Sec. VII, Chap. 3), the synagogue became all-important by the endorsement and promotion given to it by the Pharisees. Through their influence, the synagogue became the true house of worship of the people, in practice often rivaling the Temple in Jerusalem.

Unlike the Sadducees, the Pharisees opposed a rigid interpretation of the Pentateuchal law. To them the Holy Writ was a "living Torah" valid for all times, and never in conflict with the time. By using the God-given power of reason and special method of interpretation, various Pentateuchal laws could be reinterpreted and modified to harmonize with the advanced ideas of each generation. The law was not ethnic in nature and could be followed by those Gentiles who as a result of sincere conviction were ready to accept it and join the Jewish people as proselytes. The Pharisees rejected, however, the imposing of the Jewish religion by force upon entire peoples, as practiced by Hasmonean rulers.

The Pharisaic leader-scholar enjoyed among the Judaeans a status similar to that of the philosopher-statesman among the Greeks. His views, resembling those of the Stoics, were, through their pragmatism, decisive in strengthening the moral stamina of the people to overcome the general despair created by the brutality of the later Hasmonean rulers and the Roman procurators who followed them. *The Sayings of the Fathers* tell us of the lofty way of life which the Pharisees attempted to create for themselves and recommended to the people as the means to survive with dignity in this world and to gain eternal life in the hereafter. They thus were the true followers of the prophets of the First Commonwealth in their insistence that man is capable of establishing in this world an order of justice and dignity, the Kingdom of God.

While the Sadducean movement disappeared from the historical scene with the destruction of the Temple and the liquidation of the last vestiges of the Jewish civil administration in Judaea, the influence of the Pharisees survived long beyond that time. Whether the name "Pharisees" was given to them by their opponents to denigrate them, or whether it came to denote their perpetual readiness to interpret or reinterpret the Law, their principles and teachings became tantamount to normative Judaism. There may have been among them some hypocrites, and at times they may have been harsh on their opponents, but in its totality Pharisaism bequeathed a great heritage to the Jewish people and an "invisible territory" to a people destined to live scattered among many nations and cultures.

Section VI

JUDAEA UNDER ROME

Chapter 1

Early Roman Rule

After Pompey's departure from Judaea, a period of relative peace began. Hyrcanus II was high priest, while Antipater continued to be the real power behind the throne. Several attempts of Aristobulus and his son Alexander to regain power ended in failure, and both were ultimately executed by the Romans.

Meanwhile, Antipater proceeded to tighten his hold over the country by having his son Phasael appointed governor of Jerusalem, and his son Herod governor of Galilee in 47 B.C.E. While Phasael seems to have had no serious conflicts with the population of Jerusalem, Herod's rule in Galilee added turmoil to this generally troubled region. A group of patriotic fighters was active in the border region trying to wrest from Syria a certain area and annex it to Judaea. Herod, who considered these activities anti-Roman, captured the leader of the group, Hezekiah, possibly a member of a younger branch of the Hasmonean family, and executed him together with a number of his followers.

Herod's act was considered by the people to have been illegal, and Hyrcanus II found himself compelled, under public pressure, to summon Herod to stand trial before the Sanhedrin of 23 members in Jerusalem. Herod behaved during the trial in a fashion which evoked the anger of the tribunal, and it appeared that the latter would declare Herod guilty on the next day. Hyrcanus sensed what was coming, and made it possible for Herod to escape during the night.

The power of Antipater and his family was further augmented when Julius Caesar made Antipater a Roman citizen and appointed him procurator of Judaea, that is, the representative of Rome in the country. Shortly thereafter, however, a last attempt was made to unseat the Antipater family. A certain Malichus who had gained Hyrcanus' confidence, and who seemed also to have enjoyed widespread support among the population, began to gain influence. Antipater's sudden death in 43 B.C.E., possibly as a result of poisoning by Malichus' hirelings, and not without Hyrcanus' knowledge, created a realistic possibility of freeing Judaea from the grip of the Antipater family. Herod, however, the shrewdest and most aggressive among Antipater's sons, thwarted Malichus' plans, and brought about his assassination.

Yet, Herod still had to overcome another serious obstacle on his way to the Judaean throne. Aristobulus' other son, Mattathias-Antigonus, now appeared on the scene in an attempt to gain for himself the Judaean throne with the help of a mighty ally. Rome's only adversary in the Near East, never defeated by her, was Parthia. The unstable border between Parthia and Rome's possessions in western Asia was somewhere in the desert which lay between Judaea, Syria, and Mesopotamia. It was therefore a realistic idea for Antigonus to suggest that the Parthians wrest Judaea from the Romans and let him rule it as their vassal-king. The Parthians agreed, and Antigonus indeed succeeded in establishing himself in the year 40 B.C.E. as king and high priest in Jerusalem with their help. Hyrcanus was deposed from the high priesthood, and his ears were cut off to make him unfit to assume the office again. He was deported to Parthia, where he lived in high esteem among that country's Jews.

This was the most critical point in Herod's quest for the Judaean throne. But it was also an opportune moment to convince Rome to throw her full support to him. The contest between a prince of a tiny kingdom and an ambitious aristocrat was suddenly transformed into a contest between the world's greatest power and her greatest adversary. Herod knew that his salvation lay in Rome, and he immediately sailed there. In Rome, Herod was received in a friendly manner, and the Senate, convinced of his loyalty, unanimously appointed him king of Judaea in 40 B.C.E. It was clear to Herod that despite their endorsement the Romans would not fight his war against Antigonus, and that it was up to him to achieve his goal. He then shrewdly used the inner divisions in Judaea and the enormous wealth accumulated by the Antipater family to promote his plans. Upon his landing in Acre early in 39 B.C.E., he immediately set out to recruit an army of mercenaries. Some Judaeans were among his followers, as was the entire Samaritan nation, probably still resenting the destruction of their temple on Mount Gerizim by the Hasmoneans. The Idumaeans, of course, supported Herod (who possibly was their kinsman). Herod also cleverly utilized a strategic blunder made by Antigonus, and in January 37 B.C.E. he captured Jerusalem with the help of Roman units. Antigonus surrendered to the Romans and was executed. Herod thus became undisputed ruler of Judaea.

In addition to the endorsement by Rome, Herod tried to win a semblance of legitimacy by marrying, during the time Jerusalem was besieged, the Hasmonean princess Mariamme. Several years earlier he had betrothed her to himself both for his love for her and for the legitimacy she could provide him in case of his ascension to the Judaean throne. Mariamme was a granddaughter of both Hasmonean brothers Hyrcanus II and Aristobulus II, and a man married to her could hope for wide support in the nation. The consummation of the marriage to Mariamme a short while before the capture of Jerusalem added strength to the new king's position in the country.

Chapter 2

The Reign of Herod (37–4 B.C.E.)

Herod's authority as king of Judaea was ambiguous and uncertain. He was an "ally and friend of Rome," but without the right of establishing a dynasty. His position was further endangered by the rivalry between Marc Anthony and Octavian, which compelled every client king to take sides. Herod overcame most of these difficulties by his astuteness as a statesman and by his superior skill as an administrator. It was this latter characteristic which made him a valuable "ally and friend" of whoever at a given time ruled in Rome. This is why Octavian supported him and steadily increased his territory.

Within the country, Herod's rule brought many advantages to the people by virtue of his success in eliminating brigandry, and in establishing a regime of general safety on the highways, in the villages, and in the towns. Nevertheless, the masses did not consider his times a happy period in the life of the country. He was, to begin with, considered an alien, more due to his behavior than to his alleged Idumaean origin. Most of his officials were non-Jews, and his army was largely composed of foreign mercenaries. In addition, his cruelty in dealing with any kind of opposition alienated the people.

This became evident shortly after his elevation to the throne, when he began to eliminate the last Hasmoneans and their sympathizers. A number of pro-Hasmonean members of the Sanhedrin were among his first victims. But, even more shocking was the way in which he put to death Mariamme's brother Aristobulus, sometimes called Aristobulus III. Early in his reign Herod was compelled by the intrigues of Mariamme's mother Alexandra to appoint her young son Aristobulus as high priest. Being, however, determined to eliminate him, he invited Aristobulus to his palace in Jericho and had him drowned by two of his henchmen during a party of water frolics. His formal expression of grief and the magnificent funeral which he arranged for the young high priest did not, however, fool the people.

The resentment of the people was further augmented by a fiscal system which cruelly exacted high taxes not always spent for the benefit of the country, and by the ruthless confiscation of the property of the king's opponents. Sensing that under the surface of his "pax Herodiana" the pent-up hatred of the people was steadily growing, Herod set out on a program of the building of fortresses, not for the protection of the country against invaders, but for the prevention of a possible uprising against him. In addition, he reinforced several hilltop fortresses in southeastern Judaea, built by the Hasmoneans.

As time went on, Herod's fear of an uprising intensified, and he reacted to it by executing more and more Judaeans whom he suspected of conspiring against him. His fears of a conspiracy led him also to put to death many members of his immediate family. The situation in the palace was constantly tense due to the rivalries and intrigues of some of its female inhabitants, especially Herod's sister Salome and Mariamme's mother Alexandra. The first victim was the old earless Hyrcanus II, whom Herod had lured back to Jerusalem from Babylonia in 36 B.C.E., to have him under surveillance. He was put to death in 30 B.C.E. His granddaughter, the Queen Mariamme, probably the most beloved among Herod's many wives, met a similar fate. She was executed in 29 B.C.E. Her two sons were executed late in Herod's reign, and another son, Agrippa, was put to death only five days before Herod himself died. A similar fate also befell Alexandra, Hyrcanus' daughter and Mariamme's mother.

Strange as it may seem, all the time these atrocities were being committed, Herod was performing unusual acts of magnanimity in the wider Greco-Roman world. He was by choice more Roman than Jew. He had no interest in Jewish culture, and the law of the Torah was not his way of life. But he lavishly supported the Olympic games, and built many gymnasia and temples for the pagans. The two cities he built in Judaea, Sebaste on the site of Israel's former capital Samaria, and Caesarea were both largely non-Jewish cities. His contemporaries in the Greco-Roman world were so impressed by his deeds that they called him Herod the Great.

Being the greatest builder in Judaea since Solomon, Herod also proceeded, about the year 22 B.C.E., to rebuild and enlarge the Temple of Jerusalem. With the enormous increase in the Judaean population, and the countless pilgrims coming to the holy city from the Diaspora, the modest Temple built by the returnees from Babylonia in the sixth century B.C.E. became too small. Herod therefore increased the Temple mount by encircling it with a wall, and subsequently filling in the encircled areas. Thus the area on which the new Temple was built was double the size of the former Temple mount. The new Temple, sometimes called the Third Temple, and sometimes Herod's Temple, was indeed a magnificent structure. Ironically, the people kept on beautifying the new edifice for several generations, and the Temple came to be considered complete only a few short years before its destruction. Though the Judaeans were no doubt pleased by the erection of the new Temple, they still considered Herod an alien. His inability to understand the feelings of the Judaeans manifested itself when he put a golden eagle over the main gate of the Temple to symbolize his allegiance to Rome. Nothing was more abhorrent to the Judaeans than the sight of an image over the Temple of their invisible God who commanded them not to make images. Many a young, pious Judaean lost his life in an attempt to pull down the golden image. Under these circumstances, not even Herod's successful intercessions in favor of Jewish communities in the Diaspora could change the opinion the Judaeans had of him.

In his latter years Herod suffered from a grave illness. The repeated rumors of his death only show that the people looked forward to the end of his rule, which was simultaneously beneficial and tyrannical. He died in the year 4 B.C.E.

Chapter 3

The Roman Procurators

According to Herod's will, his son Archelaus was to inherit his title of king and rule in Judaea, Samaria, and Idumaea. Two other sons were to rule in the North and in Transjordan: Herod Antipas in Galilee and Peraea (a narrow strip of land east of the Jordan), and Philip in the border region between Judaea and Syria including Ituraea, whose inhabitants were forcibly converted to Judaism by Judah Aristobulus. The will had no legal validity, however, since the Roman Senate did not give to Herod's sons the right of succession at the time when it appointed their father king of Judaea. Herod's sons had therefore to go to Rome in order to obtain consent for assuming power in the areas allotted to them in their father's will. In the meantime, serious riots had broken out in various parts of the country. Inevitably the superior Roman forces easily suppressed the rebels. About 2,000 Judaeans were crucified. Roman vengeance came down especially cruelly upon Galilee's largest city Sepphoris, which was burned and whose inhabitants were sold into slavery.

The Roman government confirmed most of Herod's will. However, it did not grant to Archelaus the title of king, but made him ethnarch (ruler) of Judaea, while his brothers were given the title of tetrarch, that is, ruler of a "quarter" of the land. The rule of the three brothers was rather uneventful except for Herod Antipas' execution in 29 C.E. of John the Baptist, an event which assumed major significance in the history of early Christianity (see Sec. VII, Chap. 5), but which was probably not considered very important at the time it occurred. Like their father the two tetrarchs built new cities. Herod Antipas built the city of Tiberias in honor of the Emperor Tiberius, and Philip built Caesarea Philippi in Ituraea, so called to distinguish it from Caesarea built by Herod in Samaria.

The Roman government seems not to have been satisfied with Archelaus' performance as a ruler, and it removed him from office in 6 C.E.; he was deported to Gallia (today's France). The same fate befell Herod Antipas many years later. Only Philip, who was the most humane among the brothers, was permitted to rule his tetrarchy to the end of his life. Upon the removal of Archelaus and Antipas, and Philip's death, Judaea became a Roman province, henceforth to be governed by a Roman official with the title of *procurator.*

The period of the procurators lasted about 60 years, interrupted only by the seven years of the reign of King Agrippa I (37–44 C.E.). Five procurators ruled the country from Archelaus' removal to Agrippa's appointment, and seven between Agrippa's death and the outbreak of the war against Rome in 66 C.E. The procurators were appointed by the emperor and were directly accountable to him. Not a single one among them was able to win the confidence of the Judaean people. Most of them were dishonest men, bent on enriching themselves during the few years they expected to hold the office. In addition, they had no understanding for the peculiar attitudes and customs of the Jews, who were different from all other peoples tributary to Rome. They, therefore, often offended the Judaeans, even though this was not their intention. The period of the procurators was thus marked by rising tensions which ultimately led to the outbreak of the war.

The period of the procurators was ushered in by a census, that is, a registration of all inhabitants of the country and their property. It was customary in the Roman empire to hold a census once every five years, and now was a time for such a census. Jews, however, traditionally disliked censuses. They therefore opposed the census, and even more so because it forshadowed the imposition of new heavy taxes. It is possible that the word "census" assumed in the Hebrew dialect of that time the meaning of "penalty" or "fine" (Hebrew *qenas*). In reaction to the census, the group of aggressive fighters against Rome, known as "Zealots," came into being at that time under the leadership of Judah, a son of Hezekiah, who was executed by Herod. There is a likelihood that Judah, a scion of the Hasmoneans, aspired to the throne of Judaea. Although the Romans cruelly crucified many of the Zealots, their seemingly hopeless war against mighty Rome did not cease.

The procurators chose as their residence not Jerusalem but the coastal city Caesarea. They probably felt more secure in this largely pagan city than in the perpetually tumultuous Holy City. They also probably stayed away from Jerusalem out of the desire not to offend the Jews by displaying standards and shields on which the image of the emperor was engraved. During holidays, however, when large numbers of pilgrims converged on Jerusalem, the procurators would go there to supervise order and keep the peace. In addition to matters of internal security, the procurators controlled the finances of the country and the collection of taxes. They had the right to appoint high priests and to keep the priestly robes in their custody. Occasionally they would also initiate programs of public works. By and large, however, the Herodian civil administration continued to function, as did also the Sanhedrin, whatever its prerogatives may have been at that time.

In the year 37 C.E., an unexpected change of major significance took place. Caius Caligula, upon ascending Rome's imperial throne, appointed Herod's grandson Agrippa as king over an ever-increasing territory in Galilee and Transjordan. Agrippa was a son of Aristobulus, Mariamme's and Herod's son executed by his father in 7 B.C.E. As a child, Agrippa was sent to Rome, where he grew up among the aristocracy. The Emperor Tiberius employed him in his household as a tutor. It seems that he lived an aimless life, as one of Rome's "golden youth." His Jewish interests seem to have been nil. His closest friend at that time was Caius Caligula. When Caius became emperor, Agrippa was in jail, where he had been put by the Emperor Tiberius for having expressed in a state of drunkenness the hope for Caius' quick ascendance to the throne.

Predictably, the new emperor immediately released his faithful friend from prison. In addition, as we have seen, he appointed him king over the territory of his late uncle Philip. On his way to his newly acquired kingdom, Agrippa visited Alexandria, and was given a rousing reception by the local Jewish community. The fact that a Jewish prince, who was of Hasmonean origin, had appeared on the scene, evidently generated hope that an end might come to the detested rule of the procurators in the Holy Land. The reception in Alexandria made a deep impact on Agrippa, who suddenly became conscious of his Jewishness and of the opportunity with which destiny confronted him. Upon arrival in the Holy Land, he began to act in a manner which decisively endeared him to the Jewish population. Simultaneously he had the occasion to successfully intercede in favor of Diaspora Jewry at the imperial court in Rome.

The greatest moment in the life of Agrippa I came when Caius was assassinated in 41 C.E. Being at the time in Rome, Agrippa had the opportunity to mediate between the new Emperor Claudius and a balky Senate. A grateful Claudius then appointed him king over all the territories formerly ruled by his grandfather Herod, and the rule of the procurators came to a temporary end. The years Agrippa I reigned in Jerusalem (41–44 C.E.) became a short golden age in the middle of the 60 years of procuratorial oppression and brutality. He personally conducted himself as an observant Jew and fully respected the Jewish law in public affairs. He entrenched himself deeply in the memory of the Jewish people as a compassionate and pious king. He had serious doubts as to whether he was a legitimate king of the Jews, having been partly of non-Jewish origin, but public opinion, probably disregarding the legal aspects, declared him enthusiastically to be a "brother" (Deuteronomy 17:15).

Agrippa I enjoyed the full confidence of both Caius and Claudius, who left him a fairly free hand in managing Judaea's affairs. He nevertheless thought it wise to strengthen his position in Judaea, and began to rebuild the walls of Jerusalem. But this was precisely the thing Rome's client king was not supposed to do. Consequently, the Roman legate of Syria, who seems to have claimed authority over Judaea even when it was ruled by a king appointed by the emperor, compelled Agrippa to discontinue the work. Contemporaries were of the opinion that had Agrippa completed the wall, the Romans would not have been able to capture the city in the year 70 C.E. Agrippa died a short while after the setback with the wall, in Caesarea of an unknown cause (44 C.E.); the possibility should not be dismissed that the Romans, concerned about his political plans, brought about his death by administering poison to him.

Agrippa's son, known as Agrippa II, inherited from his father the title of king, but only a minor part of his territories in the north, where only a small number of Jews lived. His only connection with Jerusalem was the task given to him by the Romans to supervise the Temple, to appoint high priests, and to keep their ceremonial robes in his custody. In all other respects the areas inhabited by Jews (Judaea, Samaria, and Galilee) were now again under exclusive procuratorial rule.

During the 22 years between the death of Agrippa I and the outbreak of the First Revolt against Rome, the emperors sent to Judaea seven procurators. They all, except for Tiberius Alexander, a nephew of the philosopher Philo, aggravated the situation in the country by perpetually offending the feelings of the Jews. They repeatedly arrested young Jews for attempts to remove Herod's golden eagle from the Temple wall. Furthermore, the procurators sporadically offended the Jews by tolerating the deliberate destruction of Torah scrolls by Roman soldiers. The situation became especially grave in the '50s under the procurator Antonius Felix. Small wonder that the Ẓealots' call for revenge appealed to ever-growing numbers of Judaeans. Though once part of the Pharisaic movement, the Zealots were now less and less inclined to listen to the calls for moderation coming from the Pharisaic leadership. In fact, an even more radical group emerged from among the Zealots, called *Sicarii* because they carried in their robes concealed daggers with which they attacked unsuspecting Romans. The previously sporadic anti-Roman outbreaks became an almost daily occurrence. The country was rapidly approaching an open revolt against Rome.

Section VII

SOCIETY, CULTURE, AND RELIGION IN THE SECOND COMMONWEALTH

Chapter 1

Social and Cultural Conditions

The socioeconomic conditions in Judaea under Roman rule were not basically different from those under the Hasmoneans, but the social and economic contrasts now became more visible and serious. The urban centers became bigger and trade assumed a wider scope. The influx of Gentiles into the new cities, such as Sebaste and Caesarea, brought into the country additional urban elements, and the increased trade, further promoted by the general safety on the roads during the 33 years of Herod's rule, was by no means limited to the Gentile population. Suffice it to say that a major port city like Jaffa had a Jewish majority, and even largely pagan Caesarea had a Jewish community of 20,000. The fact that under Herod the sages, led by Hillel, found it necessary to introduce the *prosbol,* a major legal innovation designed to facilitate credit operations hitherto impeded by the Pentateuchal law, clearly attests to massive Jewish involvement in the expanded trade. Alongside the increased merchant class, the class of skilled workers was growing in numbers as well.

The majority of the population, however, consisted of peasants, who steadily became poorer. The harsh exaction of taxes by Herod and the procurators created an ever-growing mass of landless proletarians. In years of famine their situation became especially precarious. They streamed in large numbers to the cities, and it was mainly among them that the Zealots found followers, men driven by despair to tumultuous and radical actions.

The composite nature of the Judaean population continued to be reflected in the linguistic conditions. It was a trilingual country where Hebrew, Aramaic, and Greek were equally used. It seems that the language most common among the Jewish population, especially in the countryside, was Aramaic. Hebrew, however, was still in use among the sages to a certain degree as a spoken language. To be sure, its use in literature was by far more widespread than in everyday life. The Greek language was spoken not only by the Gentile population, but also by the higher strata of the Jewish population, including the priests. The use of Greek in the latter period of the Second Commonwealth was no longer considered among the Jews a sign of assimilation. Many Greek words penetrated the Hebrew style of the time, not only in the field of trade but also in the religious literature. Some Greek words are even found in late biblical books. The script used by the Jews was not uniform. Both the old Hebrew script and an early form of the square, or Assyrian, alphabet are found in manuscripts that have come down to us from those times.

In this period the opposition to Hellenistic culture, so strong at the time of the Hasmonean revolution, had largely subsided. No one, including Hellenized kings, such as Judah Aristobulus I, called Philhellen, or his brother and successor Jannaeus Alexander, or even the totally un-Jewish Herod, tried to impose upon the Jews Hellenistic culture by force. Nor were gymnasia, the most hated Hellenistic institution, built in the Jewish cities after the success of the Hasmonean revolt. As a result, Greek names were now used even in the circles of the sages. Some Greek customs, and the Greek style of public life, imported by the countless settlers in the new cities, were now widely adopted. Greek influences were especially noticeable in the urban centers. Even the visual arts now found limited acceptance among the Jews. Engravings and carved pictures were not infrequent, even in synagogues. The traditional Jewish opposition to the visual arts now, it seems, limited itself mainly to portrayals of the human form. Only the golden eagle placed by Herod over the Temple portals continued to be unacceptable to the Judaeans. Its character as the emblem of the Roman oppressor may have been the cause.

In the latter part of the Second Commonwealth education assumed more organized forms than hitherto. The fact that the Pentateuch imposed on every individual Jew the obligation to educate his children may have served as a hindrance to the organization of a formal school system. Only priests who had to learn the involved ritual of the sacrificial service possibly received training in an organized and formal way. A modern theory has it that the custom of initiating a child in the study of the Pentateuch by first teaching him the Book of Leviticus may have been an echo from distant times when the priests studied this book, which contains most of the laws and regulations of the sacrificial service. With the rise of the religio-cultural complexities in the period of the Second Commonwealth, however, private instruction handed down from father to son may have proved inadequate. Thus, the way was opened to a more formal and organized system of education.

Priests and levites continued to be trained in their professional schools, the former in the sacrificial laws, and the latter in music and the use of musical instruments. The first public schools were probably established for the education of children who for some reason were unable to receive parental instruction. This was done at the initiative of the Pharisaic leader Simon ben Shetah, possibly a brother of Queen Salome Alexandra. A public school open to every child seems to have functioned at first in Jerusalem, but only in the last few years preceding the outbreak of the war against Rome was a universal public school system for all children established on a countrywide basis. There are indications that High Priest Joshua ben Gamala (Gamliel) was instrumental in bringing about this fundamental educational improvement.

The elementary school, called *beth hasepher,* house of the book, was by its nature a religious school, where mainly the Pentateuch was taught. It is possible that the name "house of the book" was given to the school because in it the Book, that is, the Bible, was studied. In addition to the Pentateuch, the students were also taught arithmetic and geometry, since the knowledge of these two subjects was necessary for the performance of certain religious rites and commandments. Instruction was given in Hebrew, but Aramaic was no doubt used as frequently in the school. Simultaneously, an elaborate system of adult education was functioning. Instruction in the Pentateuch for adults was given regularly on Sabbaths, mostly in the synagogues. During the months preceding Passover and the High Holidays adult studies were intensified. The more advanced school was called *beth hamidrash*, house of interpretation. Here the Jewish law was discussed and interpreted, and out of these schools came the galaxy of brilliant sages, who became known as "Tannaim" and whose teachings found literary permanence in the Mishnah. Most outstanding among them in this period was Hillel. He was possibly an immigrant from Babylonia who was held in high esteem due to his learning, righteousness, and humility. About the year 10 B.C.E. he was elevated to the presidency of the Sanhedrin. He issued a number of ordinances of major importance, some of which gained acceptance in his lifetime, while others became part of the Jewish law in later generations. Except for short intervals, his descendants headed the Jewish community in the Holy Land as patriarchs (*nesiim*) down to the early fifth century C.E. (A detailed description of the scholarly achievements of the Tannaim and of the Jewish Oral Law, the Halakhah, interpreted and formulated by them, will be given in a future chapter.)

Chapter 2

The Literature of the Second Commonwealth

During the period of the Second Commonwealth great events occurred in the field of Jewish literature. This was the time when the Bible, largely written during the period of the First Commonwealth, assumed the form of a canonized text. Although much of the literature of the First Commonwealth perished due to illiteracy, difficulties in copying, and an inhospitable climate, a major body of literature remained to be transformed by the sages of the Second Commonwealth into the Book of Books. In addition, this period made its own significant contribution to Jewish literature. The collection of works called in modern times "Apocrypha" and "Pseudepigrapha" and "sectarian writings" constitute by themselves a literary monument of decisive importance. This was also the time when foundations were laid for the Rabbinic literature in all its ramifications. (A description of the Rabbinic and sectarian literatures also belongs to later chapters.)

Early in the period the square, or Assyrian, script was introduced into Judaea, largely replacing, but not fully eliminating, the ancient Hebrew script. It is hard to say what impact the duality of the script had on literary developments. What was surely beneficial to literature was the availability of a greater variety of writing materials. Papyrus, parchment, and to a lesser degree copper were now in use.

About one-fourth of the books which make up the Bible were written during the period of the Second Commonwealth. At the very beginning of the period the last three prophets appeared, Haggai, Zechariah, and Malachi, and their writings comprise the prophetic literature of the Second Commonwealth. A selection of the contemporary historical literature consisting of the books of Ezra, Nehemiah, Esther, and Chronicles, was also included in the Bible. While these two categories of literature are basically not different from the prophetic and historical literature of the First Commonwealth, a third category, almost unknown in earlier times, the wisdom literature, or Hagiographa, now appeared on the literary scene. Books like Ecclesiastes and Job, both possibly originally written in Aramaic, seem to express spiritual and religious complexities more characteristic of the Second Commonwealth than of the First. The same holds true also of Daniel, a typically apocalyptic book, the only one to enter the Bible.

Despite many major scholarly efforts in modern times to describe the process of the canonization of the Bible, nothing definite can be said about it as yet. It is probable that some biblical books were considered holy long before the Babylonian exile. Others did not attain the status of sanctity before the second century C.E. It can be said with certainty, however, that most of the work of canonization of the Bible was done during the period of the Second Commonwealth, that is, between 538 B.C.E. and 70 C.E. It was then that the tripartite division into Pentateuch, Prophets, and Writings was given to the Bible. In addition, action was taken, partly in conformity with Greek scholarly practice, to clearly define what is "good" literature and should be included in the canon, and what should be excluded and consigned to oblivion. The general increase of the literary output and the proliferation of sectarian literature in the form of pseudepigrapha, that is, works ascribed to revered heroes of the past, made such a review an essential necessity.

The first part of the Bible, the Torah, or the Five Books of Moses, was no doubt considered of divine origin long before the Babylonian exile. Modern theories asserting that it was Ezra who "edited" the Torah are contradicted by the fact that the Samaritans, who considered Ezra their greatest enemy, accepted the Torah as a divine book. Originally one book, the Torah was divided, possibly for reasons of scribal convenience, into five books. Hence, its Greek name, "Pentateuch." Although the Torah was universally read, studied, and interpreted, divergent versions such as the Samaritan text, the Septuagint, and texts used by the so-called Qumran community, were current during the entire period of the Second Commonwealth in addition to the standard (masoretic) text. Occasionally the sages themselves purposely changed certain words in the Torah to enhance its character as a holy book.

While the Torah and the Prophets needed little or no endorsement from the sages to be accepted as divine books, it was different with regard to the third part of the Bible, the Hagiographa, or Writings. Some of these books were written in post-exilic times and lacked the aura of antiquity, some contained ideas which were controversial. Their inclusion in the Bible even became a matter of controversy among the very sages whose authority stood behind the canonization of each individual book. Consequently, the fixation of the biblical canon should not be considered a definite action taken by the sages at a particular moment, but rather as a prolonged process of deliberation and discussion, out of which the biblical canon ultimately emerged.

In general, it is not apparent what the sages considered a valid criterion for the admission of a book into the Bible. Sometimes it must have been the literary beauty of the book which earned it survival. Another time it was the content which told about the heroic and romantic past of the people. But it was basically the fact that the Bible in its totality represented a great theological history of the Israelitic people, written with unequaled candor, that led the sages to declare it the Book of Books. After all deliberations and controversies had been resolved, the Bible consisted of a total of 39 books. For reasons not fully clear, the sages coupled together various books to make the Bible a collection of only 24 books. These consist of the Five Books of Moses, eight books of Prophetic literature, which included the historical writings of the First Commonwealth, and eleven books of the Hagiographa. The work of the sages was, however, not confined to the selection of these 24 books. They also made an important contribution in deciding what version was the correct one in cases where divergent traditions existed. Finally, they attempted to determine the chronological setting of the prophecies by adding "headlines" to certain books, or even individual prophecies.

Once the canon had attained a more or less firm shape, it became customary to view it as a unit. To manifest this, the entire collection began to be designated by the name *Hasepharim*, The Books. Greek-speaking Jews then translated the name into their language, and so the name *Bible* came into use. Later other names became popular, such as *Kitve haqoḍesh*, Holy Writ, and *Miqra*, Readings. Quite popular became the name *Tanakh*, an abbreviation of the Hebrew names for Pentateuch, Prophets, and Writings. The term "Old Testament" was introduced by the Christians to distinguish between the Jewish Bible and the New Testament. This term thus has a Christian theological connotation.

The period of the Second Commonwealth is also the time when the Aramaic translation of the Bible, popularly known as *Targum* ("translation") came into being. With a considerable part of the Judaean population speaking Aramaic, it became necessary to interpret the Hebrew Pentateuch in Aramaic, whenever it was read or studied. Thus, a certain tradition of an Aramaic translation slowly developed. This was at the beginning an oral rather than a written text. The sages looked with a certain distrust at these translations, since by nature they opened the way to different interpretations of one and the same biblical passage. The sages also wished to avoid the distinct possibility of a translation assuming a degree of holiness not unlike the original Hebrew text. Nevertheless, privately written texts of the Targum were prepared. There is evidence that in the first century C.E. a leading sage was in possession of such a written text. With Jewish lore constantly growing in size, it was no longer possible to rely on memory, and opposition to the written Targum diminished. In time, the written texts began to be used also in public. But it cannot be determined with certainty whether this latter development belongs to the period of the Second Commonwealth or to a later time.

The literature of the Second Commonwealth which was not included in the Bible is divided into two groups, Apocrypha and Pseudepigrapha. Some of these books too were written in the earlier part of the period, when Judaea was under Persian domination. Most of them, however, are products of the tumultuous times often designated as the Hellenistic period. It seems that the Apocrypha and Pseudepigrapha were written in all the three languages then current among the Jews: Hebrew, Aramaic, and Greek. They all survived only in Greek. There is a possibility that some of them were originally included in the Bible but later removed from it. The reasons for their exclusion from the Bible are not all too clear, but it is a fact that as time progressed, the opposition of the sages to this literature became even stiffer. It no longer sufficed to term them *sepharim hitsoniyim*, extraneous books, or Apocrypha, hidden books. In the second century C.E. Rabbi Aqiva went as far as to threaten those who read them with the loss of eternal life. The original opposition to this literature may have developed because some of these books, and especially the Pseudepigrapha, revealed sectarian leanings. In the second century C.E., however, it became evident that the Christian Church, by then no longer a Jewish sect, had adopted them for the purpose of proving the truth of its beliefs. Hence, Rabbi Aqiva's decisive rejection.

The Apocrypha consists of a number of historical books, the most important of which is I Maccabees, originally written in

Hebrew. In this book, modeled after the historical books of the Bible, the story of the Hellenistic oppression and the Hasmonean revolution is told in detail. The reason this book, written in the best tradition of religious history, was not included in the Bible, may be due to the disappointment of the sages with the later Hasmoneans. The Apocrypha further contain three historical novels, Judith, Tobit, and Susanna, designed to strengthen the courage and the moral stamina of the people. There are also additions to, and completions of, various books in the Bible. In the group of the wisdom literature, by far the most important is Ben Sira or Ecclesiasticus. Ben Sira is a large collection of aphorisms and maxims designed to direct man to a true understanding of life. Although the work was modeled after the biblical book of Proverbs, the attitudes of the author remind us of the skepticism of Ecclesiastes. Ben Sira, composed about 180 B.C.E. in Hebrew, was translated into Greek by the author's grandson. More than any other apocryphal book, Ben Sira was popular both with the people and the sages, and is quoted in the Talmud in the manner that genuine Biblical passages are copied. By and large, the Apocrypha attempted to discredit idolatry, which in the Hellenistic period began to make some inroads among the Jews. In view of this, the question remains open as to the true reasons for their rejection by the sages.

The Pseudepigrapha consist of a larger number of books whose authorship is ascribed to heroes of old. They deal with the past only to predict an apocalyptic future. They are written in an exalted style, and attempt to divorce the reader from reality so that he may envision a predictable, preordained future. Modeled after Jacob's testament to his sons (Genesis 49) is The Testaments of the XII Patriarchs, that is, Jacob's sons, a highly moralistic book. Several other books or fragments center around the personality of Enoch, whose ascendance into heaven (Genesis 5:24) excited the mystics of those times. The most important book of the Pseudepigrapha, however, is The Book of Jubilees, originally composed in Hebrew. In an encounter between Moses and an angel on Mount Sinai, the past and the future are told in periods of 50 years. Simultaneously, many laws are discussed, usually in a more rigid form than found in the Halakhah.

While the sages rejected this extraneous literature to such a degree that the original Hebrew and Aramaic texts disappeared, Greek-speaking Jews seem to have been interested in them. Many of these books found a place in the Septuagint, the Bible of the Greek-speaking Jews (see Sec. X, Chap. 1). They also became part of the Bible as accepted in both the Catholic and Greek-Orthodox Churches.

Chapter 3

The Religious Life

The period of the Second Commonwealth witnessed the emergence of great changes in the religious life of the Judaeans. To begin with, idolatry—which had plagued Israel's society prior to the Babylonian exile—had by now disappeared, and was replaced by an uncompromising monotheism. The Hellenistic aberration was basically more of a cultural than religious nature. In addition, the God concept became refined, and YHWH was now believed to be not only intangible, but also absolutely incorporeal. The early translators of the Pentateuch took pains to spread the idea that the God of the Bible was an incorporeal God. The God of Israel ceased also to be a strictly ethnic God and became a universal God who directed the destiny of all mankind while still maintaining His unique covenantal relationship with the chosen Israel. To manifest this, the God of Israel began to be referred to as *Adonai,* the Lord of all the world. Nonetheless, foreign influences did penetrate the religious views of the Judaeans. Typical of this was the belief in angels and demons borrowed by the Babylonian Jews from their Persian neighbors. An additional source of foreign influences were the proselytes, ever increasing in number.

Favorable to the admission of proselytes were both the readiness of the Jews to accept them and the deep interest in Judaism expressed by many Gentiles upon their encounter with the world's first monotheistic religion. The new concept of the universal God made the Jews less clannish and more ready to admit aliens into their fold. Pharisaic leaders, such as Hillel, were surely impressed by the ever-growing numbers of "Fearers of the Lord," that is, Gentiles who had become disenchanted with paganism and began to revere the God of Israel without having taken the ultimate step of formally converting to Judaism. Such men surely deserved, according to Hillel, to have their entrance into the Jewish fold facilitated. Diaspora Jewry may have been even more eager to strengthen its position by an influx of proselytes. Tradition ascribes Gentile origin to so many of the sages that it should be assumed that conversion to Judaism was a daily occurrence.

Characteristic of this period is the cessation of prophecy. The three prophets of the Second Commonwealth prophesied during the period immediately following the Restoration. It is not fully clear why precisely at the time when monotheism became firmly established and Isaiah's idea of God's universality was commonly accepted such a unique and lofty religious phenomenon as prophecy disappeared. It may well be that, as a modern theory has it, the widespread knowledge of the Pentateuch made prophecy "unnecessary." God's will and guidance could now be derived from Scriptures. The interpreter of the Pentateuch had now replaced the prophet.

In the center of the religious life of the people stood the Temple and the sacrificial service. Although the Temple service was performed exclusively by priests and levites, the Temple mightily attracted the common people. It was also for the Temple service that masses of Diaspora Jews converged on Jerusalem during the three foot-holidays. In this period laymen were no longer personally performing the sacrificial service, as so often happened during the period of the First Commonwealth. In fact, the number of priests had so proliferated that the country had to be divided into 24 regions to make it possible for more priests to participate in the service on a rotating basis. A small group of priests (*mishmereth,* shift of priests) would represent an entire region, when its turn came, in the actual Temple service. The majority of the priests of the region would remain in their home town and spend the time together with many laymen in prayer and holy meditation.

The office of the high priest underwent drastic and contradictory metamorphoses. At the beginning, the high priest was elevated to the position of head of the state, and his glory was further enhanced by the popularization of the Pentateuch, the source of his authority. During the tumultuous times of the persecutions under Antiochus IV, when high priests were appointed and deposed in quick succession, the office lost much of its prestige. The way the latter Hasmoneans grabbed the office, often against the will of the people and the sages, further undercut its authority. Under Herod and the Roman procurators, unworthy men, unfit for the high office, began to be appointed. The fact that the government had custody of the high priest's robes, without which he could not officiate on the Day of Atonement, underscores the tragic situation of the high priesthood in the latter part of the Second Commonwealth.

And yet the glory of the Temple remained undiminished. The fact that Herod found it necessary to double the size of the Temple area, although by then the synagogue had come into being, attests to continued mass attendance at the Temple. Diaspora Jewry manifested its adherence by mass pilgrimages and the payment of an annual contribution. The thorough description of the Temple and its service in three full tractates of the Mishnah (Middoth, Tamid, and Yoma) clearly indicates the high esteem that the sages had for the Temple and the sacrificial service at a time when the concept of a Jewish religion based on the study of Torah, prayer, and good deeds, was no longer a novelty.

In the times of the Second Commonwealth prayer became an increasingly essential part of the religious life of the people and assumed organized forms. During most of the period of the First Commonwealth prayers were usually offered by individuals, either in the form of supplications or expressions of thanksgiving. While such prayers presumably were offered everywhere, the logical place for their recital was the Temple. In time the custom of praying became more widespread, especially praying in public, due to the unavailability of sacrificial services. It is thus possible that group prayer services came into being in Judaea in the seventh century B.C.E., when Hezekiah and Josaiah did away with the local altars and ordered that the sacrificial service should be performed exclusively in the Temple in Jerusalem. Diaspora Jewry, having decided to abstain from building temples, had to resort to group prayer services on a permanent basis, while continuing its pilgrimages to the Temple in Jerusalem.

During the period of the Second Commonwealth the legitimacy of Jerusalem as the sole place of the sacrificial service was never questioned. The deepening of the religious feelings of the people then became a major factor in the rise of prayer services. It is also understandable that the *beth hakeneseth*—the house of assembly, synagogue—became everywhere the logical place for the public prayer services. In time, prayer services became so important that the synagogue lost its primary character as a town hall and became firmly identified with prayer services. A house of prayer was ultimately erected even on the Temple mount.

It was the importance assumed by prayer which prompted the religious leadership to give it an organized form. The Great Assembly is credited with the formulation of the series of benedictions called *amidah,* and with the blessings recited when the Sabbath begins *(qiddush)* and ends *(havdalah).* The exact time of the formulation of these benedictions is unknown. Most of the prayers were taken from the Bible. The Psalms became the natural source for the Jewish prayerbook, while important passages of the Pentateuch, such as the Ten Commandments and the *shema* were also included. A certain papyrus called after its finder "the Nash papyrus," which contains the Ten Commandments and the first portion of the *shema,* is therefore sometimes called "the oldest Jewish prayerbook." The phylacteries *(tephillin)* were worn during the morning services well before the conclusion of the period of the Second Commonwealth. Prayer was often accompanied by lifting one's arms towards heaven. Diaspora Jews usually prayed in the direction of Jerusalem.

An important part of the religious life of the people was the celebration of the holidays. We may assume that Nehemiah's attempt to enforce abstention from work on the Sabbath was largely successful. We have seen how during the persecutions of Antiochus IV pious men chose to die rather than to violate the Sabbath by fighting. Obviously, the Sabbath had become firmly established as the day of rest. The masses of pilgrims who used to arrive in Jerusalem for Passover, the Weeks holiday, and Tabernacles, added much festiveness to these three holidays. The Festival of Water Drawing on the second night of Tabernacles became a carnival-like, joyous folk festival. Equally joyful were the two new holidays introduced during the period of the Second Commonwealth, Purim and Hanukah. The only holiday which seems to have lost in importance during this period was that of the New Moon. The fact that the laws of each holiday were described in a special tractate of the Mishnah clearly attests to the major role of the holidays within the framework of the religious life.

Temple, synagogue, and holidays did not constitute the totality of the religious life of the Second Commonwealth Jew. He adhered to, and practiced, a multitude of laws and customs which regulated much of his daily life and many of his activities. The totality of these laws became known as the "Oral Law." These were thus laws not found directly in the Pentateuch but sanctioned by a tradition of practice going back many generations. Their practice was so widespread that they merited a detailed description in the Mishnah. Most of them could even be linked, one way or another, with a passage in the Pentateuch. At the beginning, the high priest was considered authorized to interpret the Pentateuch, and his interpretations, presumably, lent the Oral Law a status of validity. Later this authority became vested in the sages, and in the Great Assembly and Sanhedrin led by them. As a result of these processes the Oral Law became a mighty factor in the religious life of the people. In conclusion, although the period of the Second Commonwealth was full of turmoil and of hitherto unknown challenges, the individual Jew of this period experienced a much richer and profounder form of religious life than did his ancestor in pre-exilic times.

Chapter 4

The Withdrawal Sects

While the Pharisees and the Sadducees remained in the mainstream of Judaean life, smaller groups excluded themselves from society and became typical withdrawal sects. Foremost among these groups were the Essenes. This was a sect numbering several thousand members whose precursors, known as *hasidim*, were the bitterest opponents of Hellenism and readily sacrificed their lives for the sanctification of the Name of God (see above, Sec. V, Chaps. 1 and 2). Those among them who survived the massacres of the years 168–67 B.C.E. could not, however, adjust to the new life in Judaea under the Hasmoneans. They chose to part with society and to withdraw from it in order to be able to live a life of devotion to God, undisturbed by the hustle and bustle of everyday life. They abstained from all involvement in political affairs, and seem to have been left alone by the authorities.

The Essenes lived mostly in male communities kept together by a set of clearly formulated rigid rules of discipline. Most of them never entered marital ties, but instead adopted children of others, whom they raised according to the ideals of the sect. Some of the Essenes did approve of marital life, and their wives and children were part of the community.

Some of the Essene communities, in their isolationist fervor, settled in the wilderness. In recent times traces of such settlements have been uncovered on the northwestern shores of the Dead Sea, in the vicinity of a place known as Qumran. It seems, however, that the vast majority did live in various cities and towns, where they managed to effectively separate themselves from the rest of society. The organizational basis of an Essene group was a commune to which every member relinquished his property and delivered his earnings. In return, all that a member needed in his daily life was provided by the group. The life style of the group was semi-monastic. The white clothes they wore were uniform and the food was very simple and taken in common meals bearing the character of holy convivia. Except for mealtime, theirs was a day of work and worship. Certain scholars believe to have detected in the Essene way of life practices resembling Buddhist monasticism.

The commune was a tightly knit group, strictly obedient to its elected leaders. In addition, the individual member was expected to follow an ascetic and impeccable way of life. This high standard of morality was achieved by incessant self-training and by a complicated and tedious novitiate which lasted no less than three years. Thus, only truly dedicated men were attracted to the group and lived up to its ideals. Weaklings, who were found guilty (by a court of at least 100 peers!) of breaching the discipline, were excluded from the group.

The Essenes stood in opposition to the priestly hierarchy in Jerusalem, which they considered illegitimate. They therefore generally boycotted the Temple service and created for themselves their own ways of relating to God. To begin with, they punctilliously followed the laws of purification. Significantly, the rules of purification later recorded in the Mishnah resemble the Essene practice. They followed equally rigidly the entire body of religious customs and practices, without the elasticity applied to them by the Pharisees. Prayers were recited at various hours of the day with devotion and exaltation. But it is likely that in celebrating the holidays they deviated from the commonly accepted religious calendar by following a different, possibly ancient, solar-oriented system of calendation. Their deep sense of religiosity was also expressed in good deeds and acts of compassion and by a decisive abstention from sin and evil-doing.

A place of centrality in the life of the Essenes was occupied by the expectation of the imminent end of the days. They believed that the world surrounding them was bound to break up in a series of cataclysmic events, to be followed by a world in which a regime of absolute justice, "the Kingdom of God," would be firmly established. They hoped to play a major role in the events leading to the establishment of God's kingdom. They were to be the "sons of light" who would struggle against God's adversaries, the "sons of darkness," and ultimately defeat them.

Although relatively small in number, the Essenes created a literature of their own. To be sure, they were ardent readers of the Scriptures and wrote commentaries on them with allegorical interpretations. Their specific spiritual interest, however, made it necessary for them to supplement the Bible by the addition of new holy writings. These writings, novel in their character, often employed a hitherto unknown terminology, designed to express the sect's new views and concepts. It is not surprising that they possessed written manuals of conduct to guide themselves in their self-imposed strict discipline and ascetic life. They also composed hymns of praise and thanksgiving to be used in their worship services. Their main interest, however, seems to have been devoted to authoring apocalypses ("revelations"), in which they interpreted in their own way the history of mankind, and in which they spun their dream of events to come at the end of the days. Many a book of the Pseudepigrapha originated among them. Typical of their literature is the Book of Daniel, which for reasons unknown to us became part of the biblical canon. Additional, hitherto unknown, Essene writings uncovered in recent times are popularly known as the *Dead Sea Scrolls.*

Chapter 5

Messianic Expectations and the Emergence of Christianity

The many tribulations which befell the people of Judaea under the latter Hasmoneans and the subsequent Roman rule gave great popularity to the idea of the coming of a Messiah. He was to be an anointed king, as his title "Messiah" indicates, sent by God to redeem His people from their sufferings. The Hasmonean usurpers of David's throne and the brutal Roman procurators seemed to have been so deeply entrenched that only the intervention of a supernatural hero, the Messiah, could bring about their downfall.

It is not unlikely that already the Hebrews of the First Commonwealth were yearning for the coming of the Messiah. The frustrating weakness of the two tiny Israelitic states due to their division and their unfortunate geopolitical destiny called for the appearance of a mighty warrior who, strengthened by the spirit of God, could bring about the seemingly impossible—the unification of the country and its liberation from the yoke of the two mighty neighbors, Assyria-Babylonia in the northeast and Egypt in the southwest. Only a resurrected King David, or possibly his descendant, the people dreamed, could bring about the great miracle.

The tribulations in the later times of the Second Commonwealth surpassed by far the sufferings of previous times, and the Messianic hope became the focal point in the lives of certain segments of the people. To be sure, the vast majority put their hope for the future on the guidance of the sages who had replaced the prophets. But those circles to whom the normative Judaism of the sages did not appeal expected the imminent "end of the days" and the replacement of this troublesome world order by the "Kingdom of God," which would be established by the miraculous deeds of the Messiah.

To be sure, nobody knew exactly who the expected Messiah was going to be. Some even believed in a Messianic dualism, whereby a Messiah of priestly origin would play the major role in the drama of redemption and would be assisted in his leadership by a lay Messiah, a descendant of King David. All believed that the Redeemer would be both the political head of the nation and its spiritual leader. The triumph of the Messiah was not to be an easy one. The Gentiles, God's and Israel's adversaries, would unleash a furious attack against the Jewish people, but the Messiah would be able to repel the onslaught and ultimately establish Israel's freedom under the marvelous conditions of the "Messianic age."

The belief in the imminent coming of the Messiah was so intense that "prophets" arose who promised the return of miracles and called the people to purify themselves so that they would be ready for the great event. To this group belonged John the Baptist and a certain Theudas. John summoned the people for immersion ("baptism") in the Jordan River. He also announced the coming of the Messiah. In his appearance he possibly resembled the prophet Elijah and thus made a strong impression upon the people. His actions seem to have worried the authorities, and Herod Antipas, in whose territory he appeared, had him executed in 29 C.E. A similar fate befell the "prophet" Theudas about 15 years later.

Among the people who came to be purified by John the Baptist was Jesus, the son of a certain Miriam. It is not certain where Jesus was born. But it is relatively certain that he was born some time between the years 10 and 4 B.C.E., and most probably in the year 7 B.C.E. Practically nothing is known of his youth and early adulthood. He possibly spent a number of years during his early manhood in one of the sectarian withdrawal communes in the Judaean wilderness. He may also have worked for some time as a carpenter. A decisive change took place in his life when he was in his early thirties. It is not known whether his new career began suddenly or was perhaps developing over a period of years. In any case, after having been purified by John the Baptist in the year 27 or 28 C.E., he became a miracle worker and healer, and seems to have immediately attracted a number of devoted followers. Although he appeared in various localities in Galilee, most of his activities seem to have taken place in the town of Kephar Nahum (Capernaum).

Throughout that time Jesus taught ways of human conduct not much different from those advocated by the Pharisees. Nevertheless, he often came into conflict with Pharisaic sages, because his was a deviant form of Pharisaism. He seems to have begun to neglect, or to approve the neglect of, some religious precepts strictly followed by the Pharisees. But the latter seem to have been even more shocked by the fact that Jesus was forgiving sins, something which, according to the accepted belief, only God could do.

In the year 32 C.E., shortly before Passover, Jesus went to Jerusalem in the company of 12 of his closest disciples. At that time, possibly, he arrived at the conviction, or was convinced by his disciples, that he was to be the Messiah. Thus, when he entered Jerusalem rumors spread that Jesus was the king of the Jews. Such rumors, obviously, were bound to alarm the Roman authorities. Men who claimed to be messiahs and expected to sit on the throne of a free Judaea were no rarity. Galilee especially produced some of the most spectacular messiahs in the period of

Roman rule. Some had even been executed by the Romans because of their claims. The fact that the man who now was considered by his followers to be the messiah and the king of the Jews was a Galilean surely made the Roman authorities apprehensive.

When Jesus and his pupils went to the Temple they seem to have made certain statements, and had possibly undertaken certain actions, which put them on a collision course with the priests. Consequently, the High Priest Simon Caiaphas, an appointee and collaborator of the Romans, had Jesus arrested. During the night Jesus was interrogated by the officials of the high priest. In the morning he was brought to the Roman procurator Pontius Pilate, who had come to the city to supervise the public order during the holiday when Jerusalem was filled with pilgrims. Pilate ordered Jesus to be executed by crucifixion. The inscription "King of the Jews" was attached to the cross, possibly indicating the nature of the offense for which Jesus was executed. He was buried in Jerusalem, but probably not at the place considered the Holy Sepulchre.

Jesus' kinsmen, pupils, and a part of his followers believed that he rose from the dead on the third day after the crucifixion, and ascended to heaven. Out of this belief a new faith emerged for them, which became known as *Christianity*, that is, the messianic religion. Shortly thereafter Jesus' followers established themselves as a separate religious group, a Church. Significantly, in this early period the organization of the group and some of its practices resembled those of the Essene community which lived on the shores of the Dead Sea. The Jerusalem Church was led by Jesus' brother James, while other members of the family headed similar groups in other localities. The members of the new sect called themselves *brethren, disciples,* or *believers,* while the Jews generally referred to them as *Nazarenes,* after Jesus' alleged birthplace, Nazareth, or *minim,* heretics.

The original nucleus of the Church was composed exclusively of Jews, mostly of the lower strata of the population. Little by little, however, Gentiles began to join the new sect. Peter himself, the first among the "apostles," as Jesus' closest disciples called themselves, had admitted a Gentile into the group without insisting that he be circumcised. Although at the beginning the apostles made an effort not to alienate the Jews, and even periodically visited the Temple, laxity in the observance of certain religious practices, as well as the admission of uncircumcised Gentiles, led to a breach.

It was, however, the apostle Paul who put Christianity on the road to complete separation from Judaism. He was born Saul in Tarsus, Asia Minor, into a Jewish family which had immigrated from Galilee. His father was a Pharisee, and Saul too went to Jerusalem to study under a Pharisaic teacher. Afterwards, for reasons not fully comprehensible, he devoted himself to the harassment of Christians. It is possible that at that time he was a Pharisaic zealot. It is, however, also not impossible that his harsh treatment of Christians was a subconscious attempt to overcome his own budding religious doubts. Soon he had a decisive change of heart, and he joined the Christian community in Damascus, probably in the year 34. Following this he began to propagandize zealously the new faith. He undertook extensive journeys in Syria, Asia Minor, and Europe, preaching to Jews and even more to Gentiles. This earned him the name of "the apostle to the Gentiles." He not only absolved Gentiles from the obligation of circumcision, but freed them altogether from the duty of observing the Jewish religious law.

In Paul's theology, divine grace replaced the Law and the Law now became invalid and abrogated. His teachings found much acceptance among the "fearers of the Lord," that is, Gentiles who felt attracted to Judaism's message of morality, but remained on its periphery because they were hesitant to accept the burden of the Law or submit to circumcision. As a result, the Gentiles became the majority in the Church and ultimately their beliefs attained the status of normative Christianity. The importance of the Judeo-Christians in the Church began to diminish, and alongside its Jewish elements the new religion began to absorb many non-Jewish beliefs and practices which it adopted both from the Near-Eastern mystery cults and Greco-Roman paganism. The process of rejecting the Jewish Law as something which had outlived its usefulness and validity was accelerated, and Jesus ultimately began to be looked upon as not only the Messiah but also the son of God. Although Jewish influences continued to be noticeable in its basic religious concepts and in its liturgy, Christianity became so different from Judaism that already in Paul's last years outsiders could discern that Christianity had become a religion independent of its Jewish "mother."

Simultaneously, the Judeo-Christian Church in Jerusalem became increasingly rejected, and even considered heretical by Gentile Christianity, while its relations with normative Judaism deteriorated to such a degree that its head James was executed in 62 C.E. by stoning, the usual punishment for religious offenders. A few years later, at the time of the First Revolt (66–70 C.E.), the Judeo-Christians left Jerusalem for Pella, in Transjordan.

Jewish resentment toward the Judeo-Christians further increased during the second century. The circles which saw in Bar Kocheba the true Messiah could not forgive them the fact that they were holding on to their belief in Jesus' messiahship. For the same reason, Bar Kocheba executed many of them during the years of his revolt (132–35 C.E.). The Judeo-Christians retaliated by informing to the Romans on Jews studying Torah, which at the time was prohibited by the Hadrianic laws.

The Judeo-Christians continued to exist in a variety of small groups with divergent views. Some of them considered Jesus solely a prophet. It seems that some of them still tried to hold on to their ties with the Jewish community. The Rabbis, however, considered them heretics and sinners. They therefore inserted, late in the first century a special prayer into the Amidah (the twelfth "benediction," actually malediction), designed to drive them out from the synagogues and to proclaim their ultimate severance from the Jewish people.

During the following centuries the Gentile Christian Church continued on its course of separation from Judaism. Symbolic of this tendency were the efforts of some Fathers of the Church to transfer the Sabbath from Saturday to Sunday. This time is thus called the period of the parting of the roads. But somehow Judaism and Christianity could not become indifferent to each other.

To begin with, the Christians tried hard to prove Jesus' messiahship and divinity from the Bible. Many passages in the Bible thus became a bone of contention between Jews and Christians for centuries to come. In addition, the Church claimed, to the chagrin of the Jews, that even Abraham and Moses professed true

Christianity. The Church was ready to assign to the Jewish people a place in God's design for history only up to Jesus' appearance. However, with the coming of Jesus, the Christian theologians argued, "Israel in the flesh" ceased to be the true Israel and God's chosen people. Henceforth, the Church was to be "Israel in the spirit" and the chosen people. Against this backdrop, Christianity kept on growing in numbers, while Judaism remained limited to its ethnic following. The Roman government, by prohibiting in the middle of the second century the circumcision of converts to Judaism, unwittingly helped Christianity to absorb the masses of disenchanted pagans, and prevented Judaism from becoming a world religion.

Increasingly the enmity between the two religions, the "mother" and the "daughter," became more and more intense. Anti-Christian statements, which originated in this period, are found in the Talmud, while anti-Jewish pronouncements are quite profuse in the writings of the early Christian thinkers, called Fathers of the Church. Many Christian preachers in the eastern Mediterranean countries made the Jews a target for fierce attacks, often resulting in anti-Jewish riots. Especially violent were the attacks made against the Jews in 387 by John Chrysostom ("golden-mouthed"), the greatest Christian preacher of the Antiquity.

This new hatred of the Jew blended with old, still lingering, Hellenistic-pagan civic, social, and cultural anti-Jewish feelings, to create a new brand of anti-Semitism which remained alive during the entire Middle Ages. The Jew was caricaturized, and his religion was portrayed as a set of anachronistic, outlived, and petrified superstitions. Simultaneously, a rapprochement began to develop between the now numerous Christians and the Roman authorities. Consequently, the gospels, which were given at that time their ultimate shape, largely exonerated the Romans from the accusation of deicide—that is, the crucifixion—and the main guilt was shifted to the Jews. Early in the 4th century Emperor Constantine the Great accorded to Christianity the status of a legal religion, and openly began to favor and support it. In 321 he declared Sunday a legal holiday, and most Christians henceforth celebrated their Sabbath on Sunday. A few years later, in 325, the first ecumenical Council of the Church, which convened in Nicaea, in Asia Minor, decided definitively that the Easter holiday should always be observed on a Sunday.

Thus, by cutting itself off decisively from the Jewish calendar, Christianity severed the last frail threads which still linked it with the mother religion. Only a dozen years later, Constantius II ascended the imperial throne in Constantinople, and with him began a new era of restrictions for Jews and Judaism while the Church was now given a dominant role. Thus, in 300 years from the crucifixion, Christianity became a triumphant Church. She began to consider herself "the daughter of the mistress" and relegated the Jewish people to the status of "the daughter of the maid servant."

Section VIII

FROM THE FIRST REVOLT TO THE ARAB CONQUEST

Chapter 1

The First Revolt (66–70 C.E.)

We have seen (Sec. VI, Chap. 3) how in the early '60s the situation in Judaea was approaching the point of explosion. During the following years the situation did not improve at all. Agrippa II appointed and deposed high priests with an amazing frequency. In addition, the high priests indulged more in political intrigue than in the religious leadership of the people. Their perpetual conflicts with the lower priesthood tended to generate even more agitation. The tumultuous situation in the Temple was only a reflection of the general unrest in the country caused by Roman oppression and the activities of the Zealots, the militant nationalists, who could never become reconciled to Roman rule. The large numbers of unemployed and dissatisfied proletarians were also ready for an attempt to bring about a radical change.

It is hard to pinpoint the time when the revolt actually began. It seems that the rebellion was triggered by a visit to Jerusalem of the last procurator, Gessius Florus, during which he carried away a large sum of money from the Temple treasury and massacred a number of Judaeans. A group of angered people, led by the captain of the Temple guard, Eleazar ben Hananiah, retaliated by forcing, in August 66, the discontinuance of the two daily sacrifices paid for by the emperor. This was tantamount to formally declaring the end of Roman rule. Subsequently, the rebels captured the

Antonia fortress, which overlooked the Temple, and massacred its Roman garrison. A similar fate befell the Roman garrison stationed in the palace of the Herodians.

Meanwhile, a descendant of the Galilean rebel Hezekaiah (cf. Sec. VI, Chap. 1), who called himself Menahem, possibly to indicate a Messianic claim, succeeded in occupying the fortress of Masada, in the vicinity of the Dead Sea, where large quantities of weapons fell into his hands. When he subsequently entered Jerusalem, however, the local rebel leader Eleazar had him executed, probably sensing in him a rival. When Cestius Gallus, the Roman governor of Syria, learned of the events in Judaea, he invaded the province in the autumn of 66 with the intention of restoring order. His march through Galilee and Samaria was uneventful, but when he reached Jerusalem, he was beaten by the rebels and lost about 6,000 men, together with most of his equipment.

Conflicting contemporary reports make it impossible to determine to what degree the rebels had the support of the Jewish population during the first months of the uprising. After Gallus' defeat, however, a number of moderate Pharisaic leaders, possibly carried away by the first successes, organized late in 66 what may be called a provisional government. One of the first actions of the new administration was to appoint commanders for the various regions of the country for the purpose of preparing their defense against the expected Roman offensive. Among the commanders was Joseph ben Mattathias, later famous as the historian Flavius Josephus. He was to organize the defense of the sensitive region of Galilee, where the first attack of the Romans was expected to take place. Nothing is known of Joseph's qualifications as a warrior, and modern scholars have attempted to explain in various ways the reasons for his appointment. It is not unlikely that being related to the Hasmoneans, Joseph was sent to defend Galilee, a region where loyalty to the Hasmonean dynasty was widespread and unswerving.

Save for the appointment of commanders, the provisional government was not able to do much, since its actual power was limited by the constant rivalry of the various rebel factions in the city. The presence of about 20,000 Idumaeans, descendants of those forcibly converted to Judaism by Johanan Hyrcanus (see above, Sec. V, Chap. 3), turned out to be quite troublesome. Except for massacring many members of the higher social classes, they contributed little, if anything, to the defense of the city. Also quite limited was the actual contribution of several princes from the Jewish kingdom of Adiabene, located in the territory of ancient Assyria, who joined the defenders of the city. The appearance of these recent converts to Judaism must have been heartening in view of the practically total passivity of Diaspora Jewry, and the fact that even in Judaea many Jews remained on the sidelines.

The revolt in Judaea occurred at an inopportune time for the Roman emperor Nero. He was just completing plans for an attempt to conquer the rest of the world, and the troubles in Judaea distracted him from pursuing this major objective. To take care of the situation, he appointed in February 67 Flavius Vespasian, a senator and able commander, as governor of Judaea. While still in Syria Vespasian assembled an army of about 60,000 men, composed of several Roman legions stationed in the Near East and ancillary forces sent by Rome's clients in the region, such as the king of Nabataea and Agrippa II.

At this decisive moment it became increasingly clear that the prospects for a Jewish victory were not very good. The Jewish rebels were sorely divided among themselves, and no attempt was made to establish even a semblance of unity. In addition, guerrilla warfare had now less chance than in the Maccabean times since the country was much more urbanized and had a more extensive network of roads. Moreover, the non-Jewish population all over the country was now much larger than at the time of the Maccabean revolt, and frequent armed clashes between pagans and Jews in mixed cities resulted in the loss of many Jewish lives. In Caesarea alone some 20,000 Jews were massacred. In the possessions of Agrippa II one of his generals, a Syrian, systematically slaughtered the Jewish population. Angry pagans destroyed synagogues and sporadically compelled Jews to violate their religious precepts.

The political situation was critical as well. We have seen that the majority of the Jewish people, both in Judaea and the Diaspora, failed to join the revolt, or even to support it. The hope for Parthian intervention in favor of the Jews, always looming large in the considerations of anti-Roman rebels, now all but faded. King Vologases I (50–77 C.E.) had just concluded a peace treaty with Rome which was to last much longer than other similar agreements. Thus, when Vespasian invaded Galilee in the spring of 67, he did not encounter serious obstacles. Local freedom fighters, especially those led by the wealthy merchant Johanan of Gush Halav (Gischala), had no trust in Joseph ben Mattathias, the commander sent by Jerusalem. The forces of Vespasian and Agrippa II therefore easily overcame rebel resistance, and occupied most of the cities.

Joseph ben Mattathias found himself besieged in Yodpath (Jotapata) in midsummer 67. He must have realized at that time that the prospects of the rebels were poor, and he surrendered to the Romans after having maneuvered himself out of a suicide pact with his closest aids. Vespasian and his son Titus seem to have discovered in Joseph a potential collaborator, and they kept him in their entourage for the duration of the war. Somewhat later, Gush Halav, last to resist Roman occupation, fell, and its defender Johanan escaped to Jerusalem with a group of his followers. During the subsequent months the Romans fought a few successful sea battles against the Judaean rebels, and occupied the coastal cities. The east bank of the Jordan was also occupied without much difficulty.

All that remained now under rebel control was the city of Jerusalem and a few fortresses. The rivalry between the various rebel factions continued as before, and—to make the situation worse—a feeling of false security overtook the defenders due to a belief that the Holy City could never fall into the hands of an enemy. Such were the conditions when Vespasian began to close in on the city in the spring of 68. But suddenly news came of Nero's death, and Vespasian decided to delay the attack until the election of a new emperor. In Rome, meanwhile, two men followed each other in quick succession on the imperial throne. By now, however, it became clear that Vespasian was being considered for the throne by the legions stationed in the Near East. He therefore kept on postponing the attack on the city. His inactivity could not jeopardize his plans for the siege, since the incessant struggles among the defenders sapped the Jewish revolt of its remaining strength.

In July of 69 Vespasian was proclaimed emperor by the legions stationed in Egypt. Soon various Roman client rulers in the Near East, including Agrippa II, recognized him as emperor. It was not long before Vespasian gained universal recognition as emperor and prepared to leave for Rome, and the task of subduing the rebellion was given to Titus. The renegade Tiberius Julius Alexander, a former procurator of Judaea, was made second-in-command.

Titus approached the city with an army of about 65,000 men shortly before Passover 70. After a few unsuccessful attempts to take the city by storm, Titus decided on a course of blockading the city to starve it into surrender. True, the defenders were divided and most of the city's provisions destroyed, but the fanatical zeal of the rebels, augmented by the entrance into the city in April 69 of the popular guerrilla leader Simon bar Giora with his men, prevented an immediate Roman victory. All this time Joseph ben Mattathias, now a Roman propagandist, was urging the defenders on the walls to surrender. His words, however eloquent and reasonable, did little to weaken the desperate determination of the rebels to fight on. Little by little, however, the walls gave in, and supplies began to run so low that on the 17th day of Tammuz it was no longer possible to offer the daily sacrifices in the Temple.

The Romans could now concentrate on attacking the Temple, where large numbers of defenders had dug in. At this point the Roman high command seems to have deliberated the question of whether the Temple should be burned during the attack, or efforts made to spare it. While it is known that Tiberius Alexander was in favor of saving the Temple, Titus' attitude is not fully clear. It is certain that Titus ordered his soldiers to burn the Temple gates so as to gain entrance into the court. It is not clear who was responsible for what happened next. It is known that in the heat of the fight a Roman soldier threw a torch into a window of the Sanctuary. This caused a great conflagration, and the Temple went up in fire on the 9th of the month of Av (August) in the year 70, on the same day the Solomonic Temple was destroyed by the Babylonians 656 years earlier. Large numbers of the rebels died in the Temple ruins. But strangely enough, their two ultrafanatical leaders, Johanan of Gush Halav and Simon bar Giora, surrendered to the Romans. The Temple treasurer also surrendered and saved his life by turning over to the Romans the golden vessels of the Temple.

After the fall of the Temple, fighting still continued sporadically in various parts of the ruined city. Many of the fighters, among them a group of Essenes, died in a last stand. Late in September all resistance in the city had ceased. Titus, whom Jewish tradition blames for the destruction of the Temple and calls "the wicked," went to celebrate the victory in Caesarea Philippi, the capital of Agrippa II. During the celebrations, 2,500 Jewish captives died in gladiatorial games. Additional numbers of captives lost their lives in November in honor of Vespasian's birthday.

Yet, the war was not yet fully over. Groups of rebels still held three major fortresses, Herodium, Macherus and Masada. Longest to hold out was Masada, where a community of close to 1,000 people—men, women, and children—stubbornly refused to surrender for several years. The defenders, among whom was a group of Essenes, were commanded by Eleazar ben Yair, a nephew of "king-messiah" Menahem. The Romans laid siege to this inaccessible, over 100-years-old fortress in the southern Judaean desert in 72. It still took, however, a year, or possibly two, until the besiegers succeeded in making a breach in the wall. At this point the defenders realized that the fall of the fortress was imminent, and decided to commit suicide rather than surrender. Two old women and a few children survived to tell of the grim drama in which the last Judaean rebels succumbed.

Meanwhile the Romans were rounding up whoever had, or was suspected of having, participated in the revolt. Large numbers of captives were sent to various parts of the empire to work in the mines and at public works, or to serve on the galleys. About 30,000 were sold into slavery, a number of whom were ransomed by Diaspora communities. A certain number of rebels, including the two leaders, Johanan of Gush Halav and Simon bar Giora, were taken to Rome to march in the triumphal procession which was being prepared for Titus. Individuals who claimed Davidic origin were arrested and summarily executed as potential messianic pretenders. The Adiabenean princes who had come to Jerusalem to help the rebels were spared due to their Parthian connections, and taken to Rome as hostages. The contemporary sources speak of a total of between 600,000 and 1,000,000 victims having perished during the years 66–70. Although these numbers are probably exaggerated, the actual number of the victims was appalling.

There was no end to Roman jubilation over the victory. All three emperors of the Flavian dynasty, Vespasian, Titus, and Domitian struck special coins depicting a mourning figure to symbolize overthrown Judaea. The coins bore the legends *Judaea capta,* Judaea has been captured, and *Judaea devicta,* Judaea has been defeated. In June 71 the triumphal procession took place in Rome in which the vanquished Judaean heroes and their leaders marched, and the golden vessels of their Temple were carried. After the procession Simon bar Giora was put to death, and Johanan of Gush Halav imprisoned for life. We do not know why the life of this most troublesome leader of the rebels was spared.

In the year 80, while Titus was emperor, an arch of triumph was erected for him. This arch no longer exists. A second arch erected in his honor after his death, is still standing in Rome. On its interior walls the *menorah,* the golden candelabrum, and other objects from the Jerusalem Temple are depicted, probably inaccurately, in bas-relief. Roman Jews avoid entering the arch of Titus, the symbol of their people's defeat. The Temple vessels were kept in Rome 385 years. When Genseric, the chieftain of the Vandals, sacked Rome in 455, he carried them away to the city of Tunis, his capital. In the sixth century, the Byzantine general Belisarius captured the city of Tunis, and took away the Temple vessels to Constantinople, as part of his loot. There is a possibility that soon afterwards the holy vessels were returned by the emperor Justinian I to Jerusalem. All efforts in modern times to trace their whereabouts have proven futile.

Chapter 2

Josephus

We have seen how inefficient Joseph ben Mattathias was, both as Galilee's defender and as Roman propagandist, during the years of the First Revolt. He was much more successful, although highly ambiguous, as the historian Josephus. Joseph was born in 38 C.E. in an aristocratic priestly family which, as we have seen, was related to the Hasmoneans. We do not know much about the education he received. To judge by his writings, he must have acquired a wide knowledge of the literature of the Jews, as well as that of the Greeks and Romans. It is also evident that he was deeply impressed by the tumultuousness of the time. Thus, at the age of 16, probably dissatisfied with his life as a young aristocrat, he went to the wilderness to spend several years in an Essene-like manner of life. He spent much of his time in the company of a certain Bannus, whose character resembled that of John the Baptist. The life of withdrawal, however, also ceased to satisfy him, and he returned to Jerusalem.

In 64 C.E. the 26-year-old Joseph appeared for the first time in public life. He was sent to Rome as a member of a delegation to intercede in favor of a few rebellious young priests whom the procurator Felix had arrested and sent to Rome. Joseph's later career indicates that Rome's might, and life in the capital of the empire, made a deep impression upon him. The basic ambiguity of Joseph's character revealed itself, as we have seen, during the years of the First Revolt. The way he wiggled out of the suicide pact with his lieutenants suggests that he was less than a hero and not troubled by too many scruples. While a prisoner of war in Vespasian's camp, he tried to win the latter's favor by making propaganda for his elevation to the imperial throne. To be sure, in the beginning the Romans distrusted him, but Titus took a personal liking to him and he was able to dispel their suspicions. By then Joseph's Jewish compatriots must have become aware of his switch to the side of the Romans. Thus, when he appeared before the walls of beleaguered Jerusalem, the defenders of the city had only utter contempt for him.

The same contempt was shown to Joseph by the Jewish community of Rome when he settled in the imperial capital after the fall of Jerusalem. The Romans richly compensated Joseph for his collaboration by giving him Roman citizenship, a pension, and a large tract of the land confiscated from the vanquished Judaeans. It was probably due to the personal liking Titus took to Joseph, and Vespasian's shrewd realization that his Jewish propagandist could be of further use to him, which earned him the privilege of having living quarters assigned to him in the imperial palace. He was also permitted to bear the family name of the emperor, and under his new name of Flavius Josephus he began his new career as an author.

We do not know whether Josephus had ever tried his hand at writing prior to his settling in Rome. It is equally impossible to say with certainty what prompted him to begin his career as an author shortly after his arrival in the imperial capital. Possibly the rejection by his Jewish brethren both in the homeland and in the Dispersion directed him to seek fame in a field in which he believed he might be successful. But it is also possible that the great historical happenings he witnessed evoked in him the historian that he was by nature. Be this as it may, once he began his new career, he revealed himself to be a talented, imaginative, and prolific writer.

Although Josephus may already then have planned to write the *Jewish Antiquities,* it was only natural for him to first turn his attention to the description of the immediate past, the Jewish revolt against Rome. In writing *The Jewish War* he was influenced by a variety of factors, often contradictory. On the one hand, the historian that he was could not suppress feelings of admiration for the heroism and courage of the Jewish rebels. On the other hand, as a servant of the Flavian dynasty, he had to praise the actions of Vespasian and Titus and of his only Jewish protector, Agrippa II. There was also his natural desire to portray his own activities in a manner acceptable to both Jews and Romans. These conflicting aims resulted in a work full of ambiguities, but it was Josephus' great skill as a writer that enabled him nevertheless to create a work of major literary significance.

In the seven books of the *Jewish War*, Josephus describes the history of Judaea from the capture of Jerusalem by Antiochus

Epiphanes in 168 B.C.E. to the fall of Masada in 73 C.E. The description of the events up to the outbreak of the First Revolt is markedly different from the description of the revolt itself. It is less detailed and less dramatic, but Josephus thought it necessary for an understanding of the historical chain of events leading to the inevitable outbreak of the revolt. The years of the revolt itself he described as an eyewitness who fully perceived and was able to portray its entire dramatic and tragic grandeur.

As a servant of the Romans he had to exonerate Vespasian and Titus of any wrongdoing. To justify their actions he calls the rebels "brigands," and blames the latter (as did, to be sure, also many Judaeans) for starting the war. He also completely exculpated Titus of any blame for the destruction of the Temple. The general picture thus obtained is of a people foolishly engaging in the impossible task of rebelling against mighty Rome, and nevertheless fighting it out to the tragic end with a readiness for suffering and martyrdom. Thus, a true general outline of the events was achieved, although the author quite often strayed away from the truth, substituting for it inaccuracies and halftruths. The book was published about 75 C.E., possibly in two different versions: in Aramaic for the Jews, and in Greek for the Hellenized Jews and the Gentile world.

After having established his fame as an historian, Josephus proceeded to write a general history of the Jews from the creation of the world to the years immediately preceding the outbreak of the First Revolt. He named the book, on which he worked for many years, *Jewish Antiquities.* In this work Josephus addressed himself mainly to the Gentile world in order to create a friendlier atmosphere for the Jews of the Dispersion. Thus he stressed the fact of the Jews being an ancient people. He described in vivid colors the heroes of biblical times and embellished their personalities with beautiful legends taken from the Midrash. He failed, however, to tell his readers about the prophets, since the Jewish concept of prophecy was alien to his audience. Although Josephus seems to have worked on the book for almost 20 years, it is less of a masterpiece than the *Jewish War.* Inaccuracies and contradictions are numerous, mostly attributable to sheer negligence on the part of the author.

In the eighteenth book of *Jewish Antiquities* a passage is

found known as *Testimonium Flavianum,* that is, the testimony of Flavius (Josephus). The passage, which describes enthusiastically the Christians and their messiah, became a matter for heated discussions among the scholars. Some consider it authentic; most scholars, however, believe it to be an interpolation of early Christian copyists eager to supply information about Christianity from sources other than the New Testament. Be the truth as it may, the *Testimonium* prompted Christians throughout the centuries to preserve Josephus' writings after they had been rejected by the Jews and their Aramaic versions lost, or possibly even deliberately destroyed. The work was published some time between 93 and 95 C.E., and another edition appeared shortly before the year 100.

Late in his life Josephus wrote a passionate treatise in defense of the Jewish people and its religion. There were many anti-Semites in those times among the intellectuals both in Rome and in the colonies. They used their literary skill to attack the Jews and Judaism. They falsified the history of the Jews and spread many rumors about them in order to isolate them from their Gentile neighbors. A hotbed of such propaganda was Alexandria in Egypt. Especially vicious were the attacks of a certain Apion, which were widely copied and publicized. To counteract this propaganda, Josephus composed a small treatise in two books which he named *Against Apion.* This is the most passionate of all Josephus' works. It was as if his long pent-up love and enthusiasm for his people had suddenly exploded in the heart of the aging, alienated Jew. The fervor and sincerity of the treatise must have deeply affected the Gentile reader.

Josephus first described the Jews again, as in *Jewish Antiquities,* as a very ancient people free from the faults ascribed to it by the Alexandrine anti-Semites. He then elaborated on many of the Jewish laws and customs as being useful in the life of the individual and society. *Against Apion* thus became the first typical Jewish apologetic work, to be followed by many others in the course of the centuries.

While the treatise *Against Apion* could by its warmth and Jewish pride regain for Josephus Jewish sympathy, and even forgiveness, the "old," ambivalent Josephus appeared again in a small autobiographical tract written about the same time. A certain Justus of Tiberias, not unlike Josephus an historian and warrior, accused the latter of being disloyal to Rome during Vespasian's campaign in Galilee. These accusations were hurled at Josephus at a time, under Domitian's rule, when he possibly was no longer a *persona grata* as in the days of Vespasian and Titus. Being hard-pressed, Josephus tried in the autobiography, called *The Life,* to protect himself by resorting again to inaccuracies and by forgetting the Jewish pride he so eloquently manifested in *Against Apion.* Obviously, his return to his people in the latter work was temporary, and under pressure gave way again to a decisive pro-Roman stand.

From certain remarks in his books we learn that Josephus planned to write, or did write, various other works, including an exposition of the Jewish laws, probably much more detailed than that found in *Against Apion.* But even though several of his works have been lost, or remained unwritten, Josephus occupies a major place in the literature of the Greco-Roman world. Not being a decided phil-Hellene, he nevertheless learned much from the Greek writers who had preceded him, and especially Thucydides. Although Aramaic versions of some of his works may have existed, he was, because of the environment in which he lived the last 35 years of his life, a writer who addressed himself basically to the Gentile world. He never returned to his homeland, and lived in Rome among Gentiles, rejected by most of his co-religionists.

As Josephus' attitude to the Jews and Judaism was ambiguous, so was, and still is, the attitude of the Jewish people to him. On the one hand, he was uncompromisingly rejected as a traitor, who left his homeland in a moment of its greatest tragedy to live in comfort in the lavish surroundings of the imperial palace. And his hosts were the very Vespasian and Titus who were responsible for the dstruction of the Temple and the misery of the Judaeans. On the other hand, however, it was not easy to disown his writings, which in spite of their faults count among the great works of world literature. Furthermore, his works are practically the only source of information from which we learn not only about the course of events of that era in the Jewish past, but also of its enormous tragic grandeur.

An unknown great Hebrew author undertook to solve the

dilemma of the attitude of the Jews to Josephus by producing a "version" of his writings acceptable to them. He probably had at his disposal a manuscript containing Latin versions of most of Josephus' *Jewish Antiquities* and of the entire *Jewish War.* Using these two works, as well as other historical material, he wrote a book named *Sepher Yosippon, The Book of Yosippon,* Josephus' name as common among Greek-speaking Jews. He opened his narrative with a description of the European nations in his times. This is followed by an early history of Rome. The bulk of the book, however, deals with the history of the Jews during the period of the Second Commonwealth, up to the fall of Masada.

Here the history of the Jews, their tribulations under foreign domination, and their heroic effort to liberate their country from the Roman yoke, are described with love and warmth. Gone are Josephus' ambivalences and oscillations. Josephus' material was used to present in a beautiful biblical style the description of the heroic age in the Jewish past which the Jewish reader needed, and which Josephus failed to supply. When and where the book was written is uncertain. Theories about the author's place and time range from Byzantium (or Byzantine-controlled southern Italy) to Germany, and from the third to the tenth century. According to one medieval manuscript of the work the book was written in 953. It attained extraordinary popularity among the Jews. For many centuries now it has served as the standard, though uncritical, picture the Jews had about the great confrontation between their people and the Romans, and the loss of the Temple in Jerusalem. Even at present, when Jews no longer hesitate to read Josephus' original writings, *The Book of Yosippon,* which some consider the sole truly historical work produced by the Jews in the Middle Ages, continues to charm the Jewish reader by its warmth and beauty.

Chapter 3

The Age of Yavneh

After the fall of Masada and the pacification of the country, the Romans set out to reorganize the administration of the province. Galilee was given to Agrippa II as a reward for his loyalty, and so temporarily the territory of the province was greatly diminished. Only after 92 C.E., when Agrippa II died, did Galilee again become part of Judaea. The Roman governor continued to reside in Caesarea and now bore the title of "legate." Although Judaea was now less dependent upon the governor of Syria, the latter still had some authority over Judaea in civil matters. The tenth Roman legion was now permanently stationed in the country, and it strictly controlled what remained of Jerusalem.

The country's population underwent basic changes. The Jewish element kept on decreasing in number up to the Arab conquest. The number of Jews who perished during the First Revolt was staggering, and even more died at the time of the Second Revolt (see below, Chap. 4). The Jewish element further diminished due to mass emigration and conversion. Thus, in spite of temporary reversals of the process due to the generally favorable economic conditions, at the threshold of the Arab conquest the Jews had become a small community. First Jerusalem became devoid of Jews. True, from time to time, Jews were permitted to return to the Holy City, but their stay was always of short duration, and a permanent Jewish community was not established until after the Arab conquest. The rest of Judaea proper lost its Jewish population after the downfall of the Second Revolt. Thus, Galilee, where for a long time Jews continued to be a majority of the population, was the real scene of Jewish life in the Holy Land during most of the Roman and Byzantine periods. The Jewish element in the country was further weakened by the steady increase of the Gentile population.

The leadership of the Jewish community now passed into the hands of the sages. With the destruction of the Temple and the disappearance of the office of the high priest, a vacuum of authority was created. It was only logical for the sages to try to maintain the Sanhedrin, the other source of Jewish authority prior to the Revolt. Their attempt was largely successful, and a regenerated Sanhedrin came into being in the city of Yavneh. The man most responsible for the development of the new Sanhedrin was an elderly sage by the name of Johanan ben Zakai. Yavneh was a city located near the Mediterranean coast, northwest of Jerusalem. It was a city of mixed population, where pagans were possibly the majority. In former times the city had only sporadically been under Jewish control, but a Jewish academy of sorts seems to have existed in the town. Yavneh escaped unscathed from the ravages of the war of 66–70, and it seems that a kind of refugee camp for escapees from Jerusalem and other war victims had existed in the city or its vicinity.

It was to Yavneh that Johanan ben Zakai went when he left Jerusalem in a dramatic escape in the spring of 68 C.E. Johanan, possibly of priestly origin and Hillel's pupil, had a long career of leadership behind him. About the year 30 he was active as a teacher somewhere in Galilee. Upon returning to Jerusalem shortly thereafter, he conducted in the vicinity of the Temple a sort of an academy without walls, resembling similar Greek institutions of learning. He also served as a member of the Sanhedrin in which he held the position of *av beth din,* and possibly also that of the president *(nasi),* or acting president.

We do not know exactly what attitude Johanan had to the Revolt. His subsequent secret escape from Jerusalem by outwitting the rebels would indicate that he did not believe in the success of the Revolt. After leaving Jerusalem he may or may not have met Vespasian to ask his support for, or toleration of, the plan to establish a Jewish authority by using Yavneh's rabbinic academy as a base. It is a fact that when Johanan went ahead with his plans, he met only with Jewish opposition. Curiously, we find among his opponents some of his colleagues, and even students. Johanan's plan was to acquire for the Academy of Yavneh the status of a Sanhedrin by exerting rights hitherto vested in the Jerusalem Sanhedrin and its head, the *nasi.* Thus, he proclaimed the New Moon and issued *taqqanoth,* that is, ordinances establishing or interpreting laws in a way not fully compliant with the biblical or accepted Rabbinic law. These actions proved to be successful, and enjoyed general popular support, even though some of the sages initially opposed them. Johanan also instituted, or possibly renewed, the practice of rabbinic ordination. By vesting the exclusive right of ordination in a few Judaean academies, he established the hegemony of the Judaean rabbinic leadership over the Diaspora for a long time.

The glory enjoyed by the Academy of Yavneh as a result of Johanan's actions attracted more and more students and sages. Of special importance was the arrival of Gamaliel II, Hillel's descendant, and thus a man claiming Davidic origin. Within a few years Johanan ben Zakai thus succeeded in filling effectively the vacuum created by the dissolution of the Jerusalem Sanhedrin. A new central Jewish authority had come into being. It is not clear whether Johanan bore the title of *nasi* in Yavneh, or whether the Roman authorities gave him recognition in any form. It also seems that his successor as head of the academy, Gamaliel II, also known as Gamaliel of Yavneh, was not officially recognized by the Romans as *nasi,* in the manner his descendants were. About the year 80 C.E., when the authority of Yavneh was already firmly established and other important academies had come into being in nearby towns, Johanan ben Zakai retired from his position, for reasons not fully clear. His advanced age may have been the reason; he possibly died shortly thereafter. But then also a reawakening of old resentments against the great sage for his exit from Jerusalem in a moment of her deepest despair may have had something to do with Johanan's retirement.

Upon Johanan's retirement, Gamaliel II took his place as head of the Yavneh Academy. The fact that someone considered a scion of the House of David could be appointed *nasi* was due to a general relaxation in the relationship between the Jewish community and the Roman authorities. Gamaliel's rule was turbulent, and he often felt compelled to use the weapon of excommunication to uphold his control. He was even temporarily deposed by his colleagues. Nevertheless, during his tenure important aspects of the *Halakhah,* the Oral Law (see below, Chap. 6), were discussed and clarified. It should be noted in conclusion that during the entire period of Yavneh's hegemony the leadership of the sages was by and large of a collective nature. The relationship with the imperial government in Rome and the Jewish communities in the Diaspora was also maintained mostly through delegations of sages rather than the single-handed actions of the *nasi*.

The normalization of relations with the Romans made steady progress, especially after the Emperor Domitian died in 96 C.E. Under the Emperor Trajan, however, Judaea was shaken by an uprising against the Romans which originally had begun in the Diaspora, and which could be considered a general uprising of the Jews of the empire against the Romans. To be sure, the relations between Judaean Jewry and Trajan were not unfriendly. In fact, there are indications that the Emperor promised to rebuild the Temple in Jerusalem. It is thus understandable that the uprising in Judaea came rather late in the course of the events (late in 116 or 117), and mainly as a result of an initiative taken by Jews in the Diaspora.

In further chapters the events which occurred in this general Jewish uprising against Rome will be described, as they happened in Cyrenaica, Egypt, Cyprus, and Babylonia. In Judaea the uprising was led by the brothers Pappus and Lulianus, who had arrived from Egypt. It is also possible that the leader of the Jewish uprising in Cyrenaica, Andrew (alias Lukuas), who acted as if he were the Messiah, had invaded Judaea to liberate it from the yoke of the Romans. The activities of the Jewish rebels from the Diaspora seem not to have evoked much enthusiasm among the Jews in Judaea. In addition, some of the sages also opposed the uprising. Nevertheless, when the Roman commander Lucius Quietus arrived, a number of fierce battles were fought both in the south and in Galilee before the Romans succeeded in putting an end to the uprising and executing Pappus and Lulianus. In general, our knowledge of the course of the events is vague, as is also our understanding of the real causes for which Diaspora Jewry rose up against Rome at that time.

The economic condition of the country after 70 C.E. was better than could be expected. True, much of the arable land, and possibly all the land, was confiscated by the Romans. In reality, however, most peasants continued to work the land as renters. In time much of the confiscated land reverted to Jewish ownership by purchase from Romans to whom it was given by the government. The lot of the farmers even improved thanks to the network of roads and bridges built by the government in rural areas. Jewish agriculture thus thrived up to the time of the Moslem conquest. This is especially true of Galilee, where the Jewish rural element made up the majority of the population for a long time. Quite favorable also was the condition of the Jewish craftsmen. Fewer in number than the peasants, but well organized in guilds, they represented an important factor in the country's economy. Weaving, dyeing, and leather work were popular occupations. Products of Judaean handicraft were known in, and exported to, neighboring countries. Roman taxation was quite heavy after 70 C.E., in money, produce, and forced labor. The generally favorable economic conditions, however, made it possible for the population to pay the heavy taxes without being seriously harmed. In fact, by the year 120 C.E., the country had recovered remarkably from the devastation of the war of the years 66–70. Even the unsuccessful uprising against Trajan did not jeopardize the economic revival.

In the area of Jewish culture, too, the debacle of the year 70 had little, if any, effect. The success of the Academy at Yavneh served as a mighty stimulus to the entire educational endeavor. That higher education was undergoing a real process of democratization is indicated by the fact that in the post-Temple Sanhedrin a large number of members came from poor families. This, of course, resulted from the efforts of the Rabbis to further expand the system of public elementary education established prior to the year 70 C.E. by Joshua ben Gamala. The Rabbis now especially stressed community responsibility in this field. Most of the many other academies of learning were, of course, headed by Yavneh graduates. In addition, itinerent scholars were spreading knowledge in places where permanent schools did not exist. Materials most often used for writing were papyrus, parchment, and wood slats. The language of instruction was, no doubt, the somewhat Hebraized Aramaic generally spoken in the country. Hebrew and Greek were also used to a certain degree, however, much in the way they were employed in correspondence and legal documents. It seems that the use of Hebrew as a spoken language was waning, and the Rabbis attempted to remedy the situation. Significantly, a similar attempt seems to have been made by Bar Kocheba during the years of the Second Revolt.

While the last battles about the canonization of certain of its books were fought, the Bible continued to occupy a position of centrality in the educational system. Since the Septuagint was now widely used by the Christians, the sages encouraged the proselyte Aquila of Pontus to prepare a new Greek translation of the Bible. However, even though certain rabbis collaborated with Aquila in the work, the new translation did not become universally accepted and used. Its excessive literalness made it unattractive, and it was ultimately forgotten and lost. The Aramaic translation commonly known as *Targum Onkelos*, that is, *The Translation of Onkelos*, fared much better. It is probably a compilation made in the course of the second century C.E. from earlier popular Aramaic versions. The author of this translation also tried to be literal, but only to a degree so as not to impare its readability. He successfully tried to tone down passages presenting a corporeal God or words somehow offensive to his contemporaries. In the translation of the Prophets, evidently made by another author, an attempt was made to soften the many passages in which the Jewish people were sternly rebuked. These characteristics, and the real need for an Aramaic translation, made *Targum Onkelos* very popular with its contemporaries and hallowed by many successive generations. Babylonian Jewry also held the *Targum* in high esteem, and it is often mentioned in the Talmud.

Judaean Jewry also recovered remarkably well from the blow that the destruction of the Temple dealt to its religious life. True, as we have seen, synagogues and synagogal worship were quite firmly established long before the destruction of the Temple. Nevertheless, many people felt that with the sacrificial service gone, no way was left to them to atone for their sins. Consequently, some people continued for some time to make pilgrimages to Jerusalem and to practice a sort of sacrificial service on the Temple ruins. The Romans, it seems, did not object to such practices and did not hamper access to the city. Some priestly circles made unsuccessful attempts to conduct a sacrificial service in places other than Jerusalem. In general, hope was kept alive that the Temple would be rebuilt in the not too distant future, and the Academy at Yavneh devoted considerable time and attention to the study of laws regulating the sacrificial service.

Little by little, however, the people began to adjust to the new reality and the interest in sacrifices began to fade. Of decisive importance in this respect were the teachings of Johanan ben Zakai that good deeds do as much for the atonement of one's sins as sacrifices. No doubt the existence of an extensive Diaspora, whose worship was devoid of a sacrificial service, was also very convincing. Thus the synagogue and prayer worship became the focal point in the religious life of the Jew. To be sure, at the beginning synagogal worship tended to keep alive the memory of the Temple service. But this transitional phase was rather short-lived. During the tenure of Gamaliel II the sages of Yavneh, in response to the new situation, formalized the prayer services. True, most of the prayers were known prior to that period, but now they were standardized and made mandatory. From now on every Jew was obliged to recite thrice daily at fixed times his basic prayers, the center of which was the *amidah,* a collection of blessings expressing the beliefs, devotion, and hopes of the worshipper. The reading of portions of the Pentateuch and the Prophets was given an important devotional and educational role within the order of worship. The phylacteries, already earlier in use during prayer, were also standardized at this time as to the Pentateuchal passages to be included in them. The available evidence indicates that the observance of the Sabbath and the festivals was generally followed. This was, of course, made possible by the calendric unity which prevailed due to the actions of Johanan ben Zakai and Gamaliel II.

Greco-Roman influences could be observed in clothing, architecture, names, and even religious rites, such as the Passover Seder. Such influences, however, seem not to have been considered dangerous any longer. Nascent and rising Christianity now called for more watchfulness. Thus, by inserting an anti-Christian "malediction" into the *amidah,* the Rabbis sought, as we have seen, to draw a separating line between Judaism and the new religion. Christian successes among the "Fearers of the Lord" caused much frustration among some of the rabbis, and they were ready to abandon all proselytizing efforts among Gentiles, long before a triumphant Church outlawed them. Nonetheless, proselytes were by no means a rarity within Jewish society of the second century C.E. In fact, a sage of the stature of Rabbi Aqiba very much favored converts to Judaism.

Chapter 4

The Second Revolt (132–135 C.E.)

In 117 C.E. Hadrian ascended the imperial throne of Rome. The Jews of Judaea expected to be treated in a friendly manner by him, and rumors even spread that he was going to permit the rebuilding of the Temple in Jerusalem. Hadrian had been in the Near East during the period of the Jewish uprisings against Trajan (114–17 C.E.), and it is not unlikely that he may have looked for an opportunity for a reconciliation with the Jews.

If this was so, things began to change after the year 120. At that time Hadrian began to develop a concept of a Roman empire as a commonwealth of partner states rather than a cluster of provinces, each different from the other. Not unlike Syria's King Antiochus IV almost 300 years before, Hadrian, too, thought that a speedy Hellenization of the Near East would best lead to the attainment of this goal. This, obviously, put him on a direct collision course with the Jews of the province of Judaea. Instead of rebuilding the Jewish Temple, Hadrian now wanted to transform Jerusalem into a largely pagan city, with a temple of Jupiter in its midst. The city was henceforth to be known as *Aelia Capitolina,* Aelius being one of the emperor's names. In addition, circumcision, long abhorred by Greeks and Romans as a mutilation of the human body, seems to have been prohibited at the same time. A new legate in the person of Tineius Rufus was appointed to enforce the Hellenization policy. While direct information about Tineius' activities is vague, these must have added fuel to the already inflamed situation. The fact that Jewish tradition changed "Tineius" into "Tyrannus" clearly indicates that the Jews had no illusions about the new legate's intentions.

Judaean Jewry, which emerged from the uprising against Trajan in better shape than Diaspora Jewry, became agitated enough to try to challenge the new Roman policy by force. As in the year 66 C.E., however, most of the rabbis were against provoking an open conflict with Rome, since they realized that an uprising would again end in disaster. Hot-headed Judaeans, however, began secretly to collect weapons and build fortifications in preparation for a rebellion. Already in 128 C.E. certain areas in the country became increasingly restless, but it was not before 132 that the situation developed into a full-fledged rebellion. The uprising was headed by a certain Simon ben Kosiba, the latter word indicating either his father's name or the place of his birth.

Nothing is known of Simon's past. He was possibly a personality resembling the "judges" of Israel's early history. His subsequent activities indicate that Simon possessed the abilities of both a military commander and civil administrator. Thus, it must be assumed that he was the right man to head the uprising. He assumed the title of *nasi* (prince) to manifest his status as the political and military head of the country.

As in all the rebellions against Rome, this time, too, the Jews had initial successes, and soon a considerable part of Judaea south of Jerusalem was under Simon's control. It seems also that he established an effective administration in this area. The army at his disposal was numerous, either composed of volunteers or forcibly recruited. Simon's headquarters were in Bethar (today: Bittir), a fortress located in the mountains southwest of Jerusalem. The Sanhedrin of Yavneh and the *nasi* and his family also moved to Bethar, voluntarily or by Simon's order. Whether Simon was of Davidic origin or not, he seems to have had messianic pretensions. These claims, as well as the rebellion in general, received a collossal boost from the statement of Rabbi Aqiba, the oldest and most revered among the sages, that Simon was indeed the Messiah. Following this, Simon began to be popularly called *Bar Kocheba,* that is, Son of the Star; this, because of the belief that the verse "There shall step forth a star out of Jacob" (Numbers 24:17) refers to the King Messiah. Whether Rabbi Aqiba, being of a very advanced age, was otherwise active in the revolt, is doubtful.

Simon began attacking the Roman forces in the summer of

132 C.E. and successfully defeated the twenty-second Roman legion. It soon became clear that the uprising had taken on the character of a regular war between a Jewish army and the Roman legions. Late in 132 Simon occupied Jerusalem. Coins were issued (overstruck on Roman coins) to celebrate the liberation of the city. It also seems that the sacrificial service was renewed on an altar erected on the Temple Mount. A priest named Eleazar was possibly given charge of religious affairs. Uncircumcised people were kept out of the city. In general, it should be assumed that Simon took decisive steps to remove from the Holy City all traces of paganism introduced by Hadrian.

Simon's rule over the southern part of the province, including some regions in Samaria, seems to have remained uncontested almost a full year. To be sure, as in the year 66, no help came from the Diaspora. Rabbi Aqiva's extensive travels to enlist such assistance prior to the outbreak of the revolt evidently were unsuccessful. While some support for the rebellion developed in Transjordan and Galilee, it remains inexplicable why the latter region, a perpetual hotbed of anti-Roman feelings and actions, now remained largely on the sidelines. In Simon's favor, however, was the circumstance that—unlike the First Revolt—inner Jewish unity basically prevailed in the Second Revolt. Whatever opposition there was, it was passive. Even some of the Samaritans now joined Simon, but, of course, Christians could not support a leader who manifested messianic claims. After Jerusalem's liberation, Simon seems to have evaded open warfare with the Romans, and mostly concentrated on placing his garrisons in fortresses and fortified cities.

Roman inactivity ended in the summer of 133 when a series of skirmishes restored Galilee to Roman control. This was followed by Roman successes in the lowlands on the seacoast, and an attack on Samaria restored this area too to Roman control in the fall of 133 or in the spring of 134. Julius Severus, who had successfully defeated an uprising against Rome in Britain, was now directing the Roman counter-attack against Bar Kocheba. Severus had at his disposal about 50,000 men, who were sent to Judaea from various Roman possessions. With this army he conducted a war of atrition against Simon, and slowly but surely wrested from him fortress after fortress. Each conquest was followed by a cleanup operation to pacify the countryside. Late in 134 or early in 135 the Romans built a network of strategic roads in preparation for the final attack against the Jews. This was followed rather quickly by the conquest of Hebron and Jerusalem early in 135, but not without heavy losses to the Roman army.

Simon's last stand was the fortress of Bethar, which, as we have seen, had served as his headquarters from the beginning of the uprising. The remnants of Simon's army, still numbering tens of thousands, defended the fortress desperately, but Bethar ultimately fell on or close to Tisheah be Av 135, due to starvation, and possibly Samaritan treachery. The city was destroyed, and almost all the defenders died in the battle, including the commander-Messiah Simon ben Kosiba. A small number of the rebels escaped to the caves area in the vicinity of En Gedi, on the Dead Sea, but it took the Romans only a few weeks to put down this last resistance. Bar Kocheba's memory possibly survived in the figure of the "Messiah, son of Joseph," a Messiah who dies in the fight for Jewish redemption, whom later generations expected to precede the coming of the true "Messiah, son of David."

With the revolt out of the way, Hadrian proceeded rapidly with his Hellenization plans. Jerusalem was again made *Aelia Capitolina.* The name of the province was changed to *Syria Palaestina,* that is, the Philistine region of Syria, a name previously used only occasionally. The observance of the Sabbath and the festivals, and the study of Torah were to be punished by death. The huge number of victims who lost their lives in the uprising was augmented by the many who were executed for transgressing the new laws. Large numbers of prisoners of war and civilians were sold into slavery. Ten or more of the leading sages, including the aged Rabbi Aqiva, were brutually murdered, and entered history under the name of "The Ten Martyrs."

Many Jews adjusted to the new situation and discontinued donning phylacteries. Some even underwent surgery for the removal of the traces of circumcision. But many more chose to flee to Babylonia and other countries, where they could practice the Jewish religion openly. Thus the southern regions, which were the main scene of the uprising, no longer had a Jewish population of any consequence. The devastation was appalling. Many cities lay in ruins and about 1,000 villages had disappeared from the map altogether. Only scattered pockets of Jewish farmers remained on the seacoast and in the Jordan valley. The rabbis tried to stem the erosion of the Jewish settlement in Judaea by enacting ordinances discouraging the sale or lease of land to Gentiles. Their action was largely unsuccessful, and Judaea ceased to be for all practical purposes an area of Jewish settlement.

The academies in Yavneh and elsewhere had, of course, ceased to exist. Teachers and students were either massacred or fled to Babylonia. In a highly dramatic act, one of the sages, Judah ben Bava, succeeded in ordaining several of his students just moments before he was apprehended by pursuing Roman soldiers and put to death. Thus the chain of Rabbinic tradition remained unbroken, and learning could be restored by the ordained pupils when, due to a change in the policy of Rome in later years, they returned to the homeland from their exile in Babylonia.

Chapter 5

The Age of the Patriarchate and After

Judaea's Political Destiny After 138 C.E.

The harsh treatment of the Jews lasted for another three years, until Hadrian's death in 138. The new emperor, Antoninus Pius, returned to the traditional Roman policy of noninterference with the inner life of the Jews. The prohibition of circumcision was formally abolished, and remained in force only with regard to Gentiles converting to Judaism. The prohibitions of celebrating the Sabbath and the festivals, as well as that of studying Torah were not officially revoked, but ceased to be enforced and were ultimately forgotten. During the rule of Antoninus' successors, Jewish-Roman reconciliation made further progress, and Rome, as long as its government remained pagan, rarely, if ever, imposed any restrictions on Jewish religious practice. The *nasi* Simon II, son of Gamaliel II, incarcerated by the Romans and subsequently a refugee in Babylonia, now returned and established in Usha, in Galilee, a new academy which was clearly to be a continuation of the one in Yavneh. It was at that time probably that Antoninus Pius, as an additional concession to the Jews, gave official recognition to the *nasi.* The Roman authorities then began to refer to the *nasi* as "patriarch," a title used in previous times only informally.

The improved relations with Rome had generally little effect on the distribution of the Jewish population, and the southern part of the country remained practically uninhabited by Jews. Henceforth, Jewish settlement in the south was only of a sporadic nature. Recurring attempts to re-establish a Jewish community in Jerusalem met with a similar fate. Galilee, however, continued to be an area of Jewish mass settlement, probably up to the fourth century. Some localities, such as Sepphoris and Tiberias, became thoroughly Jewish cities, and outside of Galilee the city of Caesarea had about the year 300 a Jewish population of considerable size. There were also periods when limited numbers of Jewish immigrants from the Diaspora augmented the Jewish community. By and large, however, Palestine's Jewish population underwent a process of diminution during the entire period. The process was accelerated beginning with the fifth century, but early in the seventh century Palestine's Jewish community was still significant enough to play a certain role in the Persian occupation of the Holy Land.

The political situation of the Jews was also subject to perpetual change. For obvious reasons Antoninus Pius, even though he returned to the Jews their religious freedom, still maintained in the country a harsh administrative regime, now, only five years after the victory over Bar Kocheba. Later, however, and especially under the emperors of the Severan dynasty (193–235) a decisive thaw took place also in the political arena. Alexander Severus (222–35) was known as such an enthusiastic contributor to the construction of new synagogues, that he was nicknamed *Archisynagogus.* Small wonder that the office of the patriarch kept on gaining in importance and splendor.

A decisive change for the worse took place when Christians began to ascend the imperial throne. True, Constantine I the Great (307–37), who may or may not have been a Christian, still gave the Jewish community full protection, even though he publicly vilified it. But later Christian emperors, though still recognizing Judaism as the only legal religion besides Christianity, under clergy pressure began to curtail the rights of Jews. Theodosius II (408–50) then collected in his code of laws all the anti-Jewish legislation which had piled up until that time. These laws received their ultimate formulation roughly 100 years later in the code issued by the emperor Justinian I (527–65). In this form the anti-Jewish legislation of the late Antiquity was taken over by the Middle Ages and greatly influenced the attitude of the medieval Christian state to the Jews.

A few short-lived episodes did not influence the situation in a tangible manner. This was the case when in the years 267–79 Palestine was subject to the rule of Queen Zenobia of Palmyra, who had rebelled against Rome. Similarly, the basic Jewish situation remained unchanged when in the middle of the fourth century a group of Jews in Sepphoris seem to have become involved in an attempt of a certain Patricius, possibly a pagan Roman, to seize power. Most Jewish leaders seem to have opposed this action. When the attempt failed, only Patricius' Jewish supporters were punished.

Of no real significance, but of much greater dramatic interest, was Palestine Jewry's role in the attempt of the emperor Julian (361–63) to abolish the Christian rule of the empire. Like most contemporary neoplatonists, Julian was genuinely attracted to Judaism. After receiving in Antioch a Jewish delegation from Palestine, the emperor ordered Jerusalem to be returned to the Jews and the Temple rebuilt. He appointed a special official to execute the plan and appropriated a sum of money to begin the work. On the Jewish side, opinions were divided. While some Jews returned to Jerusalem and began rebuilding the Temple, others, among them the patriarch and many of the rabbis, were less enthusiastic, or even opposed to the plan. The latter were either afraid of a repetition of the events under Hadrian, or possibly did not wish to see the priesthood return to the control of the religious life at a time when the development of the Halakhah had reached its highest point (see Chap. 6). Julian's sudden death put an end to the episode.

In the following centuries Palestinian Jewry rather resignedly accepted the creeping deterioration of its position under the Byzantine emperors. From time to time hopes for redemption arose whenever the relations between the Byzantine and the neo-Persian empires reached a point of explosion. Hopes for redemption and the coming of the Messiah were inextricably connected with Persia, the only power which had successfully withstood Roman, and later Byzantine, pressures. It often even inflicted heavy blows upon Byzantium, and its armies came quite close to the borders of Palestine. In addition, the exilarchs ruling Babylonian Jewry were believed to be descendants of King David on the male line, and thus legitimate pretenders to the throne of a redeemed Israel. Indeed, the cryptic statement of Simon bar Yohai in the second century: "If you see a Persian horse tethered to a grave in the Land of Israel, look out for the coming of the Messiah" (Midrash rabba to Song of Songs, chap. 8), sounded equally exciting to the ears of a Palestinian Jew hundreds of years later.

Redemption from the Byzantine yoke seemed quite real when the Persians invaded Palestine in 614. Already prior to that the Jews were willing to be used by the Persians as a fifth column. Their collaboration helped the Persians a few years earlier to capture the city of Antioch. Now, when the Persians showed up in Palestine, the Jewish community in Galilee rose to their assistance. The wealthy Benjamin of Tiberias put up the funds necessary to provide the rising Jewish army with weapons. Thus, a Jewish army fought together with the Persian army in wresting the Holy Land from the Byzantines. The Jewish formations proved very helpful in capturing Caesarea, the seat of the Byzantine governor, and when Jerusalem was occupied the same year, the Persians handed over its administration to the Jews. The office of governor was held by an otherwise unknown man who assumed the name Nehemiah, presumably to indicate that his status was similar to that of the Persian-Jewish governor of the Holy City almost 1,100 years earlier. No doubt, the Jews believed that the messianic promise was to be fulfilled. They evidently believed that the time of revenge had come for all their sufferings and humiliation, and with Samaritan help began to massacre Christians.

The dream, however, was short-lived. Soon conflicts broke out between the Jews and the Persians, and in 617 the administration of Jerusalem was taken away from the Jews. During the subsequent 12 years, Persian oppression became so harsh that the Jews began to long for the return of the Byzantines. And when the emperor Heraclius recaptured Palestine, it was not without the assistance of the Jews. The despair of the Jews because of the unsuccessful messianic happening was so deep, that some of them, including Benjamin of Tiberias, converted to Christianity. At first Heraclius refrained from punishing the Jews, possibly due to their collaboration in the last stages of the war. Later, however, under clergy pressure he reversed his policy, and in the last years before the Arab conquest the lot of the Jews was quite deplorable. Thus, when the Arabs occupied Palestine between 634 and 640, the Jewish community probably welcomed them as liberators. Here and there Jews may have even cooperated with the invaders.

The Patriarchs

Against the backdrop of the political ups and downs and the constantly diminishing Jewish population, the office of the *nasi*, or patriarch, functioned with astonishing efficiency. From about 140 C.E., when the nasi Simon II returned from his exile in Babylonia, and up to the abolition of the office early in the fifth century, the descendants of Hillel were firmly established in it. The power and authority of the patriarchs had its roots in a combination of various factors. First and foremost was the recognition and support accorded them by the Roman government. The government used the office of the *nasi* effectively as an agency to collect taxes from the Jewish community. In addition, it preferred Palestinian Jewry to be loyal to an official under its control than to a charismatic revolutionary claiming to be the Redeemer, or to an exilarch residing in Babylonia and subject to the control of the Persian king of kings. But no less an important source of the power of the *nasi* was the recognition and reverence accorded him by Palestine's Jewish community.

The court of the patriarch, full of princely splendor and guarded by a garrison of foreign mercenaries, first resided in Usha, then in Beth Shearim, and ultimately in Tiberias. It was maintained by donations from the Diaspora in the Roman empire, contributed as a token of reverence. At the beginning, the patriarchs were also considered the highest authority in matters of religion and they presided over the Sanhedrin. After Judah I, learning declined in the patriarchal family, and the Sanhedrin was henceforth headed by one of the sages. Nevertheless, the authority of the patriarch continued to be decisive within imperial Jewry. This can be seen from the fact that the radical calendric reform introduced by the patriarch Hillel II was accepted with no visible opposition.

The new system of calendation, still basically followed today by the Jewish people the world over, may be considered as one of the greatest contributions made by the patriarchate. As we have seen, it was within the competence of the Sanhedrin and its head to proclaim the New Moon, the backbone of the Jewish calendar. At first distant Jewish communities were informed of such proclamations by a system of flares. Close to the year 200 C.E., while Judah I held the office of patriarch, this system had to be abandoned due to the fact that sectarian groups used the same system, and caused much confusion. Consequently messengers began to be sent to the Diaspora to inform the communities of the proclamation of the New Moon. With the seemingly endless extension of the Diaspora, and the Romans occasionally interfering with the process of proclamation, the system of messengers too became inoperative. The situation definitely called for the development of a stabilized calendar. Much preparatory work was done by the sages in the generations succeeding Judah I, and in the middle of the fourth century the patriarch Hillel II was able to introduce a full-fledged stabilized calendar.

Since the Jewish holidays are not only to be celebrated on certain days of lunar months but also during specific seasons of the year, the Jewish calendar had to be based on a combination of the lunar and solar year. Since the lunar and solar years differ by about 11 days, a cycle of 19 years was introduced, with an accumulated difference totaling 209 days. These in turn were divided into seven months, and intercalated as a Second Adar to the third, sixth, eighth, eleventh, fourteenth, seventeenth, and nineteenth year of the cycle. This calendric system secured fairly well the celebration of the holidays in their proper seasons.

Regulating the calendar was only one of the prerogatives of the patriarchs. Most of the time they were also in charge of appointing judges for the Jewish communities. They also effectively supervised the judiciary by sending out emissaries whose task it was to observe the actions of the judges. Their own court finally served as a court of appeals on judgments of the lower courts. Their additional prerogative to cancel religious bans issued by local judicial authorities effectively assured the individual the possibility of relief in cases of judicial error or injustice. Most of the judges were, of course, graduates of the patriarchal academy or the other academies.

The dynasty of the patriarchs did not produce too many outstanding men. In fact, as we have seen, during the last two centuries of the patriarchate they were no longer learned enough to head the Sanhedrin, and little by little the collective of the sages took over some of the patriarchs' responsibilities, including the appointment of judges. Sometimes a sage was able to overshadow the patriarch, as was the case with Rabbi Avahu, head of the academy at Caesarea early in the fourth century, who represented Palestine's Jewish community politically, while the patriarch Gamaliel IV remained on the sidelines. By and large the patriarchs succeeded in developing a working relationship with the Romans and diverted many hardships from Palestine's Jewish community. This was the case, for instance, with Judah II, also known as Judah Nesiah, who ruled for several decades beginning about the year 230. This was a period of many changes in the Roman empire, with a quick succession of emperors and appallingly high taxes. Judah II tried to stand between his people and the government, and although blamed for many of the hardships, it was he who successfully saved the Jewish community from catastrophic calamities. Judah III (275–320) ruled at the critical time of the change from a pagan to a Christian empire. He successfully brought about the adaptation of Palestine's Jewish community to the new situation and assisted the imperial Diaspora in the organization of an educational network.

Towering above all the patriarchs was Judah I. He was born about the time of the Second Revolt and was a young child during the period of the Hadrianic religious persecution. It was his good fortune to grow to manhood during the period of Roman-Jewish reconciliation, when the patriarchal academy was re-established, and the office of the patriarch was growing in importance. He ascended to the office of the patriarch about the year 170 and held the office for close to half a century. He made full use of the powers vested in him, as he believed that these were God-given. Some of the sages were critical both of the authoritarian way in which he conducted the affairs of the Jewish community, and of his affluent and aristocratic life style. The majority of the sages, however, supported him, since his activities strengthened Jewish unity against sectarian encroachments, and because of the decisive role he played in the standardization of the Jewish religious law, the Halakhah. He made the city of Beth Shearim his capital and the seat of his academy. His day-to-day activities were of such a great blessing to the people that some of his contemporaries looked upon him as if he were the Messiah, and a grateful posterity began to call him *Rabenu haqadosh,* our saintly master.

When the Roman empire became a Christian state, the fate of the office of the Jewish patriarch was sealed. It was obvious that the Church whose messiah claimed Davidic origin would not tolerate a major Jewish office headed by men also claiming to be descendants of King David. True, at the beginning the Christian emperors still held the *nasi* in high esteem, but it was clear that the office of the patriarch was losing its significance. An abortive Jewish uprising in 351 was used as an excuse for curtailing the authority of the patriarch, a process accelerated by the fact that in the fourth century Palestine's Jewish population had become much smaller than it was in the time of Judah I. A series of imperial ordinances issued early in the fifth century then formally abolished the office. The patriarchal treasury was confiscated, and the donations coming from the Diaspora for the patriarch were diverted to the emperor's private charity fund.

By the year 430 Palestine Jewry's autonomy under the patriarchs was a thing of the past. The Sanhedrin continued to function, but gradually lost its influence on the Diaspora. Many years later a new Jewish authoritative leader arose in the personality of the exilarch Mar Zutra III, who arrived from Babylonia and settled in Tiberias. Although he served merely as head of the academy, he and his descendants down to the Arab conquest enjoyed considerable authority within the Jewish community. However, they never obtained any formal recognition from the Byzantine government.

Economic Conditions

The economy of Palestinian Jewry experienced many ups and downs in this period. Most Jews, especially in Galilee, continued to till the soil. Although agriculture was gravely undermined by reckless Roman taxation policies, progressing inflation, especially in the third century, made it still advantageous to hold on to the land. Late in the third century, however, a new policy initiated by the emperor Diocletian brought about a decrease in Jewish land ownership with a parallel increase in the number of Jewish tenants and sharecroppers.

All this time more and more Jews flocked into the cities and into crafts and retail merchandising. There were even periods when some of the Greek merchants departed from the country and Jews were able to occupy their positions. Jewish merchant princes, small as their number was, played more than a modest role in international trade, especially in the importation of silk from China, via Persia, into the Roman empire. In summary, it may be said that although the Jewish element in Palestine by and large belonged to the lower economic strata, it had a fairly secure economic existence.

The Cultural Scene

Throughout this period the scholarly class was undergoing a process of steady growth. To be sure, the scholars were rarely if ever compensated for their academic and educational activities. Some of them, as we have seen, found employment as judges and administrative functionaries in the patriarchal administration. Most of them, however, earned their livelihood in trade and the crafts. Their only real advantage was exemption from paying taxes. In addition, efforts were increasingly made to establish charitable funds for the purpose of enabling the scholars to devote all their time to the study of Torah.

Significant developments took place in the area of culture. To begin with, the use of the ancient Hebrew script went out of vogue after the Second Revolt. The Hebrew language, as preserved in the Mishnah, was still in use in various circles, but the majority spoke Aramaic. An attempt of Judah I to promote the use of Hebrew was only modestly successful. True, the Mishnah edited in his times became a Hebrew text, but the Jerusalem Talmud, which came into being in the subsequent 150 years, is an Aramaic text.

While Aramaic and a sort of an Aramaic-Greek jargon were largely spoken in rural areas and in regions of compact Jewish settlement, the Greek language spread extensively among Jews in the mixed cities. To be sure, some of the sages opposed the use of Greek rather keenly. But an official ban on studying the Greek language and culture was never issued. For reasons not fully clear, Judah I preferred Greek to Aramaic. It seems that a sort of compromise was tacitly reached according to which only children of school age were to be kept away from studying Greek, but the aristocracy seems to have felt exempt even from this limitation. The patriarch Gamaliel V did not hesitate to engage a Gentile teacher for his children, and Homer's writings, and presumably other Greek works, were used as texts for the study of Greek culture despite a certain opposition on the part of the sages. All this resulted in the adoption of the Greek language and culture, at least to a certain degree. Some of the sages, such as Rabbi Avahu, even possessed a deep and comprehensive knowledge of Greek culture.

The study of Torah continued to occupy a position of centrality in the general cultural endeavor. We have seen that as soon as the Romans discontinued enforcing the Hadrianic prohibition on Torah study, some of the surviving sages, mostly younger men, convened in Usha, a Galilean town. In addition to issuing certain ordinances, they established there the nucleus of a new academy. Somewhat later, as will be remembered, Simon II, son of Gamaliel II (of Yavneh), arrived in Usha. In time the Usha

Academy came to be considered a successor to that of Yavneh and thus attained the rank of a Sanhedrin. Subsequently, academies for the higher study of Torah emerged in other localities of Galilee, too. But ultimately the academy of Tiberias attained a status of centrality, up to the time of the abolition of the patriarchate. No academies are known to have existed early in the period outside of Galilee, but in the fourth century Torah learning had again spread southward, and we find then major academies functioning in Caesarea and Lydda.

It seems that Hebrew was the language of study in the academies up to the death of Patriarch Judah I. With his death, however, Aramaic became more and more the language of instruction and discussion. Originally the resurrected Sanhedrin was headed by the traditional collective leadership of president, and chief justice *(nasi,* and *av-beth-din).* Under Judah I the collective leadership was abolished, to be only partly restored after his death. Judah I also concentrated in his hands the exclusive right of ordination. When Antoninus Pius (138–61) granted the scholars exemption from the payment of taxes, the Jewish academies must have experienced an increase in the number of resident sages. The student body of the academies grew further following a prohibition issued by Judah I against study in open-air schools, a custom adopted by certain sages from the Greeks.

The leading scholars in the Usha period were Rabbi Aqiva's pupils Meir and Simon bar Yohai, as well as others among those who fled to Babylonia and had now returned. The end of the second century is characterized by the decisive influence of the towering personality of Judah I in the entire academic sphere. Many more sages studied and taught in the Galilean academies up to the end of the patriarchate and later. From time to time a scholar emerged as the leader of his contemporaries, such as Johanan bar Napaha who flourished in the middle of the third century, or Avahu of Caesarea in the first decades of the fourth century.

Even though the main objective of the academies was the study and development of the Jewish law, the sciences were not neglected. In fact, the mathematical and natural sciences were much in use as ancillary disciplines in legal research. By and large, the knowledge manifested by the sages in the sciences was not much different from that of their Greco-Roman counterparts. Historiography, however, trailed far behind that of the contemporary Greeks and earlier Jewish historiography. *Seder olam raba,* a systematic chronology of world history, was the only outstanding work in this field. Otherwise, the sages seem to have been content with casual excursions into the field of history which have come down to us interspersed in the Talmud and midrashic literature.

The Religious Life

The religious life of the people, too, was not seriously affected by the Hadrianic persecution, due to its short duration. If there was any danger in the area of religious life, it was caused by the presence of huge numbers of pagan Gentiles, from whom their Jewish neighbors borrowed many superstitions and a great deal of belief in magic and astrology. The clear biblical injunctions and the efforts of the sages were never fully able to eradicate these foreign elements from the life and religious practice of the average Jew. From time to time the sages saw themselves therefore compelled to neutralize strange practices by infusing them with Jewish religious content. The many restrictions legislated by the Rabbis against social and even economic contacts with Gentiles were no doubt motivated by the desire to keep the average Jew from imitating objectionable pagan practices.

Another challenge faced by the sages was an increased tendency toward mystical speculation, and possibly also practice. To be sure, mystical speculation was a hallowed occupation, going back to prophetic times. After the destruction of the Second Temple the quest for the time of the coming of the Messiah increased, and with it came quite naturally a great expansion of mystical speculation. A sage of the caliber of Rabbi Aqiva seriously indulged in mystical speculation, and his pupil Simon bar Yohai attained a status of major importance in Jewish mysticism for many centuries to come. There is unmistakable evidence, however, that mystical speculation could be quite harmful even to sages of high stature. But the rabbis succeeded in stemming mysticism's serious deviation from the mainstream of Jewish religious thought, while simultaneously preserving it as a tolerated doctrine.

The Jewish messianic idea also experienced a period of great crisis, but came through largely unscathed. Christian claims that the Messiah had come in the person of Jesus, and the failure of Bar Kocheba, who was recognized by Rabbi Aqiva as the true Messiah, shook the messianic idea to its very foundations. It is possible that the idea of the Messiah, son of Joseph, was then conceived as a remedy. This Messiah, who is supposed to appear in Galilee, would begin the struggle for Israel's redemption, but fail and die. Only afterwards the Messiah, son of David, would appear and successfully complete the act of Redemption. If Bar Kocheba could be identified with Messiah, son of Joseph, he was destined to fail and die, and both Rabbi Aqiva's honor and the idea of the Messiah-Redeemer could be saved. The possibility should not, however, be overlooked that a Christian group created the idea of the Messiah, son of Joseph, in an attempt to introduce Jesus into the Jewish concept of the Messiah. Jesus, it should be remembered, appeared in Galilee. He was the son of a man named Joseph. He claimed to be the Messiah, and died. The messianic idea remained alive and, as we have seen, awakened again and again with great force during the recurring wars between Byzantium and Persia. The hopes for redemption were also nurtured by an extensive messianic literature which skillfully described in allegorical language the contemporary historical scene to convince its readers of the imminent coming of the Redeemer.

Meantime religious life continued to be centered in the synagogue. Even though some sages were of the opinion that it was preferable to spend money on education rather than on building synagogues, many synagogues were built all over the country in this period. The city of Tiberias had no less than 13. Significantly, the synagogues had many ornamentations, including some depicting the human form. It seems that the rabbis did not consider this a violation of the Commandment prohibiting the making of images. Be it noted in this connection that the seal of the patriarch also had an ornamentation with human features. The architecture of the synagogues reveals no specific Jewish characteristics. Most synagogues were built in the Greco-Syrian style prevalent at the time, but certain adaptations were, of course, made to satisfy the specific needs of the synagogue.

Religious services were mostly conducted in Hebrew. Special services, such as the prayer for rain, were often conducted in Greek. The *Shema* prayer originally could be recited in all languages. Judah I, however, began to insist on its recital in Hebrew. Sermons interpreting the Scriptures were, of course, delivered in both vernaculars, Aramaic and Greek. Thus, the Jews were probably not overly perturbed when Emperor Justinian I (527–65) ordered that the Bible be read in the synagogues exclusively in Greek in order to prevent them from allegedly giving corrupt interpretations to Scriptures.

Throughout the period, Gentiles kept on entering the Jewish fold. True, when Antoninus Pius abolished Hadrian's prohibition of circumcision, it applied only to Jews by birth; it still remained forbidden to circumcise pagan converts to Judaism. This, of course, both limited the number of prospective converts to Judaism and gave Christianity a great advantage in its rivalry with Judaism within the pagan world. Nevertheless, converts to Judaism were no rarity in Judaea and in the empire in those centuries of the late Antiquity. The ability of the rabbis to preach in Greek and to employ methods of discussion fashionable in the Greek world was a mighty vehicle in attracting Greeks and Romans to the Jewish faith.

All through the period of the patriarchate the number of Christians in the country was growing. To be sure, Jews and Samaritans were converting to the new faith in negligible numbers, but Gentiles living in the province of Judaea converted to Christianity in ever-increasing numbers, especially in the fourth and fifth centuries, after Christianity had become the official state religion. The Christian element was further augmented by the immigration of Christians from other countries to whom the province, and especially Jerusalem, had become a holy site. The Christians thus began to claim Judaea for themselves since the Church was now, according to Christian doctrine, the true Israel. Constantine the Great and his mother Helen undertook to give the province of Judaea a Christian character by building many churches and shrines. In the fifth century many monasteries were built to accommodate the considerable influx of immigrant monks.

Jews and Samaritans obviously looked with dismay at the Christianization of the country and the resulting tension led to riots. Early in the fifth century in the period of the abolition of the patriarchate, and possibly inspired by it, Christian mobs burned many synagogues. A few decades later Jews were massacred in Jerusalem following incitement by a monk. In the middle of the sixth century resentment against the Christians rose to such a degree that the erstwhile enemies, Jews and Samaritans, joined in an anti-Christian riot in Caesarea which resulted in the destruction of a number of churches. Jewish attacks on Christians again broke out early in the seventh century during the Persian occupation of the province. In summary, the entire period of the patriarchate was a time of steadily rising tensions between Jews and Christians in the Holy Land.

Chapter 6

The Halakhah

A major achievement of this period is the standardization of the Halakhah, the Jewish Oral Law. According to normative Jewish tradition the Oral Law was handed to Moses on Mount Sinai together with the Torah, the Written Law. The Oral Law was to serve as an interpretation of the Written Law.

Modern scholars have arrived at a multitude of divergent theories as to the origins of the Oral Law and the time of its emergence. What seems probable is that already in the period of the First Commonwealth at least some customs and religious practices later recorded in the Talmud, the great repository of the Oral Law, were followed and practiced. It may also be assumed that the *Sopherim*, scribes, expert in the text of the Written Law, who were active early in the period of the Second Commonwealth, were also versed in the Oral Law to the degree that it had been practiced up to their times. In the latter part of the Second Commonwealth the Oral Law began to play a more significant role in the religious life of the people. In fact, the Pharisees accorded to the Oral Law a status of ever-increasing significance. It was at this point that the necessity began to be felt to prove that the Oral Law is based on the Written Law. Every norm or religious practice, it was felt, should be deducible from, or implied in, a pentateuchal passage.

Soon the study of the Oral Law as a derivative of the Written Law became so important and widespread that it became necessary to formulate a set of principles by which the multitude of norms and customs contained in the Oral Law could logically be connected with the written Torah. Such hermeneutical principles, as these logical rules are called, were first formulated in the first century, B.C.E., by Hillel, one of the early great sages. These hermeneutical rules, though not directly copied from the Greeks, resemble the ways in which Greek grammarians and Roman jurists were discussing linguistic and legal issues. Later generations of sages further developed the hermeneutical principles and enlarged their number. The introduction of the hermeneutical rules established a firm framework for standardizing the Oral Law in a fairly objective fashion, simultaneously keeping the sages from resorting to far-fetched interpretations of pentateuchal texts.

The uncompromising adherence to the principle of the rule of the majority added much authority to the decisions of the Rabbis in matters of the Oral Law. Its main authority, of course, was based on the belief that its ultimate source was Divine revelation. It should, however, be emphasized that despite this the Oral Law never assumed the character of a rigid and monolithic body of rules. Thus, Galilee, which was separated from southern Jewry by Samaria, developed differing practices and traditions, and these were recorded by the Rabbis. Also, with the expansion of the Diaspora, the Rabbis were faced with an emergence of increasingly different local religious customs and practices. They accepted in principle this reality by acknowledging the validity of the idea that "the custom of a place is binding."

Even though the hermeneutical rules limited the freedom of

interpretation of the Written Law, they still left the Rabbis a comfortable possibility for legislation. As long as a law or ruling issued by the Rabbis could be at least loosely connected with a pentateuchal passage, it rarely if ever evoked popular opposition. The idea of the two-fold Law consisting of the Written and Oral had become practically universally accepted after the destruction of the Second Temple and the concommitant disappearance of the Sadducean party. When a new opposition to the Oral Law appeared in the Middle Ages in the Karaitic heresy, the Oral Law already had become a way of life for the Jewish people and could no longer be eliminated.

The actual work of interpreting the Written Law and standardizing its Oral counterpart was conducted in an institution originally called *beth midrash,* house of interpretation. This institution which had emerged in the early centuries of the Second Commonwealth was ultimately transformed after the year 70 C.E. into academies of the type of that in Yavneh. Here ordained rabbis discussed the Halakhah in the presence of a larger or smaller student body and here decisions in the field of the Oral Law were made. To be sure, mostly concrete cases were discussed but in the decisions on such cases clear general rules were implicit, to be applied countless times whenever and wherever a rabbinic jurist had to make an adjudication in an actual case before him.

The entire work of discussing, formulating, standardizing, and writing down the Oral Law lasted almost 1,000 years. Hundreds of sages, both in Palestine and Babylonia, participated in the work. It is very likely that the members of the Great Assembly discussed matters of the Oral Law, even prior to the Assembly's transformation into the Sanhedrin. Simon the Just, who lived in the fourth century B.C.E. and is probably identical with the similarly named high priest, is the first teacher of the Oral Law mentioned by name. During the 300 years between him and Hillel many other sages flourished whose main preoccupation seems to have been the discussion and formulation of the Oral Law.

It is probably these sages whom later generations called *zeqenim rishonim,* former elders. Hillel and the sages who followed him up to the time of Patriarch Judah I became known as *Tannaim,* teachers, reciters, repeaters. Their number was large, and they were a galaxy of men outstanding by their character and learning. Their discussions of the Oral Law were full of dynamic, and even passionate, moments. Often their pupils, such as those of Hillel and his contemporary Shammai, created schools divergent in thought and method. Thus, for instance, *Beth Hillel,* the House (School) of Hillel, represented a lenient, conciliatory approach in the interpretation of the Law, while the *Beth Shammai,* the House (School) of Shammai, advocated a more strict and rigid conception of the Law. Sages of later generations kept on adding their own contributions to the development of this Jewish jurisprudence. Important work was done, not without conflict and struggle, by the sages of Yavneh and the other academies in the period dominated by Gamaliel II.

Thus, legal material of many categories kept on accumulating. The time was ripe for taking stock and dividing the material in order to transform it into a systematic body of laws. The task was first undertaken by Rabbi Aqiva in the years preceding the Second Revolt. Aqiva, of unknown origin, grew to manhood totally uneducated. Under the inspiring influence of his beloved wife, Rachel, he began to study Torah and became one of the leading Tannaim, if not the greatest among them. He developed such a sophisticated and flexible method of deducing laws from biblical passages, that he was credited with building "upon each crownlet on a letter [in the Pentateuch], heaps and heaps of laws" (Babylonian Talmud, tractate Menahoth 29b). Like Hillel, Aqiva too encountered formidable opposition in the school of his contemporary, Rabbi Ishmael, who maintained that the Torah is written in a simple, commonly understood style, which does not lend itself to overly farfetched legal derivations. Nevertheless, Aqiva's work on the systematic arrangement of the Oral Law became the great achievement of his generation. The work was continued after the Second Revolt by Aqiva's pupil, Meir. It then became possible for Judah I in the following generation to compile the Mishnah and thus reach a major milestone on the road to the standardization of Jewish Law.

Modern scholarship has not yet succeeded in describing with full clarity either the nature of the Mishnah, or the method employed by Judah I in compiling or editing it. What can be said with certainty is that the Mishnah is a representative repository and summary of Jewish religious and civil law, as formulated by scholars and schools up to approximately the year 200 C.E. While former collections of the Oral Law probably represented the teachings of heads of particular schools, Judah made his collection, the Mishnah, universal by including in it the basic teachings of about half a dozen former compilations of the Law. Of no lesser importance is the division of the Law into six orders according to their subject matter already attempted by Rabbi Aqiva. To facilitate the use of the Mishnah, Judah further divided each order into a number of tractates, and the latter into chapters.

True, the Mishnah more often than not recorded divergent opinions of scholars and schools with regard to a multitude of laws, and thus could not become a "regular" code of laws. But the clear and concise formulation of legal opinions, and the division into orders, tractates, and chapters made the Mishnah a useful substitute for a formal code of laws. At the same time it left the door open to further study and discussion, so that upon it as a foundation the two *Talmudim* could be built, as well as all the subsequent Rabbinic literature. Nothing could do more to prevent Jewish law from becoming petrified, and nothing suited more the needs of an ever-expanding Diaspora with a host of divergent climatic, geographic, political, economic, social, and cultural conditions, than this "indefinite" nature of the Mishnah. Once compiled, the Mishnah displaced all previous similar collections of the Jewish law. It became a sacred text, second in importance only to the Bible.

The question of how far foreign influences penetrated the Jewish law as recorded in the Mishnah is still undecided. Some scholars are of the opinion that by and large the Mishnah remained immune to the contemporary Greco-Roman and Parthian law systems. Others instead believe that the centuries-old Jewish symbiosis with Hellenistic culture is reflected in the Mishnah. In particular they find incorporated in it concepts of Greek municipal law, as well as Greek legal terms in their original form.

In keeping with the linguistic preferences of Judah the Patriarch, the Mishnah was composed not in Aramaic but in a Hebrew interspersed with certain Greek words that had become commonplace among the Jews. This made the work accessible even to intelligent laymen long after Aramaic had ceased to be a spoken language among Jews. It is thus not surprising that more than a thousand years after its compilation the Mishnah attained its greatest diffusion as a text of popular study among Jews in many countries. Societies for the study of the Mishnah proliferated everywhere and are not a rarity even in our own times. An enthusiastic admirer of the Mishnah pointed out the fact that the Hebrew letters of the word Mishnah are identical with the letters of the word *neshamah,* soul.

Originally a tendency to perpetuate the Mishnah as an oral text was noticeable, so that it might never become a rival to the Written Torah. Some scholars even claimed to have discovered in the structure of the Mishnah certain rhythmic elements, built in to facilitate its memorization and transmission. The custom of chanting the Mishnah (as well as the Gemara) in a set way may also have served the same purpose. Nevertheless, already prior to the times of Judah the Patriarch, scholars used to prepare for themselves "private" written collections of laws. The text of the Mishnah also probably began to be privately copied after Judah the Patriarch and his associates gave the finishing touches to it.

The wish that the Mishnah should be studied and used by as many Jews as possible, and the ever-growing geographic expansion of the Diaspora, probably helped to overcome all doubts, and the Mishnah was committed to writing in Judah the Patriarch's last years, or shortly after his death. It appeared in print prior to the year 1500. Many leading scholars wrote basic commentaries to the Mishnah. The most important are those of Moses Maimonides (1135–1204), Obadiah of Bertinoro (second half of the fifteenth century), and Yom Tov Lippmann Heller (1579–1654). Translations of the Mishnah into various languages, including Latin, English, and Yiddish, were made by Jewish and Gentile scholars.

We have seen that the Mishnah was only one milestone, though a very important one, on the road to the standardization of Jewish law. It is therefore understandable that at the very moment the Mishnah obtained its formulation, it became a text which beckoned to be further studied and discussed. The natural place for such discussions was the Academy at Tiberias, where the Mishnah was edited. And, indeed, a galaxy of brilliant scholars in the generations that followed Judah the Patriarch, known as *Amoraim,* speakers, interpreters (of the Mishnah), added their own original contributions to the work begun hundreds of years before them. Their main contribution lay in the formulation of general legal principles, as against the concentration of the *Tannaim* on specific cases. Ultimately the contribution of the *Amoraim* also attained the form of a text, known as the Gemara, or Talmud, that is, the authoritative exposition of the text of the Mishnah.

While the Mishnah was created in Judaea, and only faint attempts of a similar nature were made in Babylonia, it was different in the case of the Gemara. A brilliant young Babylonian scholar, Aba Arikha, whom admiring contemporaries called Rav, The Teacher, studied in the academy of Judah the Patriarch at the time of the crystallization of the Mishnah. When he returned to his homeland in 219, he brought along the Mishnah. Rav was considered by later generations to have been a *Tanna*, and it is likely that he had some active part in the compilation of the Mishnah. Be this as it may, it is a fact that he, in an academy which he established in Sura, and Samuel, an equally brilliant scholar in nearby Nehardea, were the first in a galazy of Babylonian *Amoraim* whose scholarly discussions on the text of the Mishnah also resulted in the creation of a Gemara. It should be noted, however, that the Mishnah studied in the Babylonian academies often differed from that studied in the Holy Land. Ultimately the Gemara which came into being in Judaea became known by the names of Jerusalem Talmud, Palestinian Talmud, and the Talmud of the Westerners, that is, of the scholars of the West, as Judaea was often referred to in Babylonia. The Babylonian Gemara came to be known as the Babylonian Talmud.

As in the case of the Mishnah, it is not easy to define the nature of the Gemara. The best description might possibly be that it consists of resumés of discussions held in the academies in the Holy Land and Babylonia. It is thus totally different from the Mishnah. Judah the Patriarch in compiling the Mishnah attempted to formulate the Jewish Law and the basic divergent opinions of leading jurists and law schools. He therefore could aim at developing short, precise paragraphs. He could also formulate these without difficulty in the no-longer-spoken Hebrew language. The Gemara, instead, is a dynamic recording of discussions, debates and arguments, often conducted with passion. It is therefore natural that it came down to us in Aramaic, the language actually used in the deliberations of the academies. It is also quite natural that the Aramaic of the Palestinian Talmud is quite different from the Aramaic of the Babylonian Talmud, since the two Jewish communities used different Aramaic dialects in their everyday lives.

The Amoraim whose discussions and teachings were recorded in the two Talmudim were very numerous, and their activities stretched over several hundred years. The Palestinian Amoraim, among whom were also immigrants from Babylonia, lived and taught mainly in the academies of Tiberias, Sepphoris, and Caesarea. Practically every one among them made a more or less conspicuous contribution to the clarification of Jewish Law. Most prominent among them, however, was Rabbi Johanan bar Napaha, whose teachings occupy a considerable part of the Palestinian Talmud. Many more sages were active in the Holy Land in subsequent generations, but after Johanan, the Palestinian Talmud did not undergo any more basic literary changes. In the second half of the fourth century the schools were closed and the Palestinian Talmud concluded.

Even more numerous than the Palestinian Amoraim were their Babylonian counterparts, and their activities lasted about 150 years longer. This, and the generally more favorable conditions of the Babylonian Jewish community, are responsible for the fact that the Babylonian Talmud is much larger than the Palestinian. Also, the Babylonian Talmud contains discussions on a larger number of tractates of the Mishnah than the Palestinian. There are, furthermore, differences in the contents of the two Talmudim. The Palestinian Talmud devotes much attention to the specific agricultural laws connected with the Land of Israel and binding on Jews living in it. It also deals in detail with the sacrificial service, in the expectation of the imminent rebuilding of the Temple. Conversely, the Babylonian Talmud pays greater attention to the Jewish civil law which became the foundation of Jewish life in the Diaspora communities.

Because of the new conditions under the Christian emperors, it became necessary to "close" the Palestinian Talmud about the middle of the fourth century, while such a need began for the first time to be felt in Babylonia about the year 400. By that time so much material had been accumulated in the academies at Sura, Nehardea, Mahoza, and Pumbedita, that a selection and classification of the material into a certain order became an absolute necessity. This task was painstakingly carried out by the head of the Sura academy, Rav Ashi, during the decades of his presidency (c. 375–427). Rav Ashi in many respects resembled the personality of Judah the Patriarch, and the work that he did on editing the Babylonian Talmud is not unlike the work Judah did on the Mishnah. About a decade after Ashi's death a period of grave persecution began for Babylonian Jewry, and the sages of that generation became more and more convinced that the system of mnemotechnical devices employed in the Babylonian Talmud would not suffice to save it from oblivion. Hence, as occurred 250 years earlier with regard to the Mishnah, all doubts were put aside and the Babylonian Talmud, far superior to the Palestinian as a literary text, was committed to writing under the leadership of Ravina II, the head of the Sura academy from 474 to 499. Thus about the year 500 the gigantic work of standardizing the Jewish law, which had begun possibly 1,000 years earlier, was concluded.

Rabina II is considered the last Amora and final editor of the Gemara. Nonetheless, in the first half of the sixth century certain Babylonian scholars still could make an additional contribution to the text of the Babylonian Talmud by inserting into it a number of final editorial notes. These scholars are known under the collective name of *Saboraim,* reasoners. By the year 550 the Talmud came to a definite conclusion, and no changes were afterwards made in its text. The Talmud, too, was translated into various languages, and all through the ages commentaries were written on it by countless scholars.

To the realm of Talmudic literature also belongs a large body of Mishnah-like material that was not included in the Mishnah. No doubt, a part of this material was known to Judah the Patriarch and his associates, and was deliberately kept out of the Mishnah by them. The reasons for this may be varied. Other parts of this material were probably unknown to Judah the Patriarch. Some of it no doubt, represented local Babylonian Jewish legal tradition. This material is known under the names of *Tosefta,* Addenda, and *Baraita,* External (laws). While the Tosefta and Baraita have been, and still are, an important source of Jewish

Law, they are considered noncanonical and occupy in Jewish jurisprudence a place of lesser importance than the Mishnah.

So far the Tannaim and Amoraim have appeared to us mainly as legal authorities. But they were also men of high moral stature, who had a burning desire to lead the Jewish people to a life of righteousness. A tractate of the Mishnah, different in nature from all other tractates, and called *Pirqe Avoth, Sayings of the Fathers,* contains a collection of wondrous maxims, statements, and teachings of the Tannaim on the way of life of a God-fearing Jew. To no less a degree the Amoraim, too, considered it their duty to care for the moral edification of the people for whom they created a system of law. They achieved it mainly by means of preaching. Much in the way they attempted to prove the authenticity of the Law by showing that it was rooted in the Holy Writ, they also tried to connect their ideas about the good and moral life with the Scriptures. They did it in a series of homiletical commentaries to the Bible, called *midrashim,* the most important among which are *Genesis rabbah* and *Leviticus rabbah.*

To be sure, only the Palestinian *Amoraim* chose to present their moral and philosophical teachings in midrashim. Their Babylonian counterparts, for reasons not clear to us, abstained from doing so, and their homiletics became part and parcel of the Babylonian Gemara. This is an additional reason why the Babylonian Gemara is so much larger in size than the Palestinian. In fact, the midrashic (also called aggadic) parts of the Babylonian Talmud occupy no less than two-thirds of it. The aggadic midrashim were composed mainly in Hebrew, a language, as we have seen, no longer spoken in Galilee at the time they were written. They should thus be considered handbooks for preachers rather than texts of actually delivered homilies. A sign of the time of their composition is the presence of a huge number of Aramaic, Greek, and Latin words interspersed in the Hebrew text. Besides moral teachings and philosophical thoughts, the midrashim also contain a variety of other materials, and especially historical traditions, both true and legendary, which stubbornly lived on among the people. In conclusion it may be said that the midrashim played an important role in the centuries-long effort to create a legal and ethical framework for the life of the Jew.

When the Talmud was completed after hundreds of years of

growth, it clearly had become an instrument of Jewish unity. None of the sages and none of the various schools throughout the generations ever questioned the basic assumption that the Law was God-given, and that it assured the survival of the Jewish people. The teachings of the prophets were an ideal; the teachings of the Rabbis attempted to bring about the realization of this ideal by a process of adaptation to the realities of Jewish existence. It should not be hard to understand why the Babylonian Talmud, and not the Palestinian, became the framework of Jewish life. The Palestinian Talmud was written by an ever-declining Jewish community yearning for the coming of the Messiah and the rebuilding of the Temple with the sacrificial service. The Babylonian Talmud, on the other hand, was written by a growing and ever-developing Jewish community which was fully experiencing life in a Diaspora.

This was the time when the Jewish Dispersion had reached its full expansion in the then-known world. Jewish communities dotted the world map from Central Asia to the Atlantic ocean and from the Sahara desert to Germany. Groping to find a basis for an organized Jewish community, Jews everywhere ultimately came to find it in the "Sea of the Talmud," which thus became the true "portable territory of the Jewish people."

Almost 700 years later Rabbi Moses Maimonides described the standing of the Talmud among the Jewish people in the following words: "Whatever is . . . recorded in the Babylonial Talmud is obligatory upon the entire Jewish people, and [Jews] everywhere are dutybound to follow the customs of the Amoraim. They are also obliged to publish the ordinances [of the sages of the Talmud], since all the Jewish people gave their consent to these customs, ordinances, and institutions" (*Code of Laws,* Introduction).

Section IX

IN THE REST OF ASIA

Chapter 1

In Western Asia

It is likely that Israelitic settlements in today's Lebanon and Syria came into being in early biblical times. To begin with, inhabitants of border regions traditionally tend to spill over into neighboring countries. But it was the close alliance established by David and Solomon with neighboring Tyre and Sidon (Phoenicia), today's Lebanon, that in all likelihood resulted in the settlement there of a number of Israelites. The renewal of the alliance by Israel's Omri dynasty about 100 years later (see Sec. III, Chap. 2) probably caused an increase in the number of Israelites living in Phoenicia. Similarly, the perpetual entanglement, at times friendly and at times hostile, of the Kingdom of Israel with its northern neighbor, Aram, today's Syria, resulted in the emergence of a community of Israelites there. Israelites had possibly settled as early as the tenth century B.C.E. in the city of Tadmor, later known as Palmyra, located on the easternmost edge of Syria. Some Israelites had probably settled in the later biblical times in Asia Minor and Armenia as well.

The Jewish communities in the entire region of western Asia began to grow in numbers and importance in the fourth century B.C.E., after Alexander's conquests. The Jewish population in Antioch, the new capital of the Seleucid Syrian empire, as well as in the former capital Damascus, was quite large. The Jewish population in Asia Minor, mostly concentrated in the regions of Phrygia and Lydia in the central and western parts of the country, also increased in numbers. About the year 210 B.C.E., Antiochus III the Great, king of Seleucid Syria, transferred several thousand Jews from Babylonia to Asia Minor as military colonists to strengthen his hold over the country. The Jewish population in Armenia, in turn, grew when Armenian King Tigranes the Great invaded Syria in 87 B.C.E. and deported to his country a number of Jews. On the island of Cyprus, located in the northeastern corner of the Mediterranean, Jews began to appear probably in the third century B.C.E. In the middle of the first century B.C.E. when the island became part of the Roman province of Cilicia (in Asia Minor), the Jewish population on Cyprus had become quite large. As for the Caucasus, it may be assumed that Jews appeared there shortly after their settlement in Armenia. Its Jewish community, however, attained a sizeable strength only in the late Antiquity when Persian Jews began to arrive, fleeing from unrest in their native country, and Byzantine Jews began to immigrate due to persecution in their homeland.

The Jewish population in Syria, and in all probability in other parts of western Asia, had increased sharply after the year 70 C.E. by an influx of refugees from Judaea following the end of the First Revolt. The Jewish settlement in Asia Minor became quite dense. In Palmyra the Jewish community attained its greatest expansion in the third century C.E. when this kingdom had its golden age. The friendly attitude of Queen Zenobia to the Jews encouraged immigration, as well as conversion to Judaism.

When the Romans had extended their rule over all western Asia the region had, as we have seen, a considerable Jewish population. Certain scholars believe that it is not improbable that Syria and Asia Minor each harbored a Jewish population of about one million. Understandably, conflicts of interest often existed between the Jews and the pagan majority. At the beginning, when the population was still largely hostile to the Romans, the latter usually protected the rights of the Jewish minority. It was along these lines that King Herod was able to intervene successfully in favor of his Jewish coreligionists in Asia Minor, when they were threatened with the loss of their privileges. True, most Jews in Asia Minor did not enjoy the right of citizenship, but the fact that the Roman government reaffirmed the privileges of the Jews late in the first century B.C.E. gave them a considerable degree of security. In later times, when the population became more friendly to the Romans, Rome lost some of its interest in protecting the Jews.

A change for the worse took place in the years 66–70 C.E. when the First Revolt raged in Judaea. Despite the fact that Diaspora Jewry remained on the sidelines out of gratitude for the protection given it by the Romans, tension kept on rising between Jews and pagans. In many places, and especially in Syria, armed clashed broke out between the two groups. In Damascus thousands of Jews lost their lives in such a clash.

When the war was over the emperor Vespasian, unmindful of the nonparticipation of western Asia's Jews in the Revolt, imposed upon them, as upon the Jews of the rest of the empire, a special tax to be paid to the temple of Jupiter in Rome. This special tax, which was to replace the half *shekel* paid voluntarily each year by Diaspora Jews to the Temple in Jerusalem, was thus by its nature very insulting. In addition, it also became very burdensome, since all members of the Jewish family, often including small children, were obliged to pay it. Under Vespasian and his two sons the tax was collected with much brutality. In time the Jewish tax became an important source of income to the Roman government. It was paid to an office called *Fiscus Judaicus,* and was collected for a period of almost 300 years. It was the first tax imposed anywhere specifically on Jews, and thus had ominous implications for later times when Jewish taxes became a major source of income to the state.

When early in the second century the emperor Trajan prepared to attack Parthia, Diaspora Jewry rose in a great revolt against the Romans and their pagan neighbors, for reasons not very clear. In western Asia it was mainly Cyprian Jewry which participated in the uprising. Under the leadership of a certain Artemion, the Jews of Cyprus attacked their neighbors, and are said to have massacred the entire population of the city of Salamis. When the uprising was suppressed, many Jews lost their lives, and the rest were banished from the island. Simultaneously, a governmental ordinance prohibited the Jews from ever settling again on the island. Although the ordinance seems to have been disregarded, and Jews were living again on Cyprus in the late Antiquity, the order of expulsion, like the Jewish tax, was quite ominous. It was the first time that Jews were forbidden to live in a country, a practice often repeated in the Middle Ages and in modern times.

A decisive deterioration in the situation of the Jews in Roman Asia took place in the fourth century when Christians began to ascend the imperial throne. True, the codes promulgated by the emperors Theodosius II (408–50) and Justinian I (527–65) still accorded the Jewish religion the status of a *religio licita,* a legal religion. Also social relations between Jews and Gentiles continued in general to be friendly. But the Church, now constantly gaining strength, began to exert an ever-increasing anti-Jewish influence on both government and population. The Church councils issued many rules for the purpose of keeping Christians away from their Jewish neighbors. This produced so much hostility to the Jews and their religion that synagogue burning became a frequent occurrence, despite governmental attempts to prevent it. At the same time the government, too, began to promulgate many laws which seriously curtailed the rights of the Jews.

The greatest damage to the Jews was done by the Christian preachers. A striking example is the large, proud, and wealthy Jewish community of Antioch in Syria, which began rapidly to lose ground under the impact of the sermons of the famous preacher John Chrysostom (345–407). He, and many other Christian theologians possibly did not foresee the degree of anti-Jewish violence which was to follow their sermons depicting the Jew as a monster. And, even though Jews still served in Roman Asia in the local militias, and still participated to a certain degree in public life, the deterioration of the Jewish condition was constant and decisive. It is thus not surprising that the Jews of Syria, like their brethren in Judaea, welcomed the Muslim conquest in 635, and possibly even actively aided in it.

Jewish religious life enjoyed the protection of the government as long as pagans sat on the imperial throne, and to a certain degree, as we have seen, even under the Christian emperors. In certain cities in Asia Minor the municipal authorities, too, provided such protection. Judaism was quite popular among Gentiles. "Fearers of Heaven," that is, pagans who in practice abandoned idolatry and adhered to the Jewish way of life, without formally accepting the Jewish faith, were quite numerous. The number of proselytes was also impressive. Characteristically, many Christians too practiced various Jewish customs and even used to come to synagogues. Synagogues seem to have existed all over Roman Asia. Even under the Christian emperors, when the mob often attacked synagogues, permission could still be secured for their repair. The Bible seems to have been read in the synagogues mostly in Greek. Some Jews in Asia also considered it improper to use the Septuagint since it was now widely read by Christians. Consequently, they replaced the Septuagint by the Bible translation of the proselyte Aquila of Pontus.

Strange as it may seem to us, the emperor Justinian from time to time regulated the Jewish worship. The emperor believed that as he was the head of the Christian Church, he also had such authority with regard to the Jewish religion, which as a *religio licita* was for all practical purposes under his protection.

It is equally surprising that there seems to have been no direct religio-cultural influence of the *Tannaim* and *Amoraim* on the Jews in the rest of Roman Asia. However, names of sages in various parts of the Roman Asian Diaspora found in the Talmud suggest that the scope of such influence may have been much greater than is indicated by the available evidence.

Chapter 2

In Babylonia and the Neighboring Countries

Political Destiny

The Jewish community in Babylonia, which was destined to become one of the greatest Jewish communities of all times, came into being in 722 B.C.E. In this year, as we have seen, Assyria put an end to Samaria, the northern of the two Israelitic states, and deported tens of thousands of its inhabitants to distant regions of its territory. We know little, if anything, about the fate of these first Jewish exiles. Some of them may have assimilated with the local population and became pagans. Others, and possibly the majority, had survived as a Jewish Diaspora, when 125 years later King Nebuchadrezzar II of Babylonia began to deport to his country inhabitants of Judah, the southern of the two Israelitic states. It is not possible to estimate the total number of Judaeans deported by Nebuchadrezzar. It surely was larger, however, than the number of 15,000 suggested by certain modern scholars.

It is equally impossible to draw a precise map of the settlements to which the exiles from Samaria and Judah were directed. The fact that descendants of the exiles were found centered around the cities of Babel and Nippur would indicate that the southern part of today's Iraq was the oldest Jewish settlement in Babylonia. It may be also safely assumed that shortly after their settlement in Babylonia, some of the exiles, or their descendants, emigrated farther east and established Jewish communities in Persia, today's Iran.

We do not know when the exiles of 722 B.C.E. began to feel at home in Assyria. As for Babylonia, the integration of the Judaean exiles began to proceed rather rapidly after Nebuchadrezzar's death. Judah's King Jehoiachin was released from jail and given royal status at the Babylonian court. He seems to have been recognized by the exiles as their leader, and heads of Babylonia's Jewish community in the late Antiquity and Middle Ages based their authority on their claim of being his descendants. Simultaneously, a process of amalgamation of the Israelitic and Judaean exiles began to develop which was strongly endorsed by the prophet Ezekiel.

Economically, too, the exiles and their descendants did well. Opportunities undreamed of in Israel and Judah were now open to them. In the city of Nippur some played a leading role in the world of big business. The economic success of Assyrio-Babylonian Jewry in the sixth century B.C.E. is indicated not only by the fact that when they were given an opportunity in 538 to return to Judaea, only a minority chose to do so, but also by the fact that those who did return were able to take along thousands of slaves.

In 539 B.C.E. the Persian king Cyrus the Great captured Babylonia and the new situation was of great advantage to its

Jews. They generally enjoyed equality with the other inhabitants of the Persian empire. Cyrus' proclamation permitting and supporting the re-establishment of a Jewish commonwealth in Judaea (see Sec. IV, Chap. 1) is indicative of the high degree of favor he bestowed upon his Jewish subjects. The favorable situation of the majority that had remained in Babylonia and Persia is sufficiently shown by the fact that in the fifth century B.C.E. Nehemiah, a pious and proud Jew, could hold the sensitive office of the king's cup-bearer. Also, there is evidence that Jewish soldiers were no rarity in the Persian armies. The attack on the Jews of the empire in the time of King Xerxes (485–65 B.C.E.), reported in the Scroll of Esther, whatever its real scope may have been, was certainly of short duration and had no lasting impact on the destiny of Persian Jewry.

The situation of the Jews in the Persian empire continued to be favorable when Alexander the Great occupied the country in 333 B.C.E. As in the other countries conquered by him, Alexander included Babylonia's large Jewish population in his scheme of forging a new, unified Greco-Asian people. It is therefore not surprising that Babylonian Jews took up service in Alexander's armies. The situation of the Jews remained favorable when somewhat later Babylonia became part of the Syrian-Seleucian monarchy. During the entire Seleucian period, which lasted almost two hundred years, the Babylonian Jews had no reason to complain, for they seem not to have been affected by the harsh religious persecution which Antiochus IV inflicted upon Judaean Jewry. This was probably the reason why Babylonian Jewry failed to give a helping hand to the Hasmoneans when the latter rose to defend Jewish religious freedom in Judaea.

About 140 B.C.E. the Parthians, who had already ruled for a long time in Persia, occupied Babylonia. Luckily for the Jews, the Parthians did not identify with any specific religious cult, and pursued a policy of tolerance towards the various religions in their empire. Thus, despite the fact that Babylonian Jewry now paid the special tax imposed on all minorities, it was enjoying a period of almost perfect political tranquility. The only disturbing factor was that the compact settlements of Babylonian Jewry lay in the border region of Parthia and the Roman empire. The Jewish communities were therefore often exposed to the ravages of war.

Understandably, the sympathies of Babylonian Jewry were with the Parthians. The frequent Roman occupations of parts of Babylonia brought large numbers of Babylonian Jewry under Roman rule for periods of longer or shorter duration. Most of the time, however, Babylonian Jewry remained firmly within the orbit of the Parthian empire.

How relaxed Parthian rule was in the area of compact Jewish settlement can be seen from the following episode. About the year 20 C.E. two young Jewish men in Nehardea, the brothers Hanilai and Hasinai (the historian Josephus calls them Anilaeus and Asinaeus), established themselves as rulers over Nehardea and its vicinity. Of low social origin, they attracted to themselves a number of people from the lowest strata of the population, and organized an armed gang, the activities of which, if we are to believe Josephus, closely resembled those of King David and his followers during the period preceding his enthronement in Hebron (see Sec. II, Chap. 1). As time progressed, the brothers began to deport themselves more and more as responsible rulers of the region. At first the central Parthian government seems either to have been unaware of what was going on, or to have believed it to be inconsequential. Only the satrap (governor) of Babylonia became worried. He attacked the brothers, but was defeated. At that point, the Parthian government seems to have realized that it could use the two brothers and their army to check rebellious satraps in the region. Having thus gained the support of the Parthian king, Hasinai and Hanilai were soon able to extend their control over a large area in Mesopotamia. Drunk with power, however, the brothers began to commit acts repulsive to the Jewish population, and Hasinai was poisoned in a family quarrel. Now the general situation of the Jewish feudal state began to deteriorate quickly, and it lost its usefulness to the Parthians. A Parthian expeditionary force defeated Hanilai's army, and he lost his life at the hands of local pagans. As always in such a situation, the Gentiles attacked the Jews and massacred many of them. Many of the survivors then fled from Nehardea to other cities in Mesopotamia.

Babylonian Jewry's basic loyalty to the Parthians was never more effectively demonstrated than in the years 114–17 C.E. In these years the emperor Trajan made Rome's most dramatic attempt to conquer Parthia and so fulfill the old dream of reaching India. Early in the war the Roman legions stormed into Babylonia and occupied practically the entire area of Jewish settlement. But then Babylonian Jewry rose and attacked the Romans from the rear. This Jewish uprising broke out at the time when, as we have seen, the Jews of Judaea and of the island of Cyprus rose in rebellion as well. We shall further see that simultaneously the Jews also rebelled in various Roman possessions in North Africa.

It is doubtful whether all these Jewish uprisings were a planned Jewish conspiracy against Rome, but their effect greatly contributed to the failure of Rome's ambitious expedition. The uprising in Babylonia was cruelly suppressed by a Roman army under the leadership of Lucius Quietus, a fact long remembered among the Jews. Roman incursions into Babylonia, which met with Jewish resistance, occurred in later times too. Characteristically, Babylonian Jewry remained faithful to the Parthians even during the invasions of emperors from the Severan dynasty who, as we have seen, treated Judaean Jewry with much favor. The friendly attitude of the Parthians resulted in a considerable geographic expansion of Babylonian Jewry. The Jewish communities in Persia and Media, identical with today's Iran, which came into being in preceding centuries, now became quite numerous.

In the years 223–26 C.E. a great change took place in Persia which strongly affected the destiny of its Jewish community for centuries to come. Ardashir I, a regional potentate in Persia, succeeded in deposing the Parthian dynasty, and he established the Neo-Persian empire. Unlike the Parthians, Ardashir I strongly identified with the Parsiist religion and, even though the legal basis of the Jewish community had not fundamentally changed during the entire 400 years preceding the Arab conquest, in reality the Jewish condition had greatly deteriorated. Gone was the tranquility in the life of Persian-Babylonian Jewry, hitherto disturbed only by Roman invasions. The *magi,* the priests of the Parsiist religion, wielded a decisive influence in the court of the Sassanians, as the new dynasty was called, and this resulted in anti-Jewish riots and persecution, totally unknown under the Parthians.

The Jewish leadership in Babylonia was aware from the very beginning of the change that took place. In an act of adjustment to the new reality, Samuel, the leader of the academy in Nehardea, then formulated the principle of "the law of the land is the law." This principle made it obligatory upon the Jews of the empire loyally to obey the laws promulgated by the king of kings. In practice this principle was mostly operative with regard to taxation and the acquisition of property. Significantly, the office of the exilarch lost some of its importance, and governmental control over the Jewish communal institutions increased. Characteristic of the new situation, also, was the fact that the Babylonian Jews no longer actively participated in the recurring wars with the Romans. They were now reduced instead to the status of victims living in a perpetually turbulent border region.

In practice the fate of the Jews now depended on the personal attitude of the king and the actual influence of the magi. Thus, when in the second half of the third century the influence of the latter on the government increased, a period of discrimination toward the minority religions began, which lasted till about the year 290. True, the Jews suffered less than the Christians. This was nevertheless a time of hardship for the Jewish community, especially because it followed the destruction of the Jewish community in Nehardea in 262 by the invading army of King Odenathus of nearby Palmyra. During the long reign of Shapur II (309–79) the situation of the Jews greatly improved due to the friendly attitude of the king.

The fifth century, however, became the most tragic period in the history of Babylonian Jewry. Under the reigns of Yazdegerd II (438–57) and his son Peroz (459–84), the Jewish community was hit with a series of laws which in effect declared Judaism an illicit religion and made Jewish religious life all but impossible. Peroz survived in Jewish tradition as Peroz *reshia,* the wicked Peroz. Hardest hit was the Jewish community of Isfahan about the year 470, for reasons not fully clear. At that time, the four-hundredth anniversary of the destruction of the Second Temple, expectations were high for the coming of the Messiah. We do not know exactly what happened in Isfahan. Rumors, true or false, had it that the Jews assaulted two magi. As a result riots broke out in which about half the city's Jews lost their lives. In addition, many Jewish children were handed over to the magi to be forcibly raised in the Parsiist religion. All over the country synagogues were destroyed. The exilarch was executed and it seems that his office was then temporarily abolished, to be restored only decades later.

Some scholars believe that a certain Mar Zutra, of the exilarch's family, then rebelled against the Persians and established in Mahoza, the Jewish section in the capital city Ctesiphon, a Jewish "state" which existed about seven years. While it is possible that some sort of a Jewish messianic uprising did take place, it is unlikely that the Persians would have tolerated an independent Jewish "state" next door to their capital city. During the sixth century the Persian Jews again enjoyed more tranquil times. The only exception was the Jewish community of Mahoza which was massacred in 590 during the general upheaval resulting from the assassination of King Hormizd IV. When the Arabs conquered the Persian empire a few decades later, the Jews seem to have demonstrated a sort of neutrality bordering on friendship, but not the enthusiasm with which their brethren in Judaea welcomed the new conquerors.

Exilarch and Communal Organization

Little is known of the Jewish communal structure in Babylonia during the entire period of the Achaemenian, Seleucian, and early Parthian kings. Tradition has it that the descendants of exiled King Jehoiachin of Judah (see Sec. III, Chap. 4) had served as heads of the Babylonian Jewish community almost from its inception. No evidence, however, is available on the functioning of such leaders, later called *rashe golah,* or *reshe galutha,* heads of the captivity, at least to the second half of the first century C.E. It was possibly King Vologases I (51–77 C.E.) who initiated the office of the *reshe galutha,* referred to in modern historical literature as *exilarchs.* It is not unlikely that the destruction of the Temple in Jerusalem in the year 70 C.E. and the temporary dissolution of the Sanhedrin created the vacuum in which the emergence of a new Jewish authority of major significance became possible.

Be this as it may, about 100 years later the office of the exilarch had become firmly established. The authority of the exilarchs rested on the fact that they presided over a Jewish community rising in numbers at a time when Judaea's Jewish community was diminishing in size, as well as on the claim that they were descendants of King David. Furthermore, it was universally conceded that the authority of the Babylonian exilarchs was superior to that of the Palestinian patriarchs, since the former were believed to be descendants of the House of David on the male line, while the latter descended from it on the female line.

The authority of the exilarchs was immensely enhanced by the support given to them by the government. It was in the interest of the government to have the large Jewish community be ruled by a local dignitary, rather than it being loyal to the Palestinian patriarch, who depended on Rome. In addition, the exilarch could also be conveniently used as an agent for the collection of taxes from the Jewish community. Under the Parthian kings, governmental support for the exilarch was uninterrupted and unconditional. Under the Sassanians, this support was at times wavering or missing, but was always reinstated. The office thus survived into the period of the caliphate, when it attained additional significance and glory.

Formally, the exilarch enjoyed the status of a vassal prince or a governor of a semi-autonomous province, and was a member of the state council. He resided in Mahoza, a locality in the immediate vicinity of the capital city of Ctesiphon. His lifestyle was that of a prince, and he had the privilege of keeping a military retinue. In addition to administering affairs common to all Babylonian Jewry, he had the authority to appoint judges in the local communities. He himself together with a number of outstanding legal scholars constituted a sort of Jewish supreme court. It is likely that his authority was also recognized by Jews living in the Persian empire outside of Babylonia. Since all Jewish communal life was based on the mishnaic law, the exilarch had to use immigrant rabbis from Palestine as officials of his administration and judges in the local communities.

The immigrant rabbis were of course dependent on the exilarch and were therefore by and large loyal to him. However, when a native class of rabbis came into being about the middle of the third century C.E., a rivalry between them and the exilarchs developed. The exilarchs also had to fight the opposition of the local Jewish nobility, which saw in them a threat to their own privileged status. All this, together with the anti-Jewish attitude of some Sassanian kings of the fifth and sixth centuries brought about an erosion of the real power of the exilarchs in the latter Sassanian period. There were times when no exilarch was in office, and there were times when delegations of rabbis, rather than the ruling exilarch, were interceding in the royal court in behalf of Babylonian Jewry. In general, the office of the exilarch was much more tightly supervised by the government during the Sassanian period than during the Parthian.

It is impossible to form a clear picture of the organizational structure of the local community. Some kind of communal council consisting of seven members or more seems to have existed. Its main functions were probably limited to supervising the schools and the charitable funds. But the judges appointed by the exilarch seem to have wielded the real power. Their authority derived both from being appointees of the exilarch and from being versed in the Jewish law. They not only discharged the duties of the judiciary, but also supervised commerce, trade, and ritual slaughter. They enforced the law by a system of fines and punishments, short only of the death penalty which was the prerogative of the exilarch and his high court. Excommunication, however, was under certain conditions within the competence of the local judges. The frequent conflicts between the lay leadership and the rabbinic judges attest to a perpetual state of tension in the local community. A number of voluntary societies cared for areas of communal life not controlled by the lay and judicial authorities.

Economic Life and Social Stratification

The Jewish population in Babylonia steadily increased in numbers, both by natural growth and mass influxes of refugees from Judaea. Especially large was the influx of Judaeans after the First and Second Revolts and late in the fourth century when Christian rule had become firmly established in the Roman empire. Some estimates have it that in the Sassanian period as many as two million Jews lived within the confines of the Persian empire. It is not unlikely that at that time about one half of the entire Jewish people lived under the Sassanian kings. Most of the Jews lived in Babylonia, today's Iraq. Such cities as Nisibis in the Parthian era, and Nehardea in later times, had heavy concentrations of Jews. Sura, Pumbedita, and Mahoza were likewise "Jewish" cities. The bulk of the Jewish population, however, seems to have lived in smaller towns and rural areas.

Most Jews were either farmers or artisans. To be sure, the farmers had to pay unusually heavy taxes, which drove many of them into ruin. The burdensome contributions imposed by the frequently invading Roman armies dealt additional blows to the Jewish farming class in Babylonia. The exceptional fertility of the soil, however, made farming nevertheless attractive. Even peasants who had lost their land due to taxation or other adverse factors still found it profitable to till the land as tenants or sharecroppers. The variety of crafts practiced by Jews was very large, and even included the manufacture of weapons for the Persian army. Significantly, over 100 of the Amoraim made their living as craftsmen or farmers.

Some Jews, though not many, ascended to the higher rungs of the economic ladder. We have seen that already in the early Achaemenian period some Jews had played an important role in the economy of southern Babylonia. In later times, too, a number of Jews were active in the field of international trade, especially in the transit trade of silk from China to the Roman empire. Other Persian Jews succeeded in amassing large landholdings. An owner of such a large estate was, for example, the founder of the Academy at Sura, Aba Arikha, also known as Rav.

Against this backdrop, social differentiation among the Jews appears to have been mild. The fact that so many rabbis practiced the crafts and farming indicates that manual labor was not considered a demeaning occupation. It further shows that poverty was not a factor in preventing talented and ambitious people from entering the prestigious circle of the aristocracy of learning. A small group of Jews attained the status of knighthood and were integrated into the Parthian nobility. For obvious reasons their influence within Jewish society was considerable.

Although the Jewish nobility, as well as the exilarchal family, cultivated relations with the non-Jewish nobility, the Jewish masses lived by and large well separated from the non-Jewish population. To be sure, most of the time the relations between Jews and Parsees were not unfriendly. The fact that there were religious differences, however, that most Jews lived in compact masses, and that the Jewish community was economically largely self-sufficient, made a closer relationship between Jews and Gentiles both unlikely and unnecessary. Be it noted, however, that the relations between the Jews and the Christians living in the empire were not devoid of a certain degree of hostility.

The Cultural Scene

Practically nothing is known of the cultural life of Babylonian Jewry in the Achaemenian and Hellenistic periods. If there is truth in the tradition that Hillel was a native of Babylonia, it would indicate that in the first century B.C.E. cultural interest had arisen there to the degree of stimulating young people to go to Judaea for the purpose of acquiring Jewish knowledge. If there was any Jewish cultural life in Babylonia during the succeeding 200 years, it surely depended largely on the cultural resources of Judaean Jewry.

A local brand of Jewish culture began to develop in Babylonia about the middle of the second century C.E. as a result of the arrival of large numbers of refugee scholars who escaped from Judaea during the period of the Hadrianic persecutions. True, a part of them returned to their homeland after the cessation of the persecutions. But those who remained were able to establish a base for Babylonia's Jewish cultural life. The scholarly excellence achieved by Samual of Nehardea, who probably never visited the Holy Land, indicates that about the year 200 C.E. it had become possible to acquire in Babylonia Jewish knowledge equal to that available in the Galilean academies. Thus, beginning with the early third century C.E., when Samuel and the partly Judaean-educated Rav dominated the Jewish cultural scene in Babylonia, this country had become a Jewish cultural center equal to that of Palestine. Furthermore, when with the progressive diminution of Palestine's Jewish population its Rabbinic academies began to experience a process of decline, Jewish cultural life in Babylonia began a process of almost steady growth.

This growth was in part made possible by continuous arrivals of larger and smaller groups of Palestinian scholars, as well as by an ever-growing network of Jewish elementary schools. The admonitions of the religious leadership to establish elementary schools were so frequent and insistent, and the educational programs prepared by the rabbis so excellent, that despite some neglect on the local level, the elementary schools took firm root in the Babylonian Jewish community. With the establishment of an academy for advanced studies in Jewish law by Samuel in Nehardea, this type of school too became not only a familiar sight but the most glorious characteristic of Babylonian Jewry of that period.

We have seen (Sec. VIII, Chap. 6) that in these academies scholars known as Amoraim discussed the Mishnah and created the Gemara. These schools, including the one in Sura established by Rav in the first half of the third century C.E., and that which was organized in Pumbedita closer to the year 300 C.E., also provided the exilarchs with men trained in the Jewish law for service in their administration and judiciary. In return, the exilarchs supplied the academies with much of the funds needed for their maintenance. The organizers of the school in Pumbedita at first made an effort to be financially independent. Ultimately, however, this school, too, had to accept exilarchal subsidies and control. Although the academies were subsidized by the exilarchal treasury, the many hundreds of students, as well as the scholars connected with the academies, had to care for their own maintenance at least in part. This is why, as we have seen, so many of the rabbis earned their livelihood as artisans and farmers. In the fourth century, however, more public attention began to be given to the economic needs of the scholars. They could now receive stipends either directly from the academies or from special funds set up for the promotion of learning. In addition, scholars were more and more exempted from the payment of taxes. This privilege was used by so many scholars that it ultimately began to evoke public resentment.

Despite exilarchal patronage, the academies were run along fairly democratic lines. To begin with, admission was open to everybody regardless of his social status. The same was true with regard to promotion inside the academy, which was accorded along strict lines of achievement and seniority. The basic democratic character of the academies was further strengthened by the decisive influence of the scholars on the election of the academy heads. Despite the fact that due to adverse political conditions some, or even all, academies were closed from time to time, they always re-opened and remained an institution of decisive importance in Jewish life in Babylonia. Be it also noted that the academies were largely confined to Babylonia proper, and only a few existed in the other parts of the Persian empire.

A unique system of education for lay adults, unknown in Judaea, also developed in Babylonia. Twice a year, during the month of Elul early in the fall, and the month of Adar early in the spring, the main academies would interrupt their regular instructional program and open their doors to thousands of lay people coming to study the Law. This institution was called *kallah,* a word the meaning of which has not yet been clarified. Nor do we know when the *kallah* came into being. Be this as it may, by the year 300 C.E. the institution was well-established. A few leading scholars of each academy, probably those privileged to sit in the first row, served as "heads of the *kallah.*" Their exact duties, however, are also unclear.

Two things seem to have been happening during the *kallah:* the regular students of the academies prepared themselves through intensive study for a rigid final examination for the semester, and a daily discourse was given for the benefit of the visitors. The *kallah* seems to have had a powerful attraction and survived into the geonic period. Significantly, at the conclusion of each *kallah* the heads of the academies announced which tractate of the Mishnah would be studied during the forthcoming *kallah* so that the participants would have an opportunity to properly prepare themselves for the next semiannual great adventure in learning. Although a specific tractate of the Mishnah was the subject of study at the *kallah,* it should be assumed that during the Elul *kallah* attention was given to the laws of the High Holidays and Tabernacles which followed immediately, while the laws of Passover were reviewed during the Adar *kallah.*

The main subjects studied in the academies were centered

around Jewish law and religious thought. We have no exhaustive evidence as to the status of the sciences within Babylonian Jewish society. It should be assumed that the decline of Hellenistic culture during the Parthian period must have been in general detrimental to the sciences. But the fact that a teacher of the stature of Samuel was highly versed in medicine and astronomy would suggest that the sciences were not outside the realm of interest of the Jewish scholar and student in Babylonia. This is further indicated by an impressive quantity of statements on various aspects of the sciences profusely interspersed in the Babylonian Talmud.

We have seen (Sec. VIII, Chap. 6) that by the middle of the sixth century the Saboraim, Reasoners, gave the final editorial touch to the Babylonian Talmud. The talmudic era in the cultural history of Babylonian Jewry thus came to an end, and was followed by the geonic era, which began several decades later, and which will be described in a later chapter. Meanwhile, in the second half of the sixth century, Babylonian Jewry manifested its interest in some other areas of Jewish culture and made then a considerable contribution to Jewish liturgy and homiletics.

The Religious Life

Nothing at all is known about the religious life of the tens of thousands of Israelites who in 722 B.C.E. were deported from Samaria to Assyria. It was observed above that some of them were lost altogether to idolatry. It was different with the exiles from Judaea to Babylonia over 100 years later. It seems that there was a desire among them to build in their new home a Temple where a sacrificial service, presumably on the model of that in the Jerusalem Temple, could be instituted. The view prevailed, however, that no sacrificial service could be practiced outside of Jerusalem, and the plan was given up. Instead, houses of worship were established, and it is possible that the words "little sanctuary" in Ezekiel 11:16 refer to a synagogue.

Prayer thus began to play a major role in the religious life of the community, and some beautiful liturgical compositions then written have been preserved in the contemporary Hebrew literature. Fasting as a means of supplication became quite popular. It should also be assumed that the custom of sending contributions to the Temple in Jerusalem came into being soon after its rebuilding. It is somewhat puzzling that in the first century C.E., when Pharisaism became the decisive ideology in Judaean Jewry, its influence was less than conspicuous in Babylonia. Especially so since its teachings were suitable for a Jewish community in the Diaspora, devoid of a sacrificial service. Nevertheless, we will have to assume that Babylonian Jewry in its early period had received much religious guidance from Judaea, as indicated by its total dependence on Judaea in matters of calendation for hundreds of years to come. Attempts in the second and third centuries C.E. both by immigrant and local rabbis to introduce the proclamation of the New Moon independently of the Judaean leadership, ended in failure.

Local religious leadership began to take hold in the age of Rav and Samuel. The activities of these two giants could not fail to firmly establish a basis for the religious life of Babylonian Jewry. It was Rav, especially, whose actions were all-important. He made lasting contributions to the standardization of the High Holidays services, and issued a series of religious ordinances which closed the gap that may have existed between Babylonian and Palestinian Jewry in the area of religious life. His extensive travels to the communities in the Persian empire further aided in the stabilization of religious unity of its Jewry. Of decisive importance was the fact that the sages whose discussions in the academies resulted in the creation of the Gemara were at the same time the religious leaders of Babylonian Jewry. Thus, Babylonian Jewry, which about the year 200 C.E. may still have had a fluctuating system of religious practice and an equally unsolidified order of prayer, was the first and foremost beneficiary of the standardization of the Halakhah. It was indeed the period following the conclusion of the Talmud that witnessed the synagogue service attaining its final shape. It is worth noting that the use of *tephillin,* phylacteries, during prayer was in vogue already at an earlier age in Babylonia.

True, neglect of religious observance was not unknown, especially among the aristocracy. Signs of moral laxity, too, appeared here and there, mostly toward the end of the Sassanian period. Superstitious beliefs and practices, probably mainly borrowed from the Parsees, could also be noticed. Likewise, some kabbalistic practices, including mortification of the body, must have accompanied mystical speculation which had invaded the academies. By and large, however, Babylonian Jewry emerges from the contemporary literature as a community firmly adhering to normative Jewish religious experience.

Some Smaller Jewish Communities

In Northern Mesopotamia, on the upper Tigris, lay the Parthian satrapy Hadayab, also known as Adiabene. A Jewish population had in all probability lived there, as in all areas adjacent to the great Jewish center in Babylonia. What makes Hadayab unique is the fact that about the year 40 C.E. King Izates, his mother Helena, and brother Monobazes converted to the Jewish faith. This conversion was probably a result of Jewish missionary activities in the region. The royal house may also have been at least in part motivated by the desire to gain the support of the mighty Jewish community in neighboring Babylonia.

Be this as it may, Queen Helena and her sons seem to have taken their Judaism quite seriously. The queen made a pilgrimage to Jerusalem, and the royal house of Adiabene sent aid to Jerusalem during the First Revolt, at a time when Diaspora Jewry disappointingly remained on the sidelines. The attachment of Adiabene's royalty to Judaism is further attested by their desire to be buried in the Holy Land. The sepulcher in Jerusalem presently known as "tombs of the kings" is probably the place of their burial. The conversion of the royal house seems not to have deeply affected the country, and the population remained largely pagan. Nor does Jewish culture seem to have penetrated Adiabene to any remarkable degree. In fact, Christianity was making rather rapid progress, among Jews as well as pagans.

Practically nothing is known of Jewish expansion from Persia into neighboring Central Asia, China, and India during the Antiquity. While China's and India's organized Jewish communities do not appear until well into the Middle Ages, it is not unlikely that Persian Jewry did spill over into these countries already in the Antiquity. The same holds true of Bukhara and its region in Central Asia. The tradition of Bukharan Jewry that it descended from the "ten lost tribes" also hint at its origin during the Antiquity.

Chapter 3

On the Arabian Peninsula

The Emergence of a Jewish Community in Northern Arabia

Although no evidence exists of a Jewish settlement in northern Arabia (Hejaz) prior to the first century B.C.E., it is likely that already in the period of the First Commonwealth Hebrews began to spill over into this region from the Negev. The existence in the Negev and southern Transjordan of the Arab kingdom of Nabataea in the period of the Second Commonwealth no doubt facilitated the settlement of Judaeans in Arabia. It is thus not surprising that many inscriptions in northern Arabia dating back to the first century B.C.E. indicate the presence of Jews in the region. It is also likely that the cultivation of the palm tree, so characteristic of northern Arabia, was introduced by Judaean immigrants from palm-tree-growing regions near Jericho. The political disasters in Judaea, such as those following the First and Second Revolts (70 and 135 C.E.), drove additional numbers of Judaeans to seek refuge in nearby northern Arabia. The development of numerous Jewish settlements was facilitated by the lack of an organized state in this scarcely inhabited area. Somewhat later, Jews also began to arrive from Babylonia. They settled on the east coast of the Peninsula and on the Bahrein islands. The persecutions in Persia during the second half of the fifth century brought additional Jewish immigrants into northern and northeastern Arabia.

As a result of all these developments, by 500 C.E. the Jewish element had attained a dominant position in the region. Like the Arabs, the Jews were organized in clans or tribes. In addition, they seem to have constituted the majority in the most important northern cities, Teima, Khaibar, and Yathrib, (now known as Medina). The Jewish tribes, about 20 in number, cultivated the land and practiced the crafts and commerce. The Jews seem to have economically excelled over the Arabs, and the latter learned from them more efficient ways of agriculture and the rudiments of trade. Among the Jewish tribes were "men of the sword." Their custom of building castles on mountain tops gave them additional security as well as more healthy living conditions.

The lifestyle of the Jews was basically not different from that of their Arab neighbors. Culturally, however, they stood far above them. The Jews, like the Christians, impressed Mohammed as being "people of the book." A certain degree of Rabbinic learning was no doubt imported from both Palestine and Babylonia. Significantly, the Quran attests to the presence, early in the seventh century, of Rabbinic scholars in Yathrib. But even in the general culture of the region the Jews excelled. The Jewish tribes produced a remarkable number of poets who wrote in Arabic. One of them, Samaual (Samuel) ibn Adiyah, was famous in the first half of the sixth century C.E. for both his excellent verses and noble character. The emergence of Jewish poetry in Arabic indicates that this was the language in use among the Jews during the sixth and early seventh centuries. Prior to that the Jews of northern Arabia spoke Aramaic like their brethren in Palestine and Babylonia.

The better economic and health conditions enjoyed by the Jews served as a mighty attraction to the Bedouins living farther south. Many of them then began to move northward. In time the Bedouins became so numerous that the Jewish tribes lost their dominant position. About the same time an autonomous Jewish merchant colony on a nearby island in the Gulf of Aqaba, once under Persian sovereignty, fell under the control of the Byzantines and lost its autonomy. All this weakened the position of the Jews and was to a great degree responsible for the catastrophe that befell them when Mohammed, the new prophet of the Arabs, turned against them.

The Jewish Community in Himyar-Yemen

A Jewish settlement had also existed in southern Arabia in pre-Mohammedan times. It is impossible to determine with certainty how and when this settlement came into being. One theory has it that at first Jewish merchants from the Persian empire repeatedly visited the country, and that ultimately some of them settled there permanently, and so laid the foundation for a Jewish community. Later, possibly in the fourth century C.E., a movement began among the Arabs of Himyar (a state geographically more or less identical with today's Yemen) to convert to the Jewish faith. It is not clear whether the Jewish settlers from Babylonia or some Palestinian Jewish immigrants actively promoted the Jewish religion, but it seems that Judaism gained in popularity. The Jewish community had by then become sufficiently numerous to arouse the envy of a visiting Christian missionary. There are indications that Judaism even penetrated one of the ruling families in Himyar late in the fourth century.

During the fourth and fifth centuries the already Christianized Ethiopians made attempts of varying success to occupy the kingdom of Himyar. The Jewish communities seem to have survived the turmoil of the Ethiopian occupation and Judaism may have been the source of a movement of liberation from Ethiopian yoke early in the sixth century. A Himyaran prince, Yusuf Asar Dhu Nuwas, who had converted to Judaism about the year 517 succeeded in liberating the country and re-establishing Himyar's complete independence. Following his example, many more Himyaran Arabs converted to the Jewish faith. It is, however, impossible to say whether their number was large enough to have made a Jewish kingdom out of Himyar.

A Jewish king on Himyar's throne was, however, unacceptable to the Christian world. Thus, after a period of less than ten years of independence, Himyar and its Jewish king had to face a new Ethiopian invasion, supported by the superior forces of the Byzantine empire. In a fierce battle which took place in 525, the invaders gained a decisive victory. King Yusuf fell on the battlefield, and Ethiopia was able to rule Himyar again for another half century.

What happened to the Jews under the new Ethiopian occupation is unknown. Some may have been massacred, some may have fled to join the Jewish tribes in northern Arabia, and some may have retreated into the mountainous regions in the interior. At any rate, there is no evidence of the existence of a Jewish community in Himyar-Yemen at the time the new Muslim faith began to spread in this region. It is thus impossible to say whether a "silent" Jewry existed in southern Arabia for the next several hundred years until the community of the Yemenite Jews appeared again on the map of Jewish history in the tenth century.

Mohammed's Encounter with Arabia's Jews

Historians of religion are still debating the question as to what degree Mohammed's religious ideas were influenced by Judaism. It is clear, however, that upon arriving in Yathrib in 622 the new prophet made a serious attempt to win the local Jewish population over to his new religion. The first encounter with the Jews seems to have been not unfriendly. To begin with, the idea of the oneness of God must have come to the attention of the Arab neighbors of the Jews. This, no doubt, facilitated Mohammed's efforts at converting the Arabs of Yathrib to his new monotheistic faith. In addition, Yathrib's Jewish tribes were allied with the Arab tribes that supported the prophet. He possibly also had an opportunity to meet the Rabbinic scholars who then lived in Yathrib. It is thus understandable that Mohammed was ready to make a number of religious concessions to the Jews, including the recognition of Jerusalem as the place to which prayer should be directed, in order to win for his cause the culturally superior Jewish community in north Arabia. In general, be it noted, he tried to present his message as a continuation of that of the prophets of Israel.

When only a handful of Jews joined him, however, Mohammed realized that his hopes were in vain. He also became aware that the Jews of Yathrib were now conspiring against him with his enemies in Mecca. He therefore turned against the Jewish community in 624 and after a fierce struggle put an end to its existence. Many Jews were massacred and many fled, and their land was given to Mohammed's followers. The Jews of Khaibar and other towns were for the time being left alone, and a sort of pact was concluded between the Muslims and them. We shall see later that not before long they too were eliminated. After Mohammed's death a document was found which allegedly contained his last will. This document proclaimed Hejaz a country in which only the religion of Islam could be practiced.

Section X

IN AFRICA

Chapter 1

In Egypt

The Jewish Population

We do not know whether some Hebrews remained in Egypt at the time of the Exodus. The proximity of the country to Judaea makes it likely that Judaeans emigrated there, at least in small numbers, already during the period of the "Judges." In the tenth century B.C.E., it can be said with certainty, a nucleus of a Jewish settlement had come into being, composed of political emigrés from Israel who were in conflict with the regime of King Solomon. It is likely that during the entire period of the First Commonwealth additional groups of political emigrés and war refugees came from Israel and Judah. A good example is the group of refugees, including the prophet Jeremiah, who left for Egypt after Gedaliah's assassination (cf. Sec. III, Chap. 4). Jewish immigration considerably increased later, as is manifested by the existence of a Jewish military colony in Elephantine, an island on the upper Nile, imported from Judaea by one of the Pharaohs for the purpose of guarding the border against raids from Nubia.

New opportunities for large-scale immigration of Judaeans opened with the conquest of Egypt by Alexander the Great in the year 332 B.C.E. and the founding of the city of Alexandria. It is not known whether Judaeans were among the original settlers in Alexandria. Soon, however, they became a considerable part of the population. All other parts of the country were virtually dotted with Jewish communities. In the first century B.C.E. at the time of the Roman conquest, about one million Jews were living in Egypt, constituting over 12 percent of the total population. They lived in about 80 communities, mostly located in central Egypt, yet the majority lived in the city of Alexandria.

In the following period many conflicts and clashes developed between the Jewish and Gentile populations, and Egypt ceased to be attractive to Jewish emigrants from Judaea. In fact, the Jewish population, and especially that of Alexandria, began to decrease drastically in number even prior to the ascendance of Christians to Rome's imperial throne. Beginning with the Christian period, when the bishops of Alexandria became the dominant power in the city, the Jewish population underwent a process of rapid decline. There may have even been times when no Jews at all lived in Alexandria. The same process of decline took place in other Egyptian cities as well.

In the sixth century C.E., conditions somewhat improved and the existence of Jewish communities in Egypt is again attested to. Early in the seventh century, when the Persians occupied Egypt for a short period, the Jewish population further increased in numbers. Thus, when the Muslims conquered Egypt in 639 they found in the country a sizable Jewish population.

Jews also already lived in the period of the First Commonwealth farther south in the land of Cush, meaning either today's Sudan or Ethiopia. The presence of Jews in Ethiopia is also attested to in the fourth century C.E. These Ethiopian Jews were possibly the ancestors of the community of black Jews, known as Falasha, discovered in the nineteenth century.

Political Vicissitudes

Virtually nothing is known directly about the political fate of the Jews in Egypt up to the time of the Persian conquest in 525 B.C.E. The continuous stream of Jewish immigrants would, however, indicate that they were generally treated well by the government of the Pharaohs. It may even be assumed that the Jewish community enjoyed the confidence of the government, in view of the fact that Jews were employed as mercenaries in military units guarding the borders. As for the period of the Persian occupation (525–404 B.C.E.), there is no reason to suspect that the Jews in Egypt were treated in a less friendly manner than in other Persian possessions. The Jewish military colony on the island of Elephantine, which was entrusted with the task of guarding the southern border against incursions from Nubia, was officially known as a "Jewish force," and some of its officers were Jews.

The friendly attitude of the governments was, however, not always shared by the Egyptian population. The profound religious differences by themselves could have been a source of friction between the Egyptian majority and the small Jewish minority. In places of more dense Jewish settlement, such as the island of Elephantine, anti-Jewish sentiments seem to have been quite strong, and the continuous existence of the Jewish community was dependent on unwavering governmental protection. In fact, when in 411 B.C.E. this protection was temporarily withheld, serious anti-Jewish riots broke out in Elephantine, during which the temple of the Jews was destroyed.

Under Ptolemaic rule, which began close to the year 300 B.C.E., the political situation of the Egyptian Jews greatly improved. The Ptolemies were a small group of foreign invaders who found in the Jewish minority a natural ally. The situation of the Jews was most favorable under King Ptolemy VI (181–145 B.C.E.). Not only was Jewish immigration encouraged, but Jews began to play an even greater role than hitherto in the military. Jewish mercenaries also served, in accordance with general Ptolomaic policy, in exclusively Jewish units. Two members of a Jewish priestly family, Hananiah and Hilkiah (Helkias) even attained the rank of high commanders in the Egyptian army. True, Jews were not generally given the right of citizenship in the Egyptian *polis,* and only a small number of them managed to secure it for themselves. This was, however, far outweighed by the fact that Jews were granted the privilege of living by their own ancestral laws.

The favored position of the Jews, however, had some negative aspects. It evoked, as we have seen, resentments among the Egyptian population. Popular resentment was also fanned by the tendency of the Jews to live in separate quarters, as well as by the anti-Egyptian Exodus stories, now widely known from the Septuagint, the Greek translation of the Bible. When the Romans conquered Egypt they found themselves opposed by the majority of the population. This, of course, placed the Jews squarely on the side of the conquerors and simultaneously in a state of greater friction with the Egyptians. Nevertheless, Roman policy tended to dissociate itself more and more from the Jews.

Julius Caesar, who was greatly helped by the Jews in establishing order in the country, confirmed their basic rights in 47 B.C.E. Emperor Augustus, however, initiated an ambiguous Jewish policy. On the one hand, he confirmed the traditional rights of Alexandrian Jewry. In practice, however, he set out on a clear pattern of curtailing these rights. The Jews were almost completely eliminated from the administration and military, and had to pay a burdensome poll tax. In general, the Jews were assigned to a status equal to that of the descendants of the ancient Egyptians, who constituted the lowest class in the population. An equally ambiguous and wavering policy was also pursued by Emperor Claudius (41–54 C.E.).

Such a policy could only encourage popular enmity to the Jews. Gentile opposition to the granting of citizenship rights to even small numbers of Jews in Alexandria and elsewhere now became violent. Anti-Jewish riots, sometimes assuming the character of pogroms, became frequent, and the Jews had to appeal again and again for Roman protection. The riots between the years 38–41 C.E. were especially serious. To be sure, the Jews also rose from time to time to attack their Gentile neighbors. In the years 66–70 C.E., when the First Revolt was raging in Judaea, clashes between Jews and Gentiles were the order of the day in Alexandria. A staggering number of Jews lost their lives during these four years. A temple built by a refugee high priest from Judaea more than 200 years earlier in Leontopolis was destroyed. The special Jewish tax imposed by Vespasian was collected in Egypt, too, and proved to be as irritating as elsewhere.

The anti-Jewish riots were accompanied by an outpouring of anti-Semitic literature. It was especially during the first century C.E. that such literature proliferated. The general aim of this literature was to prove that the ancient as well as the contemporary Jews were of a base character and therefore inadmissable to civilized Hellenistic society. Chief among the anti-Semitic writers was a certain Apion, whose vitriolic attacks on the Jews were matched by his skill as an author. The literary attack on the Jews was of such serious nature that it had to be countered by the major literary talent of the philosopher Philo of Alexandria and of the historian Josephus.

It was this complex and continuously deteriorating situation which became the backdrop of the tragic events of the years 115–17. The general Jewish uprising in the Roman provinces in the Near East and North Africa during these years brought Egyptian Jewry to an almost complete breakdown. This uprising, which, as we have seen (Sec. IX, Chap. 1) brought disaster to Cypriot Jewry, seems to have begun in Egypt and elsewhere in the form of a clash between Jews and Gentiles. Significantly, the Roman authorities in Alexandria at first attempted to restore order by punishing both Jewish and Gentile rioters. Soon, however, the events took on the character of a Jewish uprising against Rome, probably under the impact of a Messianic movement which emerged among the Jews in nearby Cyrene.

The battles fought by the Jews against both the Roman legions and Greek and Egyptian militias spread from Alexandria to the countryside and became more and more fierce. The Jews demolished a number of pagan temples, and the Gentiles destroyed Alexandria's great synagogue, famous for its size and artistic beauty. When the Romans finally subdued the Jews, it became clear that the Jewish community was destroyed to an unprecedented degree. Provincial Jewry had all but disappeared, and the traces of the destruction could still be seen a generation later. What remained of Alexandrian Jewry hardly resembled the once wealthy and proud Jewish community. Its remnants now lived in a small settlement built in the vicinity of the city with the consent of the Romans.

Though Egyptian Jewry never recovered from the disaster of the years 115–17, it continued to exist as an organized entity for several hundred years more. Of course, the Christianization of the Roman empire in the fourth century resulted in an additional deterioration of the Jewish condition in Egypt. Characteristic of the situation is the fact that in 410 the bishop Cyril was able to effect the expulsion of the Jews from Alexandria even though the civil authorities tried to prevent it. The rest of the fifth century and the sixth century was a generally uneventful period in the history of the now greatly diminished Egyptian Jewry. It still enjoyed basic protection on the part of the Byzantine empire, but clearly shared the unhappy fate of Jewish communities living in a hostile Christian environment. It was mainly due to the imperial protection that Egyptian Jewry managed to survive to the time of the Muslim conquest.

Community Government

Even though the Jews of Alexandria, and presumably elsewhere in Egypt, were usually permitted to live scattered among the other inhabitants, they still chose to separate themselves and dwell in quarters of their own. At least two of the five quarters in Alexandria had a Jewish majority during the Hellenistic period. While it is debatable whether Alexandria's Jewry was organized in the form of a *polis* fully independent from the general city administration, it is certain that it enjoyed a great degree of autonomy. During the Ptolemaic period and the beginnings of Roman rule Alexandria's Jewry was headed by an ethnarch, whose princely status and authority, at least in part, resembled that of the patriarch in the Holy Land and the exilarch in Babylonia.

In the year 10 or 11 C.E., however, Emperor Augustus abolished the office of the ethnarch and replaced it by a Council of Elders (*gerousia*) composed of 71 members. Obviously, an attempt was made to imitate Judaea's Sanhedrin, which at that time was a fully developed legislative and judicial institution. While it is not possible to fully assess the scope of authority of the Alexandrian *gerousia,* it is known that it administered the judicial and fiscal matters of the Jewish community and controlled its charitable institutions. There are indications that in provincial communities, too, *gerousias* were in charge of Jewish affairs. It should be assumed that in larger communities, and especially Alexandria, representatives of the synagogal congregations were sitting on the council.

The law by which the Jewish communities conducted their

affairs was basically not different from the general Hellenistic law practiced in Egypt. Nothing else could be expected of so thoroughly Hellenized a Jewry as that of Egypt. The only exception was the area of Jewish marital life, which was governed by Jewish law.

Economic and Social Conditions

During the entire period of the Antiquity the Jews of Egypt seem to have been active in most areas of economic endeavor. Here and there, however, Jewish participation in a given area seems to have been limited, while simultaneously heavier Jewish concentration can be noticed in other fields.

During the sixth and fifth centuries B.C.E., the period of increased Jewish immigration, Jews could make a living by entering the government service or being active in commerce. Most conspicuous, however, was the service of Jews in the army as mercenaries. The Ptolemaic period witnessed the entrance of increasing numbers of Jews into agriculture. True, agriculture was often connected with military service, but Jews active in agriculture could be found all through the time down to the sixth century C.E. in roles not connected with the military. We find Jews among the large landowners. Many, many more of them, however, could be found among the peasants, tenants, and sharecroppers. Jews were also represented among the cattle breeders. Curiously, while the bulk of the Jewish population lived in northern Egypt, and most of the provincial communities could be found in central Egypt, Jewish agriculture seems to have been mostly concentrated in the south. This can possibly be explained by the presence of many Jewish military colonies in the southern border region. It was Ptolemaic practice to grant arable land to the military.

The Jews were quite numerous in the crafts. It is likely that a considerable part, if not the majority, of Alexandria's Jews were craftsmen. They were at least numerous enough to organize their own guilds and occupy separate pews in the city's gigantic synagogue. The available information leaves no doubt that Jews were found in practically all the crafts.

Smaller numbers of Jews were active in commerce and

money-lending. Under the Romans Jewish participation in commerce became all but impossible. Commerce was restricted to the *collegia mercatorum,* merchant guilds, which were cult-related and therefore closed to the Jews. It should nevertheless be assumed that some Jewish merchants must have found it possible to practice their business without enjoying the protection of the guilds. In fact, occasionally there may even have been some advantage in being a free agent, not subject to the rules and regulations of a guild. Be it also noted that the continuous curtailment of Jewish rights under the Romans had a generally unfavorable impact on Jewish economic activities. Money-lending was never an important occupation among the Jews of Egypt. Most Jewish loan transactions were carried out on a person-to-person basis rather than in a broad framework of banking.

Government service was in principle open to the Jews during the entire Ptolemaic period. In practice, however, it was mostly in tax collecting and custom farming, areas detested by both Jews and Gentiles, where we find Jewish officials. We have seen above that under the Romans Jews were practically eliminated from the officialdom.

Socially, most Egyptian Jews belonged to the lower middle class. The limited number of wealthy Jews, especially in Alexandria, may have given the impression that the Jews were an affluent society. But this cannot overshadow the fact that the bulk of the Jewish population—artisans, government officials, and farmers—enjoyed only a moderate income. True, most Jews seem to have lived, except in times of political crisis, under conditions of economic stability. But their lifestyle was by no means one of affluence.

The Cultural Scene

The Jewish settlers who came to Egypt in the sixth and fifth centuries B.C.E. spoke Aramaic, and Aramaic continued to be the language of Egypt's Jews till the period of the Ptolemies. There is no doubt, however, that the Jewish settlers used the Egyptian language in their contacts with their Egyptian neighbors and to a certain degree among themselves. Egyptian names, too, appeared among the Jews. With the advent of the Ptolemies, the Greek language began to spread more and more among the Jews, and in time probably eliminated the use of Aramaic altogether. The processes of linguistic Hellenization and the assumption of Greek names were rapid and thorough in the city of Alexandria. In the provincial communities, however, the Jews continued to speak in the Egyptian language, in use among their native Egyptian neighbors. Even a few hundred years later, as is attested by the Rabbis, Jews were still using the Egyptian language even in their religious services. It should be noted, however, that a Jewish-Egyptian cultural symbiosis never came into being, no doubt due to the low social status of the native population.

The fact that the majority of Egyptian Jewry lived in totally Hellenistic Alexandria imposed upon Egypt's Jewish community the character of a thoroughly Hellenized society. Nonetheless, the Jewish acceptance of Hellenistic culture was not without reservations. Hellenistic culture was cult-related and permeated with the belief in the Greek deities. Polytheism was repugnant to the Jews, and they therefore created their own brand of Hellenism. Since there are no traces of the existence of Jewish schools, Jewish children probably attended Greek schools and gymnasia. The knowledge of the Hebrew language had diminished to such a degree that in the second century B.C.E. it had become necessary to translate the Bible into Greek.

Characteristically, there are indications that the Greek style used by Alexandrian Jewry was similar to that employed in the Greek translation of the Bible, known as the Hellenistic Canon, or Septuagint. *Septuagint,* meaning "seventy," is the name given to the translation due to a tradition disseminated at that time that it was prepared by 72 sages who came from Judaea. It seems that at first the Pentateuch, and possibly also Joshua were translated, while renditions of the Prophets and Hagiographa were added at a later date. A part of the apocryphal and pseudepigraphal literature (see Sec. VII, Chap. 2) was also written in Greek in Egypt in Ptolemaic times.

Egyptian Jewry's literature not directly linked to the religious life has also come down to us only in Greek. In most cases only names of authors are known, or only fragments of their writings have survived. Solid historical tradition has it that there were among the Egyptian Jews many poets, playwrights, and historians. A prolific playwright in the first century B.C.E., Ezekiel, was known as "the writer of tragedies." The fragments of his play *Exodus* which have survived attest to his talent as dramatist and the affinity of his style to that of the Septuagint.

The virtual disappearance of the Greco-Jewish literature makes it impossible to properly evaluate its importance and influence on Jewish life. It may, however, be said that the philosophical literature of Alexandrian Jewry was probably of greater significance in the framework of Greco-Jewish culture than its poetry, historical literature, and drama. Regrettably, the philosophical literature also remained only in fragments, mostly preserved in the writings of later classical authors. Such was the case, for example, with the writings of Aristobulus of Paneas. Aristobulus lived in the first half of the second century B.C.E. and was an adviser on Jewish affairs to King Ptolemy VI. He was the author of a great work, written in the form of a dialogue between himself and the king, in which he gave an exposition of Jewish law and the Jewish past.

The only author whose works have survived almost in their entirety is Philo of Alexandria. Philo, whose Hebrew name was possibly David, was born about the year 20 B.C.E. into an aristocratic family. He received a thorough Greek education, probably in Alexandrian Greek schools. His erudition in the classical literature and especially in the writings of the philosophers was phenomenal. His Jewish erudition was less thorough. While his familiarity with the Septuagint version of the Pentateuch was great, he was less versed in other parts of the Bible, and he had almost no knowledge of the Jewish Oral Law. Equally limited was his knowledge of the Hebrew language.

Philo was an observant Jew, and he is known to have made a pilgrimage to Jerusalem. In the tradition of his family he involved himself actively in matters of Jewish communal life. During the great confrontation between Jews and Gentiles in Alexandria in 38 C.E., he joined the delegation sent by the Jewish community to Emperor Caius, so lending to it his immense prestige as an author. His deep interest in the well-being of his Jewish brethren is indicated by the fact that he authored two treatises describing from the Jewish point of view the events of 38 C.E. and the embassy to Caius. Philo died about the middle of the first century C.E.

Philo was a prolific writer, and the bulk of his writings is related to Judaism. Many of his works aim at presenting to the non-Jewish world a true picture of the Pentateuchal law, in order to save it from being maligned by contemporary anti-Semitic authors. Foremost among these writings is a special, brief treatise on the Decalogue. Similarly, he presented the Jewish past in the form of biographies of the Patriarchs and Joseph. In his biography of Moses, his greatest work, he clearly addressed himself to the Gentile world. A collection of philosophical treatises loosely linked to Genesis may have originally been a series of sermons delivered in one of the synagogues. Philo also authored a number of treatises, some in the form of dialogues, which dealt with general philosophical concepts and issues, and had little or no connection with Judaism.

While Philo's attitude to the various philosophical schools is still a matter of debate, it is certain that he firmly believed in the allegorical nature of the biblical narrative. He probably knew earlier Jewish attempts at interpreting the Holy Writ by way of allegory. In general, however, his contribution of an allegorical interpretation of the Pentateuch is original.

The use of allegory brought Philo both triumph and tragedy. His triumph was that in a period of a serious literary attack on the Jewish people, he was able to present to the intellectuals among his contemporaries the Jewish past and the Jewish law in a way which was bound to evoke a favorable response. His tragedy, however, lies in the fact that during the period of the early great confrontation between Judaism and Christianity, the Fathers of the Church skillfully used his allegories in an attempt to prove the truth of their cause. This made allegory, and with it Philo's writings, suspect in the eyes of the Jews. His writings thus remained outside of the realm of Jewish literature for a millenium and a half. It was only in the 16th century that one of his treatises was translated into Hebrew and thus made accessible to the Jewish reader. Only in the aggadic Midrash, itself by definition dedicated to allegorical exegesis, can Philo's influence be noticed here and there.

Philo's death signified the end of Egyptian Jewry's cultural heyday. The continuous deterioration of the Jewish condition under Roman rule, coupled with the rise in the tension between the Jews and the Greek population, brought about a partial disengagement of the Jews from their cultural symbiosis with the Greeks. In addition, the Roman administration was now limiting the admission of Jews to the gymnasia. Study at a gymnasium was a prerequisite for obtaining citizenship, and the government wanted to limit the number of Jews entitled to citizenship. This, too, of course, put a wedge between Jews and the Hellenistic culture. But it was the calamity of the years 115–17 C.E. that put a definite end to Alexandria as a great center of Jewish Hellenistic culture. What followed then was merely a faint echo of Alexandrian Jewry's great cultural past. But the cultural life of the new small Jewish community was probably more Jewish in practice than hitherto.

The Religious Life

The immigrants from Judaea who arrived in the sixth and fifth centuries B.C.E. attempted to organize their religious life in Egypt along patterns known to them from their homeland. Thus, the prophet Jeremiah, forcibly taken to Egypt by Judaean refugee soldiers, continued to prophecy from his new domicile in northern Egypt. Similarly, the military colony in Elephantine, established prior to 525 B.C.E., built a temple for the practice of a sacrificial service.

To be sure, the temple of Elephantine was architecturally different from the Jerusalem Temple, as was the sacrificial service practiced in it. In addition to sacrificing to YHWH, offerings were also made to other gods and goddesses. The Elephantine Jews obviously adhered to the "popular" form of Judaism, which stubbornly coexisted alongside the pure Judaism upheld by the prophets. That Anath, a goddess of war, was worshipped could only be expected of a community of soldiers. The daily religious usages and customs of the Elephantine Jews, including such a sensitive area as the marriage law, differed drastically from that of the Pentateuch and of what later became known as "normative"

Judaism. There is no evidence that they celebrated Jewish holidays other than Passover. Characteristically, the Elephantine Jews had their priests, but no prophets. Their temple had existed for more than 100 years, when in 411 B.C.E. it was destroyed in an anti-Jewish riot. It was rebuilt, without the cooperation, or even in the face of opposition of the high priest of the Jerusalem Temple which is not surprising. The second Elephantine temple was still in existence in 398 B.C.E. It is not known how long it lasted.

Curiously, some 250 years later another Jewish military colony chose the sacrificial service as its way of worshipping God. About the middle of the second century B.C.E. a Judaean priest named Onias, probably a son of High Priest Onias III of the Jerusalem Temple, acquired a pagan temple in Leontopolis, in northern Egypt, and transformed it into a Jewish temple. Onias had immigrated from Judaea together with a number of Jews who hired themselves out as mercenaries to the Ptolemies. He introduced in the Leontopolis temple a sacrificial service probably identical with that of the Jerusalem Temple. But although Onias belonged to the legitimate line of high priests, the authorities of the Jerusalem Temple never accorded the Leontopolis temple their recognition. Nor did the Leontopolis temple gain acceptance within the general Jewish community of Egypt; its authority remained limited to its immediate vicinity, known as the "land of Onias." The Leontopolis temple existed for over 200 years and was closed by the Roman authorities in 73 C.E.

By and large, at least with the beginning of large-scale Jewish immigration under the Ptolemies, Egyptian Jewry adhered to a religious life centered in the synagogue. Archeologists have found in Egypt traces of synagogues dating back to the middle of the third century B.C.E. Indications are, however, that synagogues existed in Egypt even in the previous century. Alexandria had many synagogues, of course, located in the various quarters inhabited by Jews. There was also one synagogue which surpassed all others in splendor and size. It is said to have been so large that worshippers could hardly hear the chanting of the cantor, and had to be signaled to their responses by a flag waved from the pulpit.

The daily religious observance of the Egyptian Jews differed, like that of the Elephantine Jews, from the "normative" Judaism practiced in Judaea, but probably to a much lesser degree. The tendency of Egypt's Jewish theologians to interpret the Torah in an allegorical way naturally caused a laxity in the observance of the Pentateuchal law. The deviation from the Law was often accompanied by such dubious practices as the invocation of pagan gods on gravestones, charms, and amulets. It is important to note, however, that provincial Jewry adhered to traditional Jewish observance to a greater degree than the urbanized and more Hellenized Jewry of Alexandria. There were also groups which adhered to the rigidity of the Law in an extreme way, reminiscent of the contemporary Essenes in Judaea. But one theory has it that this Egyptian withdrawal sect, known as Therapeutoi, was in fact an early group of Christian monks.

We have seen that due to its linguistic integration Egyptian Jewry read the Bible in Greek. It is characteristic that as it differed in religious usage and custom, so too does Egyptian Jewry's Septuagint have many passages which differ from the text in the Hebrew Bible. The Septuagint also differs structurally from the Hebrew text, insofar as various apocryphal and pseudepigraphal books are interspersed among the traditional books of the Bible. The scroll of Esther, at least, was read in the native Egyptian language. Much of the synagogue worship was surely conducted in the vernacular, a practice endorsed for Diaspora Jewry by the Rabbis.

The Egyptian-Jewish theologians-philosophers presented the God of Israel in their writings as a Universal God. They further attempted to show that the Jewish Law was not at variance with the standards of morality accepted in the Greco-Roman world. They did this not only for apologetical reasons, but also in order to attract proselytes to the Jewish religion. Philo, like the Pharisees in Judaea, was much in favor of accepting proselytes. Proselytes, indeed, seem to have been no rarity among Egyptian Jews.

While the Hadrianic religious persecutions seem not to have affected Egyptian Jewry, the situation worsened considerably with the advent of the Christian empire in the fourth century. We have seen how the bishop of Alexandria was able to banish the

Jews from the city in 410. The situation surely did not improve under Byzantine rule. Under these conditions defection to Christianity was increasing. Almost on the eve of the Arab conquest an entire Jewish community of about 400 people converted to Christianity. In fact, conversion to Christianity must have been a major factor in the continuous diminution of the size of the Jewish population in the centuries preceding the Arab conquest.

Chapter 2

In the Rest of North Africa

The Jewish Population

There is no way to determine the exact dates when Jewish settlements began to form in the various countries of the North African coast. The widespread medieval tradition that considerable numbers of Jews had settled there cannot be substantiated, but it is likely that in biblical times a small number of Hebrews did settle there. When the Ptolemies occupied Cyrene and its region in the fourth century B.C.E., Jews began to arrive there from Egypt. In time this area came to house a substantial Jewish community. While the Jewish population of Tripolitania remained rather sparse, Jews flocked in large numbers into the city of Carthage farther west and into the other parts of today's Tunisia after the Roman conquest in 146 B.C.E. Jewish immigration from Egypt and Judaea became especially intensive in the first and second centuries C.E. The Jewish population may have been further increased by the conversion to Judaism of a number of local Phoenicians. Later, in the second century C.E., Morocco too became an area of Jewish settlement.

While the Jewish population of Cyrene greatly diminished in the wake of the uprising against the emperor Trajan in 115–17 C.E., the Jewish population in the other parts of Roman North

Africa seems to have increased. When in the fourth century Christianity became the dominant religion in the empire, however, many Jews left the coastal areas and moved southward to the Berber tribes. This Jewish community in the inner regions of North Africa later increased in number due to frequent conversions to Judaism among its Berber neighbors. There are indications that here and there entire tribes of the Berber population converted to the Jewish faith. When the emperor Justinian I, upon conquering North Africa in 533, outlawed the Jewish religion there, many more Jews fled southward. About 100 years later the Jewish community in Morocco received a large number of refugees from Visigothic Spain, where the Jewish community was exposed to brutal religious persecution.

The Political Conditions

Little is known of the political destiny of North African Jewry in the early period of Roman rule. The leading Jewish communities were Cyrene and Carthage (later known as Tunis).It must be assumed that Roman rule was by and large benign. Further, no information is available which would indicate the existence of friction between the Jews and their Berber neighbors. The apparent tranquility of the Jewish community was also due to the general economic prosperity of its members, mostly farmers and craftsmen.

The sole exception seems to have been the city of Cyrene and its environs. The perpetual conflict between Jews and Gentiles in nearby Egypt caused tensions here as well, tensions unknown in the Jewish communities farther west. In the year 73 C.E., serious unrest developed among the lower strata of the Jewish population, incited by refugees from Judaea. The Roman authorities easily suppressed the uprising. In the process, many wealthy Jews, who took no part in the unrest, were also massacred. Far more serious were the events which took place in Cyrene in 115–17 C.E. In fact, what is sometimes called the general Jewish uprising against Emperor Trajan (cf. Sec. VIII, Chap. 5; Sec. IX, Chaps. 1 and 2; and Sec. X, Chap. 1) began in the city of Cyrene. A certain Lukuas-Andrew, who may have believed himself to be the Messiah, attacked the pagan population, massacred many, and destroyed pagan temples. Andrew possibly planned to transform Cyrene into a Jewish state. When he was defeated by the Roman army, however, he left Cyrene and invaded Egypt, as we have seen, and possibly also Judaea. Although a Jewish community later existed in Cyrene again, it never regained the position it held prior to 115 C.E.

With the Christianization of North Africa, the condition of the Jews deteriorated. In the last decades of the fourth and early in the fifth century many laws were issued curtailing their rights. A certain improvement in the situation of the Jews was noticeable during the hundred years of Vandal rule (429–533). The Vandals were Arian Christians and their attitude to the Jews was friendlier than that of rulers belonging to the universal Church.

Hard times arrived for North Africa's Jewish community when in a series of attacks between 533 and 548 the Byzantines succeeded in occupying the land. The fact that the Jews were suspected of aiding the Vandals created among the Byzantines an atmosphere of hostility towards the Jewish community. Although Emperor Justinian I tolerated the existence of Jewish communities in his other possessions, he embarked on a different policy in North Africa. An imperial order issued in 535 outlawed Judaism and condemned all synagogues to be converted into churches. True, the order was executed only partially. It sufficed, however, as we have seen, to prompt many Jews to flee southward to the Berber tribes, among whom Judaism was quite popular.

Byzantine rule over North Africa was broken after about 100 years by the advent of the Muslims. Before the Muslims had firmly established their control over Northwest Africa. they had to overcome the resistance of a coalition of Jews and Berbers in today's Algeria. The coalition was led by Dahya (or, Dehiyya) Kahina, possibly a Jewish queen from a priestly family who ruled a Berber tribe in the Aures mountains. It was only after her defeat and death about the year 700 that the Muslims could complete their conquest of North Africa.

Communal Organization and Religious Life

Not much is known directly about the communal organization and the cultural and religious life of North African Jewry in the Antiquity. With regard to Cyrene it may be said that as early as the first century B.C.E. it had well-organized Jewish communities which in all likelihood resembled those of Egyptian Jewry (cf. Sec. X, Chap. 1). The same holds true of Jewish cultural life, as Cyrenian Jewry was always strongly influenced by its immediate neighbor to the east. In fact, the higher strata of Cyrene's Jewish urban population culturally were thoroughly Hellenized. Jewish religious life in Cyrene was centered around the synagogue. No information is available as to the existence of temples with a sacrificial service. Instead, Cyrenian Jews supported the Temple of Jerusalem with lavish donations. The existence of synagogues in Cyrene and its environs is attested to beginning with the first century B.C.E.

While the Cyrenian Jews, like those of Egypt, generally spoke Greek, the Jews of Carthage spoke Latin. The same should, of course, be assumed with regard to the Jews in the western part of North Africa, today's Algeria and Morocco. Western Roman culture was prevalent in this region, as is manifested by a Jewish burial site in today's Tunisia which resembles the Jewish catacombs in Rome (cf. Sec. XI, Chap. 2).

Jewish religious life in the western parts of North Africa, though unknown to us in detail, must have been quite intensive. Talmudic scholars are known to have lived in the city of Carthage. Judaism also demonstrated a great power of attraction among the Gentiles. Not only were there certain Judaizing sects, possibly of the "Fearers of the Lord" type, but some Berber tribes had accepted the Jewish faith. This was true of tribes living in the interior of the country, as well as of some living in the coastal regions.

A great blow was dealt to the religious life of North African Jewry when the country was conquered by the Byzantines in the sixth century. As we have seen, in 535 Emperor Justinian I ordered that Judaism be outlawed and synagogues converted into churches. To be sure, the order was carried out only in part, and the restrictions on Judaism were relaxed later in the century. With the advent of the Muslims in the seventh century, the Jews, it must be assumed, regained full religious freedom. In the region of today's Algeria Judaism possibly even had attained a position of prominence during the time this area was under the control of the Jewish queen Dahya al-Kahina. With her death, Judaism declined and many members of her tribe converted to Islam.

Section XI

IN EUROPE

Chapter 1

In Southeastern Europe

The Jewish Population

It is not unlikely that Judaeans began to settle in Greece at the time of the downfall of the state of Judah (586 B.C.E.), or shortly thereafter. If Sepharad mentioned by the prophet Obadiah (1:20) is identical with the city of Sparta, and there is no reason to reject such an identification, it would be safe to assume that a considerable Judaean population had been living in southern Greece in the sixth century B.C.E. By the year 300 B.C.E., at any rate, a Jewish community was well established there. Jews came to Greece both from nearby Asia Minor and from not so distant Judaea. Jewish communities on the Greek islands, such as Crete, Delos, and Paros, whose existence is attested to at a later time, probably date back to the earliest period of Jewish settlement in Greece.

In the second century B.C.E., a period of many Jewish-Greek encounters, both peaceful and hostile, Jewish communities were to be found all over Greece, including such leading cities as Athens, Philippi, Delphi, Sparta, Corinth, and Thessalonica. The Jewish communities further expanded geographically and numerically after Rome became mistress of both Greece and Judaea. It was only natural that at a later date groups of Jews spilled over from Greece into the nearby Rome-controlled Balkan countries, such as today's Bulgaria and Rumania. Some of the Jews came to these Roman possessions, as elsewhere, as mercenaries in, and suppliers to, the Roman legions. After its establishment, Constantinople became the seat of a major Jewish community.

Prior to that, in the first century B.C.E., or possibly even earlier, Jewish communities came into being on the Crimean peninsula and on the northern shores of the Black Sea, today's southern Ukraine. They were established by arrivals from Greece and Asia Minor. The number of Jews in this region was later increased by an influx of immigrants from Byzantium and Persia due to religious oppression, and from Armenia due to the general turmoil prevalent there. The barbarian invasions in the late Antiquity did to the Jews in this area the same damage as to the rest of the population. By and large, however, the Jewish settlement survived them. Thus, in the waning years of the Antiquity the entire area of southeastern Europe, including the Greek islands in the Mediterranean, had become a permanent point on the map of the Jewish Diaspora.

Political and Economic Conditions

During the many centuries preceding the ascension of Christians to the throne of imperial Rome, the history of the Jews in southeastern Europe was rather uneventful. True, the Jews did not possess full civil and political rights due to the pagan nature of the *polis,* which was the basic governmental institution. But in general the situation of the Jews was favorable and their economic condition satisfactory. Although here and there large numbers of Jewish slaves could be found, slavery was not the characteristic social position of the Jews. Jewish slavery here probably resulted from the wars and revolts in Judaea, and in time disappeared. Religious oppression was all but absent, as was usually the case in pagan societies.

All this changed drastically when the Roman empire became a Christian state. When Constantine the Great (307–37), who, himself, possibly never converted to Christianity, began openly to favor the Christians, the situation of the Jews began to deteriorate. Contemporary Greek Christian theologians developed a violently anti-Jewish literature, which, in the tradition of certain books in the New Testament (e.g., John 8:44; Revelation 2:9 and 3:9) described the Jews as a people of God killers in conspiracy with Satan. They called the Jewish house of worship "synagogue of Satan" and heaped many other insults upon it. This literature, which created a frightening image of the Jew, could not fail to influence the attitude of the Christian emperors to their Jewish subjects. A sole exception were the emperors who followed the Arian heresy; their attitude toward the Jews was invariably less hostile.

The formal curtailment of Jewish rights in Byzantium (as the eastern part of the Roman Empire was called) made rapid progress, and resulted in the withdrawal of citizenship rights from the Jews and their exclusion from government service, the army, and the legal profession. The Jews were, however to continue serving in certain burdensome governmental offices shunned by everybody. Not only did they lose the privilege of claiming exemption from such duties on religious grounds, which they had possessed in former times, but they were even prohibited from obtaining the meager advantages enjoyed by Christian holders of such offices. The partial restrictions on holding slaves also dealt a severe blow to the economic freedom of the Jews.

This changed situation was reflected in the codes of the emperors Theodosius II (408–50) and Justinian I (527–65). The code of Theodosius issued in 438, and that of Justinian codified about 100 years later, repeated all the insults produced in the literature of the theologians. The many restrictions the codes imposed upon the Jews legalized a situation which had been developing de facto since the times of Constantine the Great. And yet both codes tried to retain for the Jews and the Jewish religion some degree of security in face of the relentless efforts of the Church to degrade them and to incite the populace against them. Evidently, the tradition of the Jews having been citizens of the empire had not been completely forgotten. Only this can explain how the Byzantine Jews could still have involved themselves to a degree in the political life of the empire during the fifth and sixth centuries. It is not without significance that a certain rapprochement developed between the Jews and pagans who were now also a persecuted religious group. The political degradation of the Jews reached its peak during the second half of the sixth and the first decades of the seventh century, not least because of the general weakening of the imperial power. The most blatant expression of the situation was an attempt in 632 to forcibly convert all Jews to the Christian faith. This attempt, like others to follow, was unsuccessful. Byzantine Jewry thus survived into the Middle Ages. But it survived as a group despised by both Church and state, and deprived of most of its ancient rights.

The Religious Life

We do not know whether and to what degree the early Jewish settlers in Greece and the other Balkan countries developed any form of Jewish culture of their own. If there was any Jewish cultural life, it was by far inferior to that which came into being in Hellenistic Egypt (see Sec. X, Chap. 1). The only thing that can be said with certainty is that the Jewish immigrants assimilated linguistically, and the specific Jewish languages, Hebrew and Aramaic, were quickly forgotten among them.

Nonetheless, the Jews of Greece and the Balkans, as well as those on the Crimean peninsula, possessed a communal organization, headed by officers called *archons.* The existence of synagogues is documented as far back as the second century B.C.E. Traces of synagogues have been found in many localities both on the Greek islands and on the mainland. It goes without saying that the synagogues were much more numerous than the score the existence of which in the first century C.E. can be documented. How services were conducted in these synagogues is unknown. There is a likelihood that certain customs and practices were borrowed from pagan neighbors, especially in the remote regions of the Black Sea. This may have gone so far as to give to Jewish life a touch of religious syncretism.

In later times, when more Jews arrived from Judaea, either as prisoners of war or as immigrants, Jewish religious life began to conform more and more with normative Judaism. It is even safe to assume that religion came to occupy an ever-increasing part in the life of the Jewish community. Only such an intensive Jewish religious life could have become popular enough among the Gentiles to attract the many of them who either began to emulate the

Jewish way of life or who took the decisive step to convert to Judaism.

This intensive Jewish religious life was given a hard blow when Constantine the Great began to demonstrate his favoritism to Christianity. His prohibition of proselytization among Gentiles put an effective halt to the spread of the Jewish faith. Under the following emperors, as we have seen, a situation developed in which Judaism had to fight for its very existence. The main problem in the religious life was to retain the synagogues as Jewish houses of worship and to save them from forcible conversion into churches, or destruction by hostile mobs. The attitude of the Byzantine emperors and their codes of law to the synagogue was ambiguous. It was clear to the Jews that no permission would be given to erect new synagogues. But even the repair of old synagogues, seemingly guaranteed by law, was often in practice prohibited. And yet Judaism retained in Byzantium the status of a legal religion. Theodosius II even continued to recognize Jewish judicial autonomy in cases exclusively involving Jews. Strange as it may seem, Justinian I claimed the right to regulate matters of worship in the synagogue precisely because Judaism was the only legally recognized religion next to Christianity. But it remains open to doubt whether Justinian interfered more than occasionally in matters of Jewish worship.

The arrival of many Judaeans in the period of Roman rule seems to have brought back to local Jewry the knowledge of the Hebrew language and its use in religious worship. It is thus understandable that, while certain Jews in the sixth century preferred to read the Bible in the synagogue in a Greek translation, others insisted on using the Hebrew text. In the sixth century Byzantine Jewry also began to form its own order of prayers, known as the *Mahazor Romania,* or the Romaniote prayerbook.

Chapter 2

In Rome and Italy

The Jewish Population

Jewish settlement in Italy, like that in neighboring Greece, possibly dates back to the earlier years of the Second Commonwealth. By the third century B.C.E., however, Jewish communities existed in all likelihood in various localities on the peninsula, and especially in the south and on the islands of Sicily and Sardinia. During the next two centuries the Jewish population greatly increased in numbers. A steady flow of Jewish immigrants began to stream to Italy from Judaea after its occupation by the Romans in 63 B.C.E. Many of the new Jewish arrivals may have been brought to Italy as captives by the various Roman commanders. True, most of the about 100,000 Judaean captives reportedly brought to Italy with the downfall of the First Revolt (70 C.E.) were either sold or sent to other countries, or assimilated into the households of their pagan owners. But it is likely that many were ransomed by Italian Jews and numerically augmented the Jewish community.

The friendly attitude to the Jews manifested by Julius Caesar and the first emperors, coupled with vast economic opportunities, served as a mighty attraction to many in perpetually war-torn Judaea. Thus, Italy became during the imperial period a major area of Jewish settlement. The Jewish population, whose numbers it is difficult to estimate, lived in about 40 localities. The city of Rome, of course, harbored the largest Jewish community. Estimates of its size range from 12,000 to 60,000. It is worth noting that during the imperial period, if not prior to it, Jews began to spill over from Italy into Pannonia, more or less identical with today's Hungary. Their number was large enough to necessitate the establishing of communities and the building of synagogues.

In the third century, when the decline of the Roman empire set in, Jewish immigration greatly diminished. Furthermore, it should be assumed that the Jewish population declined in number due to the general turmoil prevalent in the country and emigration to other regions in Europe. In addition, an inner shift of the Jewish population from the north to the south took place. The invasions of Germanic tribes affected first and foremost the north. It is thus understandable that many Jews sought refuge in the more stable south. The attempt of a Langobardian king in 661 to forcibly convert the Jews under his rule also, no doubt, resulted in the diminution of the Jewish population in northern Italy. It was then that Naples began to play a greater role in Italian Jewry than formerly. In general, despite its setbacks Italian Jewry remained a major community on the map of the Jewish Diaspora in the period of the waning Antiquity.

Political and Economic Conditions

As long as the Jewish population in Rome and Italy was small, no "Jewish question" seems to have existed there. Rome's treaties with the Hasmonean rulers of Judaea (see Sec. V, Chap. 2) must have created a friendly atmosphere for the Judaeans living in Italy. The expulsion of Judaeans from the city of Rome, reported to have taken place in 139 B.C.E., may have affected only certain members of the community who possibly engaged in Jewish religious propaganda.

When in the first century B.C.E. Roman rule established itself firmly in Asia Minor, Syria, and North Africa, their dense Jewish settlements allied themselves closely with the new conqueror, as we have seen, who protected them against excesses on the part of the native population. These developments strongly affected the situation of the Jews in Rome proper in a very advantageous way. This was clearly manifested by the fact that while Julius Caesar outlawed all Near-Eastern cults, he exempted from the prohibition the Jewish religion and its worship. Augustus, the first emperor, continued this basically friendly Jewish policy. To be sure, the favorable treatment of the Jews and their numerical growth began to evoke ever-increasing resentments among the population.

These resentments found clear expression in the literature of the time. As prominent an author, orator, and statesman as Cicero spoke about the Jews (in 59 B.C.E.) with a mixture of hatred and fear resembling utterances of modern anti-Semites. Small wonder that the Jews flocked to the support of the rising imperial power, opposed by the same patrician circles which nurtured most of the anti-Jewish feelings. True, Augustus (27 B.C.E.–14 C.E.) and his successors did not have much personal affection for their Jewish subjects. Under Tiberius, Caius, and Claudius, the Italian Jews experienced some difficulties, including the temporary removal of parts of the community from the city of Rome, again probably caused by missionary activities or conflicts with newly arisen Christianity. By and large, however, the relations between the imperial government and Italy's Jews were not unfriendly, despite the rising tension between Romans and the Jews in Judaea.

The friendly atmosphere in which the Jews lived was also responsible for their basic integration into the economic life of the country. Most Jews seem to have earned their livelihood as merchants, and most had probably attained a comfortable degree of economic prosperity. Nothing is known of any economic restrictions imposed upon the Jews during the pagan imperial period. Significantly, the less fortunate among the Jews were eligible to receive welfare on a par with the non-Jewish poor.

Ultimately, however, the tensions in Judaea, especially after the death of King Agrippa I in 44 C.E. (cf. Sec. VI, Chap. 3) could not avoid bringing about a deterioration in the condition of Italian Jewry. Two additional factors now worked against the Jewish interest. The Romanization of the colonies in Asia and Africa made great progress, and the Romans no longer needed the support of the Jewish communities in those diasporas. Simultaneously, the Jewish population in Italy increased in number and thus began to attract more attention. The anti-Semitic literary attack on the Jews then became much more violent, and the alleged alien character of the Jews was put into focus. The first century C.E. satirist Martial even tried to convince the Romans that the body of the Jew emanated an offensive odor. The philosophers describing themselves as Stoics also manifested hostility to the Jews, accusing them of trying to attract Greco-Roman society to Judaism. One of the more famous among them, Seneca (4 B.C.E.–65 C.E.), Nero's teacher and a high official in his government, went so far as to call the Jews the most accursed and criminal people.

And in Italy, as elsewhere in the empire, the First Revolt added to the tension between Jews and Gentiles. Titus' triumphant march into Rome, in which leaders of the Judaean uprising were led in chains, and the very large numbers of Judaeans brought as slaves, lowered the prestige of the local Jews. And yet as long as Vespasian and Titus were alive no definite deterioration of the political status of the Jews took place. In fact, some Judaean "loyalists" even attained high position in the capital. A deterioration of the Jewish condition took place under Emperor Domitian (81–89 C.E.), mostly due to the brutality of his character. The introduction of the special Jewish tax was, of course, humiliating. In practice, however, burdensome as it was, it merely replaced the contributions previously paid by the Jews to the Jerusalem Temple.

Under the emperors of the second and third centuries, the legal and social status of Italian Jewry largely remained the same. During the years 115–17 C.E., Italian Jewry remained tranquil, while most Jews of the Diaspora rose against the empire and contributed to the failure of Trajan's major campaign against the Parthians (see Sec. IX, Chaps. 1 and 2, and Sec. X). Nor did Italian Jewry aid the Judaeans in any way during the Second Revolt (132–35 C.E.). The venomous attacks of the historian Tacitus, and the accusations that the Jews deliberately separated themselves from the rest of the population, and should therefore be considered haters of the human race, were basically no different from similar attacks of anti-Semitic writers of former generations and failed to permanently harm the interests of Italian Jewry.

The unfriendly personal attitude of some of the emperors was countered by the outspoken friendliness of others. Especially friendly to the Jews were the emperors of the Severan dynasty. Alexander Severus (222–35) was so outspokenly pro-Jewish that, as we have noted, some called him *archisynagogus,* head of the synagogue. Steadily, the number of Jews who were able to acquire Roman citizenship kept on growing. True, with governmental office becoming more and more burdensome, Jews were increasingly drawn into the service of the state and the municipalities. Yet they were exempted from performing services which led to the violation of the Sabbath or had pagan cultic connections. At the end of the third century, Italian Jewry found itself again protected by the benign attitude of the great emperor Diocletian (284–305).

Things began to change for the worse with the reign of Constantine the Great and the new official status given to the Christian religion. True, anti-Jewish violence was not as intensive as that perpetrated by the Christians in the Near East. But the curtailment of the rights of the Jews, as defined in the code of Emperor Theodosius II (see above, Chap. 1) became the norm in Italy too.

The abolition of the western Roman empire when the German Odoacer was proclaimed king in 476 caused no real change in the status of Italian Jewry. Under the next ruler, Theodoric the Great (487–526), the rights of the Jews were not only preserved but they gained much by the general tranquility of the country under this just king. The situation remained basically the same in the course of the sixth century. The various Germanic rulers still considered the Jews Roman citizens and did not curtail any of the rights conceded to them by the Christian emperors. In Naples, Jews were still involved in the city administration, and participated in its defense when the Byzantines attacked. The Byzantine conquest, of course, meant in practice harsher treatment of the Jews, even though Emperor Justinian's code basically confirmed Theodosius' Jewish legislation (see above, Chap. 1). The invasion of the Langobards in 568 also at first brought no great change. Like Theodoric, the Langobardian kings were Arians, and like all Christian sectarians treated the Jews leniently. It was only after their conversion to Catholicism that in 661, as we have seen, a Langobardian king decreed the forced conversion of the Jews to Christianity. Like many similar edicts in other countries, however, this decree was only partially enforced. Thus, although many were baptized and many lost their lives, a Jewish community continued to exist in northern Italy.

During the sixth century, the influence of the bishops of Rome, the popes, kept on growing in importance. It was Pope Gregory I, the Great (590–604), who first clearly formulated the Jewish policy of the Papacy. While condemning in quite abusive language the Jewish religion, Gregory I strongly insisted on securing protection for the Jews and their houses of worship. He, in fact, compelled the clergy in Palermo (Sicily) to compensate the

Jews for a synagogue forcibly taken away from them. Thus, the popes too became a source of protection for the Italian Jews during the period of invasion and turmoil, up to the time when the kings of Frankland established order in the country in the middle of the eighth century.

The effort of the Christian emperors, their Germanic successors, and the early popes to preserve a measure of protection for the life, property, and religion of their Jewish subjects, as sincere as it may have been, was seriously weakened by the abusive language most of them chose to use with regard to the Jewish religion. Gregory the Great himself used the word *vomit* in a letter to describe the Jewish religion. This ambivalence of attitude toward Judaism became one of the sources of the continuous violence perpetrated against the Jews in the following epoch, the Middle Ages.

Community Government, Culture, and Religious Life

The paucity of sources does not permit us to clearly describe ancient Italian Jewry's communal organization. It is certain, however, that such an organization, *universitas,* did exist. In fact, this communal organization was recognized in the first century B.C.E. by the nascent imperial power as an ancient and recognized institution, and therefore legitimate. How this organization governed itself, is not clearly known. Some scholars believe that in the city of Rome it was a loosely organized council, *gerousia,* representing the many congregations in the city. Other scholars believe that the originally democratic structure of the *gerousia* gave way in imperial times to a hereditary and aristocratic one. Simultaneously, some kind of an autonomous Jewish judicial system was in existence, which survived the imperial period and gained recognition from Theodoric the Great. Jews here, as in Alexandria, seem to have preferred living in quarters of their own.

Culturally, the Italian Jews of the Antiquity seem to have been fully integrated. They spoke Latin, as is indicated by the Latin names they bore. As early as the first century B.C.E., the Sicilian Jew Caecilius Calactinus made a name for himself in

Rome as a rhetorician and historian. He is occasionally called the first European-born Jewish author. It may well be assumed that more Jews, whose traces were not preserved, distinguished themselves in Roman literature. Jews may also have played a role in the visual arts, as may be indicated by the ornamentations found in Rome's Jewish catacombs. The cultural integration of the Jews within Roman society is no less indicated by the fact that elements of Jewish magic became part and parcel of Roman magical literature of the second and third centuries C.E. That a purely Jewish literature in Greek and Latin also developed in Italy is exemplified by the writings of Josephus and his adversary, Justus of Tiberias (cf. Sec. VIII, Chap. 2).

And yet genuine Hebraic culture was no stranger to Roman and Italian Jewry. The frequent arrivals from Judaea could not help but infuse genuine Jewish culture continuously into Roman Jewish society. This is best indicated by the personal influence of the Judaean sage Mattiah ben Heresh, who settled in Rome after the Second Revolt, and the importance of the *yeshivah* which he founded. The Judaean sages would not have given so much recognition to the Roman yeshivah had it not risen to the rank of an outstanding institution of learning.

The religious experience of Italian Jewry was not much different from that of its sister communities in other parts of the Roman empire. True, extreme phenomena were not missing. On the one hand, we find Jews who adopted pagan customs and, on the other hand, Jews who abstained from consuming even certain food not definitely forbidden by the Rabbis. The multitude of the Jews, however, followed the kind of normative religious practice centered around the synagogue. There is evidence of the existence of hundreds of synagogues all over the peninsula and in Sicily throughout the centuries. The community of Rome had well over ten synagogues. Synagogues were headed by officials whose title was *archisynagogus,* but it is not clear whether their functions were administrative or religious. Another functionary of the synagogue was the sexton.

Whether the Italian communities had religious leaders whose authority and functions resembled those of rabbis cannot be proven with certainty. Theudas, who in the second century C.E. introduced in Rome certain ritualistic innovations, may have been a rabbi whose authority was recognized by the entire Jewish community. It is likely that the Italianic order of prayers followed by Italian Jewry down to the present had its inception before the Antiquity came to an end. All the time, the synagogue was tacitly, and later actively, protected by the Roman government. There is no evidence that under the republic and the pagan emperors synagogues were destroyed, taken away, or their service harassed. Augustus' decree making the theft or profanation of Torah scrolls a severely punishable sacrilege sufficiently manifested imperial determination to give protection to the synagogue worship.

Although Italian Jewry's religious life was exclusively synagogue-centered, it had a sincere attachment to the Temple in Jerusalem. The flow of contributions for the support of the sacrificial service was untiring and generous. Emperor Augustus' protection for this "sacred money" destined for Jerusalem indicates how important the Jerusalem Temple loomed within Italy's Jewish community.

Despite the hatred of Judaism manifested by so many statesmen, philosophers, and authors, the Jewish faith exerted a mighty attraction to the Romans. In fact, Judaism was quite popular in the imperial court and among the aristocracy. The number of "Fearers of the Lord," that is, men and women who had abandoned their loyalty to the pagan religion and adhered to some tenets of Judaism without formally converting to it, was quite large. Poppea, the wife of Emperor Nero, is said to have been one of them. Some of the "Fearers of the Lord" had their children join Judaism formally. The number of formal converts to Judaism was surprisingly large, and included aristocrats and members of the family of Emperor Domitian. Characteristically, all this seems to have happened without noticeable proselytization on the part of the Jews.

The government looked askance at the spread of Judaism among the Romans. Emperor Domitian imposed heavy fines upon the converts and occasionally ordered the execution of some of them. Emperor Antoninus Pius (138–61 C.E.), in an attempt to counteract the movement, prohibited the circumcision of boys born of non-Jewish parents. But many nevertheless continued to convert to the Jewish faith. How serious the movement was can be seen from a satire by the poet Juvenal (c. 65–140 C.E.), in which he mockingly attacked the converts to Judaism. Significantly, in later times, when Christianity began to make inroads in Roman society, pagan thinkers began to consider Judaism as an "ally" in their even greater opposition to the daughter religion. A conspicuous example of this new attitude was the interest in Judaism manifested by Emperor Julian (see Sec. VIII, Chap. 5). At the same time, some Jews abandoned Judaism to serve Roman gods. It must be assumed that their number was larger than is indicated by direct evidence.

With the advent of the Christian empire it became harder to practice the Jewish religion, despite the governmental protection still extended to it. The number of synagogues became smaller and smaller due to the prohibition against building new ones and the obstacles which had to be overcome in repairing old ones. In addition, many synagogues were destroyed in the course of the fifth and sixth centuries due to the many invasions and wars. While, as we have seen, Pope Gregory the Great ordered compensation to be paid to the Jews for a synagogue confiscated by the clergy, compensating the Jews did not become common practice. Similarly, Gregory's admonition that Jews should not be forcibly baptized, if we judge by later times, was more often disregarded than obeyed. Despite all this, however, Judaism persisted in Italy into the late Antiquity as a religion recognized by both the state and the nascent papacy.

Chapter 3

In Western Europe

The Jewish Population

Of all the countries in Western Europe, Spain was the first to become an area of Jewish settlement. It is not unlikely that already in the times of the First Commonwealth some Israelites in the company of, or following, Phoenician seafarers settled in Spain. The fact that the author of the book of Jonah, who lived no later than the third century B.C.E., had his hero, the prophet, travel to Tarshish (Jonah 1:3), most probably a locality in southwestern Spain, clearly indicates that traveling to Spain was not out of the ordinary in the period of the Second Commonwealth.

Nonetheless, and despite the multiplicity of the traditions about the great antiquity of Spain's Jewish community, it is not before the times of Roman rule that the existence of such a community can be ascertained. At the time Judaea had become a Roman colony in 63 B.C.E., Spain had already become one of the most important and prosperous Roman colonies in the West, and Roman rule began also to entrench itself in Gaul (today's France), Germany, and England. Thus, Jewish mercenaries and army suppliers began to arrive with the Romans in the entire area of Western Europe. Traces of the presence of Jews in Roman army camps in England have also been found by archeologists. Jews likewise came with the Roman legions to certain countries in Central Europe, such as Bohemia, Moravia, and Austria.

While Jews had appeared in virtually the entire area of Roman rule in Western Europe, there were enormous differences in the density of the Jewish population. It is correct to say that the density of the Jewish population decreased in a northward direction. In Spain (including today's Portugal), with its Mediterranean climate and immense economic possibilities, Jews settled in ever-increasing numbers. In addition, following the First Revolt, many Jewish captives were brought to Spain either directly from Judaea or from among the about 100,000 originally brought by Titus to Italy (see above, Chap. 2). The Jewish population in southern France, where the climate was equally clement, was also fairly dense. The valley of the Rhone in time became a favored area of Jewish settlement. In fact, it may be assumed that the two sons of King Herod deported by the Romans to Vienne and Lyons in the years 6 and 39 C.E., respectively (see Sec. VI, Chap. 3), brought along a number of Jews large enough to have formed the nuclei of future organized Jewish communities. Further north, however, the Jewish population was scarce and its communities quite distant from one another, though imperial documents reveal the presence of a Jewish community in Cologne on the Rhine in 321 C.E., and archeological evidence suggests the existence of a Jewish community in Treves (Trier). But the Rhineland was a remote area in the empire and much less attractive to Jewish immigrants. As for England, it may be said with certainty that the arrival of Jewish mercenaries and army suppliers did not result in the establishment of a permanent Jewish community. It finally should be noted that Jewish communities in Western Europe, wherever they did come into being, were usually formed in the centers of the Roman administration. Having come as soldiers and suppliers to the armies, the Jews had naturally to reside in the vicinity of governmental centers.

It may be assumed that during the entire period of Roman rule, Western Europe's Jewish population kept on growing both by natural increase and immigration. At the beginning of the fourth century, Spain had a considerable Jewish population. The number of Jews in France probably rose too. Curiously, the instability and turmoil created by the many invasions of the Germanic tribes into Gaul and Spain seem not to have caused any serious decline in the numbers of the Jewish population. Thus, Arles in the fifth century and Clermont and Marseilles in the sixth century had become seats of sizable Jewish communities.

As for Spain, its Jewry would not have occupied such a place of centrality in the deliberations of the Church councils during the seventh century had it not been at that time of a quite considerable size. In the Rhineland, however, the small Jewish community seems to have undergone a decline in the period of the invasions. The only time in the late Antiquity that Frankland (composed of central and northern France, as well as of parts of Germany) received an influx of Jews was early in the seventh century when thousands of Jews fled there from the persecutions of the Visigothic kings who controlled Spain and southern France. This increase, however, may have been short-lived.

The attempt of King Dagobert I (628–638) of Frankland to forcibly convert all the Jews of his realm to Christianity under the threat of expulsion in 633 surely resulted in a diminution of the Jewish population. Similarly, the repeated persecutions in Visigothic Spain during the entire seventh century, as will be seen further, cut—at least temporarily—the size of Spain's large Jewry.

Thus, at the end of the Antiquity Western European Jewry had reached a point of considerable numerical decline.

Political Conditions

Almost nothing is known directly about the civic status of the Jews and their political condition in Western Europe during the period of the heyday of the Roman empire. It may, however, be said with certainty that something of the sort of a "Jewish question" did not exist. Basically, the situation of the Jews was probably not different from that of their brethren in Italy, the center of the empire. Significantly, the Jews in Western Europe did not evoke the type of social resentment so strongly expressed in Italy's Latin literature (cf. Chap. 2, above). With the advent of the Christian emperors, the situation of the Jews deteriorated, as elsewhere. This is manifestly indicated by the order of Constantine the Great in the year 321 revoking the exemption from holding the burdensome office of decurions (members of the city council) hitherto enjoyed by the Jews of Cologne on the Rhine.

What the Jews could expect of the Christian states is shown by the decisions of the Church Council held in Elvira, in southern Spain, early in the fourth century. Here, where the largest concentration of Jews in Western Europe existed, Jews seem to have had close social contacts with the Gentiles. This was not to the liking of the Church, and the Council of Elvira took steps to isolate the Jews from the Christians. While it seems that the Church did not succeed in achieving this objective, it must be assumed that in the course of the fourth century the Spanish Jews began to be subjected to the limitations of Jewish rights introduced by the Christian emperors in all their dominions. It is worth noting that in Minorca, one of the Balearic Islands, a Jew held a governmental office other than the decurionate. Only early in the fifth century, we learn, was holding such offices by Jews prohibited.

Beginning in 412, with the invasion of the Germanic tribe of Visigoths, a new era started in Spain. Roman rule in Spain had begun to disintegrate several decades earlier, and the Visigoths were able within a few years to extend their rule over the entire Iberian peninsula and the southern part of Gaul. The Visigoths were Arian Christians, and like most sectarians manifested a friendlier attitude to the Jews than Christian rulers connected with the universal Church. Their code of laws (*Lex Romana Visigothorum*), issued in 506, accorded the Jews a legal status similar to the one formulated in the *Theodosian Code* (cf. above, Chap. 1). In practice the situation of the Jews may even have been better, since there is no evidence of any serious persecution of the Jews until the end of the sixth century. Only when King Reccared converted to Catholicism late in this century did a distinctly hostile anti-Jewish policy begin to emerge. The Church councils held in the course of the seventh century issued a flood of ever-harsher anti-Jewish laws. Their influence on the destiny of the Jews was even more serious due to their dual nature as Church councils and state diets. Several times the kings ordered the Jews to be forcibly baptized or expelled. True, these orders were not always fully carried out, and sometimes altogether rescinded, but they nevertheless caused many Jews to emigrate, as we have seen, and compelled many others to choose the tragic and bizarre existence of *marranos* (crypto-Jews).

The situation of the Jews became even more deplorable late in the seventh century when it became clear that an Arab invasion from North Africa was imminent, and the Jews were suspected of conspiring with the enemy. The possibility should not be discarded altogether that some Spanish Jews indeed helped the Arabs in their designs for the conquest of Spain. Such a reaction on the part of the Jews to their brutal persecution could after all be expected. Be this as it may, King Egica (687–701), in an attempt to punish the Jews, deprived them in 694 of their liberty and declared them slaves "in perpetuity." Luckily for the new slaves, Spain was occupied by the Arabs only 17 years later, and the servitude of the Jews came to an end.

Further north, Roman rule was replaced by the Germanic kingdom of Franconia, which included central and northern France and western Germany. The Jewish population here, as we have seen, was much smaller than that in the Visigothic kingdom, and in language and appearance was not much different from their Romanized non-Jewish neighbors. It is thus not surprising that the Germanic rulers at first treated the Jews on a par with the Romans. Jews held various government offices, including judgeships. In fact, the final ouster of Jews from public office did not come until the early seventh century. Whether Jews served in the military is uncertain. Unlike the Jewish condition in the Visigothic kingdom to the south, the Jewish condition in Frankland did not basically deteriorate even when Merovingian King Clovis converted to Catholicism about the year 500, probably because of the relatively small size of the Jewish population. Only the Church councils became more bold in their attempts to isolate the Jews and to make it impossible for them to keep slaves.

In the second half of the sixth century, the influence of the Church on the kings of the ruling Merovingian dynasty increased, and the situation of the Jews began to deteriorate more visibly. Pressure for conversion to Christianity began to be exerted on individual Jews and on entire Jewish communities with increasing frequency. But as we have seen, it was not until the reign of King Dagobert I that Frankland's Jewry as a whole was hit with a persecution of major proportions. In view of the sudden increase of the Jewish population due to the influx of refugees from Visigothic-controlled Spain and southern France, and possibly to emulate the anti-Jewish policy of the Visigoths, Dagobert I, too, made an attempt to forcibly baptize all his Jewish subjects. And, as we have seen, Dagobert's attempt did constitute a serious setback to Frankland's Jewry. The latter part of the seventh century, however, seems to have again been more tranquil for Franconia's Jews. Thus, unlike the Jews of Spain at the time of the Arab invasion, Franconian Jewry lived under not-unfavorable conditions at the time of the changeover to Carolingian rule.

The Economic Scene

During the period of Roman rule in Western Europe, trade and agriculture were the main fields of Jewish economic activity. We have seen that especially in Gaul and Germany the first Jewish arrivals, besides the mercenaries, came as merchants supplying the Roman armies with their necessities. There are indications that in addition to the merchants a number of Jewish artisans had arrived with the Romans. In time, agriculture became a major Jewish occupation in all Western Europe, and especially in Spain. Spain had become the granary of the Roman empire, and much of its growing wealth was derived from agriculture. It is therefore not surprising that many Jews entered this field of economic endeavor.

Things began to change when the Roman empire turned Christian. Cultivation of the soil without employing slave labor was not profitable. Thus, when the Church councils began to pressure for banning the Jews from trading in, or holding, slaves, or employing Christian laborers, Jewish involvement in agriculture had by necessity to recede. It is worth noting that the hostile attitude of the Church affected Jewish agriculture in Gaul to a greater degree than in Spain. This was due to the fact that while in Spain many Jews tilled the soil by themselves, Jewish landowners in Gaul mostly relied on hired non-Jewish labor. Thus, while in Frankland Jewish agriculture came to a virtual end, it survived much longer in Spain, even after the Visigothic kings embraced Catholicism.

The Jews who were driven out of agriculture now turned mostly to commerce. True, Syrian merchants were the main element in Western Europe's commerce in the late Antiquity, but theirs was by no means a monopoly, and ample space was left for Jewish enterprise. The Jewish role in the supply of luxury articles to the ruling circles and the nobility, lay as well as clerical, clearly began to emerge. To be sure, late in the sixth and during the entire seventh century legal obstacles to Jewish commerce increased. But somehow the Jews managed to circumvent these by various means, not excluding bribery. The commercial opportunities may even have attracted additional Jewish immigrants to Frankland in the seventh century. Money-lending, however, in those times often associated with commerce, was still rare among the Jews. Similarly, the practice of medicine was still infrequent among them.

In summary, despite the shrinkage of Jewish agriculture and the virtual ouster of the Jews from the slave trade, Jewish economic activity in the waning years of the Antiquity remained, especially in Frankland, fairly resilient. It is worth noting that neither in Spain nor in Frankland were any special Jewish taxes, later so detrimental to Jewish economic endeavor, imposed up to the end of the Antiquity. We thus have to conclude that in Western Europe economic factors did not lie at the root of the religious persecution of Jews in the late Antiquity.

Community Organization, Culture, and Religious Life

The fact that the early Jewish arrivals in Western Europe settled, as we have seen above, in towns which grew up as Roman administrative centers, greatly facilitated the emergence of local Jewish communal organizations. We have no way of describing in detail either their early activities or structure, but it can be said that the expansion of Jewish agriculture in Spain, with its inevitable result of partially scattering the Jewish population, did not hamper the growth of the Jewish communal organization. In the third century C.E. Spanish Jewry had a network of well-organized Jewish communities. If we judge by the title *archontes* carried by the leaders of the communities, the Spanish communities probably were modeled after their sister communities in Italy and North Africa. The judicial autonomy enjoyed by Spain's Jewish communities under Visigothic rule probably dates back to the Roman period.

That Jewish communal organizations existed in the Rhineland in the first half of the fourth century is attested to by the fact that decrees of Constantine the Great addressed themselves directly to officers of the Jewish community in Cologne. Here, too, the titles of the officers suggest that the communal organization resembled those of Italy, North Africa, and the Eastern Mediterranean. It is possible that the Jewish communal organization in Gaul and Germany survived the turmoil of the Germanic invasions. Jews participated in the general exodus from the cities, which occurred during the invasions, to a much lesser degree than Gentiles. This continuous concentration of the Jewish population in urban centers probably lent strength and permanency to its communal organization.

The high degree of Jewish consciousness suggested by the

strength of the Jewish communal organization, did not prevent the Jews from far reaching integration within Roman society in Western Europe. In all likelihood Latin and its early derivatives were in use among the Jews. Similarly, about one-third of the names common among them were Latin. Many other names were Latinized versions of, or translations from, Hebrew names. Social relations with Gentiles, even after many of the latter had accepted Christianity, were close and friendly. In fact, Jewish integration within the general society was so obvious, that in the eyes of the Germanic conquerors they were, as we have seen, undistinguishable from the Romans. Regrettably, no information is available on the existence of Jewish schools, or of the emergence of a Jewish-Latin literature. However, the tendency of the Jews to live in urban centers suggests, at least, the possibility that specific Jewish educational and cultural facilities were available to them.

Even less specific is our knowledge of the religious beliefs and practices of Western Europe's Jewry in the Roman period. The fact that considerable numbers of Spaniards of Phoenician origin converted to the Jewish faith would indicate that the Jews were not lax in practicing their religion. Whether the *archisynagogi* in Cologne on the Rhine in the first half of the fourth century were religious functionaries or lay heads of the Jewish community is not clear.

A definite increase in the intensity of Jewish religious life manifested itself in the post-Roman period. The observance of the dietary laws was widespread, and was insisted upon even in the company of Gentiles. Evidence of the existence of synagogues becomes more abundant in the sixth century. Indeed, Judaism had by then become so strong that the Jewish religious leadership, whatever its nature may have been, seems not to have been concerned about the close social relations between Jews and Gentiles, including churchmen. It even happened, as surprising as it may sound, that a Jew recited a psalm in Hebrew at a funeral of a churchman. Be it noted, however, that the far-reaching integration within Gentile society had its usual pitfall in the form of intermarriage, a process accelerated by an excessive number of males among Jewish immigrants.

The most remarkable phenomenon in the field of religion was the resistance of the Jews to attempts at their forcible conversion both in Frankland and Spain. Many fled, as we have seen, in different directions to evade baptism. Still more probably preserved their Jewishness clandestinely. If this were not the case, King Swinthila of Spain would have had no reason for permitting in 621 the return to Judaism of those forcibly converted under his predecessor Sisebut. The strength of the Jewish faith was further manifested by the fact that precisely during the period of the forced conversions Jewish proselytizing activities took place which were not lacking in positive results, especially among the lower strata of the population. The only time Judaism was really vanquished was when in 694 King Egica not only declared all Jews to be slaves, but took their children from them to be raised in Christian homes. While probably all the enslaved Jews again practiced Judaism openly after the Arab conquest 17 years later, most of their children must have been lost by then to the Jewish faith. In the final analysis, however, Judaism survived this first concentrated assault perpetrated against it by Christianity in Western Europe to a greater degree than could possibly have been expected.

Section XII

THE ANTIQUITY: EPILOGUE

The historical course of the Jewish people during the Antiquity stretched over a period of more than two and a half millennia. During this period the Jews experienced a series of remarkable developments rarely encountered in the history of other peoples. They started out as a tiny clan on the Persian Gulf and went on to become one of the few peoples whom history credits with forging the civilization of the Western World. Even when the clan of Abraham was transformed in the period of the Exodus into a people, the Hebrews were still numerically insignificant. They, nonetheless, went on to become, despite a rather generally unfelicitous historical course, a people of millions by the time the Antiquity was waning. Estimates of the number of Jews living within the confines of the Roman empire range from five to seven million. The Jews may thus have numbered about ten million in their totality.

Simultaneously with numerical growth, the Jewish people experienced a major geographic expansion. Deportations by various conquerors, and—to a greater degree—emigration in search of better opportunities, scattered the Jews to most lands which in the Antiquity constituted the civilized world. The historians Strabo and Josephus in the fist century C.E. and the Father of the Church, Jerome, about the year 400, stressed the fact that the Jews were living all over the world known to them. The Jewish people had thus outgrown its original structure of a group living within the confines of its own territory to become a world people.

Of major significance also were the religious processes which took place within the Jewish people. Having been the first to arrive at the idea of the oneness of God, the Jews then produced prophecy with its unequaled religious, moral, and social message. Simultaneously, the psalms were created to give the ordinary man a way of profound and direct communion with his God. The prophetic writings, the Psalms, and other parts of the Jewish literature of the First and Second Commonwealths then went on to become the Book of Books, the Bible. We have seen how out of the religious entanglements of the Second Commonwealth there emerged beside normative Judaism, the Christian sect, which in time became the main religion of the Western World.

Nonetheless, Judaism too in its own way became a world religion. When the great process of dispersion began, the Jews created new forms of worship which made it possible for them to serve God without an altar and sacrifices. Jerusalem continued to be the religious center of the Jewish people, first as the site of the Temple, and later as the focal point to which every Jew turned in prayer.

With the expansion of the Diaspora and the overthrow of the territorial base in Judaea, new frameworks for ethnic existence were devised in the form of the Jewish communal organization. The communal organization had as its basis the Jewish Law as it developed in the period of the Second Commonwealth and thereafter. The Jewish Law proved to be a strong and workable instrument for the preservation of a Jewish separateness, sufficient to secure the existence of the Jewish people. The Law was, indeed, "a portable territory" of the Jewish people.

The early separation of the Judaeo-Christian sect, and the distinctly Gentile character assumed by the Church, made it possible to preserve Judaism as the national religion of the Jewish people. The Jewish religion thus became a decisive unifying factor for all Jews in the vastness of the Diaspora. The basic unity of the Jews living at the end of the Antiquity in the successor states of the Roman empire is clearly manifested by the structural similarity of the Jewish communal organization all over North Africa and in Europe. Great structural similarity also existed in the centrally organized Jewish communities in Palestine and Babylonia, both of which were led by dynasties, the patriarchs and the exilarchs, deriving their authority from the accepted belief of their Davidic origin. The close relationship of the sages of Palestine with the sages of Babylonia served as an additional factor of unification between the Jewries of the Persian empire and the

Jewries of Byzantium and the West. Thus, on the threshold of the Middle Ages, when they had to face great and hitherto unexperienced historical challenges, the Jews were a people of many millions united by common historical memories, a common religious and civil law, and a well-functioning communal organization.

INDEX

Geographic names which appear very frequently—such as Israel, Jerusalem, and Judaea—have not been indexed.

A

B

C

D

E-F

G

H

I

J

K-L

M

N

O-P

Q-R

S

T

U-V-W-X-Y-Z